Philoponus
On Aristotle Physics 3

Philoponus
On Aristotle
Physics 3

Translated by
M.J. Edwards

B L O O M S B U R Y
LONDON • NEW DELHI • NEW YORK • SYDNEY

Bloomsbury Academic
An imprint of Bloomsbury Publishing Plc

50 Bedford Square
London
WC1B 3DP
UK

1385 Broadway
New York
NY 10018
USA

www.bloomsbury.com

First published in 1994 by Gerald Duckworth & Co. Ltd.
Paperback edition first published 2014

British Library Cataloguing-in-Publication Data
A catalogue record for this book is available from the British Library.

ISBN HB: 978-0-7156-2616-0
PB: 978-1-7809-3434-1
ePDF: 978-1-7809-3435-8

Acknowledgements
The present translations have been made possible by generous and imaginative funding from the following
sources: the National Endowment for the Humanities, Division of Research Programs, an independent federal agen
of the USA; the Leverhulme Trust; the British Academy; the Jowett Copyright Trustees; the
Royal Society (UK); Centro Internazionale A. Beltrame di Storia dello Spazio e del Tempo
(Padua); Mario Mignucci; Liverpool University. The general editor wishes to thank
Dr Istvan Bodnar, Dr Gillian Clark, Mr D.B. Fleet, Professor David Furley, Dr A.R. Lacey,
Professor D. Russell and Professor A. Rijksbaron for their comments on the translation and Dirk Baltzly and Ian
Crystal for their help in preparing the volume for press.

Typeset by Ray Davies

Printed and bound by CPI Group (UK) Ltd, Croydon, CR0 4YY

Contents

To my family
and to Mali

Introduction

Physical theory

Richard Sorabji

1. Aristotle on change and infinity

The subject of Book 3 of Aristotle's *Physics* is the nature of change and its seat and the character and possibility of infinity. Change is something which Aristotle has to discuss in a book on physics or the philosophy of nature, for in Book 2 he has defined nature as an internal source of change. As for the seat of change, it is essential for Aristotle to locate change in the patient, not in the agent, for he needs to make room in Book 8 for a divine mover who is not himself a seat of change.

The second half of Book 3 is devoted to infinity. Philoponus suggests this is because change is itself infinitely divisible. Aristotle's conception of infinity is particularly brilliant and it is one that is widely taught to school children nowadays. It might be summarised by saying that infinity exists as an expandable finitude. However large a finite quantity you have taken, you can always take a further finite quantity, but you never reach infinity in the sense of a more than finite quantity. This fits very well with the modern idea of approaching a limit or getting as close as you like. It also applies very neatly to the infinity of future time. Future years may at best constitute an expandable finitude, but will never become a more than finite number. Aristotle's conception of infinity applies less well however to past years, if there has been an infinity of those. Aristotle sometimes puts his point by saying that infinity is potential, never actual. An actual infinity would be a more than finite quantity. Another claim that he repeatedly makes is that an infinity cannot be traversed or gone right through to the end. One of Aristotle's objections to an actual infinity is that if there were a more than finite number of anything, then even a part of that actual infinity could itself be infinite in the same sense. It seems to him impossible that the part could be no less infinite than the whole. We ourselves are prepared to accept that the odd numbers may constitute an infinity no less than the entire set of whole numbers. But Aristotle objects that you would have more than one infinity here. To pursue our example, you would have the infinity of odd numbers and the infinity of even numbers and how could there be more than one infinity? This objection is given at *Physics* 3.5, 204a20-6 and it is taken up by Philoponus at 388,15; 412,14; 415,5. Aristotle cleverly shows that his conception of infinity is the opposite of his conception of a whole. With an infinity you can always take more outside what you have so far taken. But when you have the whole of something there is nothing left outside.

2. *Philoponus on infinity*

Philoponus is at his best on the subject of infinity. Aristotle had allowed that time was infinite but denied infinity to place. Philoponus denies infinity to both. Though steeped in pagan Neoplatonism, he was a Christian and therefore wanted the universe and time to have a beginning and an end. He turns the tables on the pagans by showing that Aristotle's concept of infinity guarantees that time and the universe had a beginning. If they did not, there would be an actual infinity of past years. Moreover, that infinity would have been traversed or gone right through. Again, that infinity could be, absurdly, increased. If there has been an infinity of years up until now, how many will there have been by next year? Infinity plus one. And how many months will there have been, or days or hours? Multiples of infinity, the very thing which Aristotle had ruled out. Furthermore, mere portions of these past years would be as infinite as the whole, which is something Aristotle ruled out again. These arguments by Philoponus are found here in 428,13-430,10 and 467,15-468,4.

In this last passage Philoponus has a very interesting idea about numbers. The Greeks did not recognise negative numbers, but Philoponus seems to recognise something analogous if only to dismiss it as impossible. He is discussing whether there could be an infinity in both of two directions. The infinity of numbers goes only upwards in one direction from one, he says. If there were an infinity of numbers in the opposite direction, it too would have its terminus at one and then we should get what Aristotle forbids, an infinity that had been completely traversed by the time it reached one. This is not of course to recognise negative numbers, but it is to conceive something analogous.

As regards the finitude of place, it was much harder for Philoponus to maintain it than for Aristotle, for Philoponus conceived place as a three-dimensional space which was empty 'so far as its own nature was concerned', though never empty in fact. The question therefore arises why such a space, empty in fact, should not extend beyond the spherical mass of the universe. Aristotle was able to exclude this because he denied that there was such a thing as three-dimensional space. According to him, the place of a thing is not a three-dimensional space which it occupies but is merely the surface of its immediate surroundings. There is therefore no place outside the spherical mass of the physical universe because that mass has no physical surroundings. Philoponus cannot use this rationale for denying infinite space. What he does therefore is to argue that we can conceive that place or space, just like body, has an outer surface of its own which constitutes its outer limit. Or if we cannot conceive this, at least we can conceive that place or space derives an outermost surface from the body which it houses. The place of the world therefore can have an outermost limit and need not extend to infinity. This argumentation is given in Philoponus' commentary on Book 4 at 582,19-583,12.

In the present commentary on Book 3, another very useful aspect of Philoponus' discussion is his survey of the views taken on infinity by the presocratic philosophers. These are especially fully discussed at 386,14-398,16.

3. Dynamics

There is a curious passage at 428ff. where Philoponus argues that two bricks of the same weight, when stuck together, will weigh somewhat more than twice what each weighs separately. I believe this is connected with something he says much later in his commentary at 683,1-25. He there argues against Aristotle, quite correctly, that if you double the weight of something, you will not *double* the speed of fall. He urges that you can see this for yourself if you make the experiment. So far we may congratulate him. Unfortunately, he does think that the doubled weight will fall *slightly* faster. This is something which it would have been hard to check by observation, even though it would have been easy to observe that the speed of fall was not twice as fast. I think that Philoponus' idea that the doubled weight will fall slightly faster is what he is trying to express in our passage when he says that the two equal weights when fastened together will have slightly more than twice the original weight. He is thinking that their downward tendency will be slightly greater – not of course twice as great.

In a later part of his commentary at 642,3ff., Philoponus introduces a concept which, in its medieval context, Thomas Kuhn has regarded as a scientific revolution. He introduces the idea of an impetus, or an internal force impressed from without, and uses it against Aristotle to explain why a projectile continues to move after it has left the hand of the thrower. Aristotle had answered this in a quite different way, on one interpretation by saying that the pockets of air behind the projectile turned into unmoved movers to keep it on its way. Impetus theory is not applied to projectiles in the present book but it is applied to the motion of the fire belt. Philoponus inherits from Plato and Aristotle the idea of a spherical universe. The Earth is at the centre surrounded by the waters of the ocean. These in turn are surrounded by air and then by a belt of transparent fire to which Aristotle added a spherical belt or belts of a fifth element, aether, which rotate carrying round the heavenly bodies. Aristotle believed that the belt of fire rotated as well as the belts of aether. He inferred this from the motions of comets which he believed to be located in the fire belt. He therefore raised the question why the fire belt rotates. Philoponus gives different answers at different stages of his thought, but in the present book he argues that the fire belt is moved by an impetus or force impressed from the rotating heavens. Though at other stages of his writing he thought of the rotation of the fire belt as natural, he here prefers the idea that the rotation is supernatural. The idea of the supernatural had been introduced in the different context of the resurrection by Origen as an alternative to Aristotle's options of natural or contrary to nature.

4. Thought experiments

It will already be clear that one of the talents of Philoponus is devising thought experiments. His mistake over the speed of fall of the two weights fastened together may have been due to genuine observation rather than thought experiment. But the impossibility of an infinity of numbers running in two directions did involve a thought experiment. We find others too, involving moving the earth or expanding it or the impossibility of putting out a flame by cooling all air surrounding a city out to the furthest limits. These experiments can be found at 422,23ff.; 443,1ff.; 449,6ff.

5. Traditional and novel ideas in Philoponus' commentary on Book 3

The most striking of the pro-Christian and anti-Aristotelian ideas in this book of Philoponus is the insistence that time and the universe had a beginning. This corrects some of the more traditional ideas that are found in the very same book of his commentary. At 340,31 he mentions without comment the incompatible idea of Aristotle that the heavens are made of a beginningless and unending substance called aether. At 377,26 he refers without demur to Aristotle's divine prime mover. In Aristotle this god is responsible for the beginningless and endless rotations of the heavens but, on the other hand, is not a creator at all. This second difficulty, not the beginninglessness but the non-creativity, had already been overcome by Philoponus' teacher

Ammonius, who interpreted Aristotle's god not only as a mover, but also as a creator (*poiêtikon*), responsible for the beginningless and endless existence of the orderly world (see Richard Sorabji, *Matter, Space and Motion*, ch. 15).

At 473,22 Mark Edwards suggests that Philoponus may be insisting upon the harmony of Plato and Aristotle. This was also a view of his teacher Ammonius, who was indeed harmonising Aristotle with Plato when he claimed, incredibly, that Aristotle's god was a creator. Philoponus would have had less incentive to make Aristotle respectable by harmonising him with Plato once he had decided to launch his anti-Aristotelian and pro-Christian ideas.

The bulk of the *Physics* commentary is dated to AD 517 by a reference at 703,16-17. But it has been argued by Verrycken that Philoponus revised the *Physics* commentary, inserting some of his novel ideas after AD 529. It was in the latter year that he launched a full-scale attack against pagan Neoplatonism in his treatise *Against Proclus on the Eternity of the World*. On this reconstruction, the infinity arguments in favour of a beginning of time and the universe will have been later additions (see Koenraad Verrycken, 'The Development of Philoponus' Thought and Its Chronology' in Richard Sorabji, ed., *Aristotle Transformed: The Ancient Commentators and Their Influence*, London and Ithaca NY 1990).

6. The structure of Philoponus' commentary

It has been argued by Étienne Évrard that Philoponus begins his comments with a *protheôria* or discussion of doctrine and then returns to the beginning of the same passage to discuss the text. A lemma, or quotation, from Aristotle begins the *protheôria* and a series of lemmata introduce the portions of the text. Sometimes these lemmata overlap one another, a fact which the editor of the Greek text, Vitelli, has not understood. In three places the quotation has been written out properly as a lemma in the present translation where Vitelli did not present it as such (344,8; 462,1; 486,16). Évrard also finds that the combined *protheôria* and discussion of portions of the text added together would have taken about an hour to deliver. The commentary therefore corresponds to a series of hour-long lectures and gives us some idea of what went on in the classroom at Alexandria (Évrard, *L'école d'Olympiodore et le composition du 'Commentaire à la Physique' de Jean Philopon*, dissertation, Liège 1957).

Philoponus' language and the translation

M.J. Edwards

By Aristotle's own assertion, the subjects of the third book of his
Physics are *kinêsis* and *to apeiron*, and each presents a problem for
his translators. The term *kinêsis* signifies both change within an
object and change in its relations with other objects, so that growth
and colouration must be treated on the same footing as locomotion.
Still less translatable is the word *apeiron*, which, connoting merely
that which has no limit, covers both the infinite and the infinitesimal,
together with a variety of senses that make it ambiguous even for a
Greek.

Although in many contexts the word 'infinite' might be preferable,
I have tried to use 'unlimited' consistently as a rendering of *apeiron*.
Many of the arguments in Philoponus exploit the correlation between
this word and *peras* (limit), which has *perainô* as an associated verb.
Since there is in English a verb 'to limit', and no one word that
signifies 'to be infinite' only my translation would make sense of the
argument to a Greekless reader. In turning the vocabulary of Philoponus into English, I have attempted, in so far as it is possible, to
preserve the same root wherever he uses words that are etymologi-
cally related. Where a Greek verb lends itself to compounds, I have
looked for one of equal versatility in English. Neither of these proce-
dures can be carried through consistently: the idiom and grammar of
the two tongues differ greatly, we have not so many cognates or such
freedom in making compounds, and many words in Greek have a
semantic field exceeding that of any possible English synonym. One
feature of his style which I have not attempted to reproduce is his
fondness for playing on words. As Philoponus himself observes, the
trope is at least as old as Aristotle, who had slightingly declared that
the use of Mind in Anaxagoras' philosophy was 'mindless' and his
attempt to locate the unlimited 'out of place' (see 397,14; 448,13).
Philoponus borrows the former pun and adds a joke of his own when
he inquires how the Pythagoreans 'were moved' to make false infer-
ences about nature (364,23). At times his choice of vocabulary anticipates the refutation of Aristotle's opponents. When he 'interweaves'
a syllogism (474,28), it is as an antidote to Melissus, whom Aristotle
upbraided for erroneously 'spinning flax with flax' (478,20). In one of
his rare ascriptions of an *apodeixis* or proof to Aristotle, Philoponus
implicitly contrasts the successful methods of his subject with the
geometrical 'proofs' that their very advocates had failed to use correctly (483,20; 483,2). If there is any philosophic principle at work
here, it is perhaps the one laid down by certain commentators on

Plato that the structure of philosophy should reflect that of the world. Philoponus thus reminds us that not only syllogisms, but all objects are produced by the 'interweaving' of form and matter (394,29). It is no surprise that the *Physics* is both continuous (415,21) and limited (484,5), since extension of the analogy would suggest that the same criteria make objects real and syllogisms true.

Philoponus ('the lover of work') deserves his other nickname, 'the Grammarian', when he offers us five senses of *apeiron*. He also seems to assume an etymology which relates this to its cognates: *apeirêkos* (inexperienced), *aporeutos* (pathless) and *aporia* (difficulty). We apply the word 'unlimited' (*apeiron*) as a result of inexperience (*apeirêk-otes*: 410,10) or when we travel in pathless regions (409,18). No wonder then that philosophers who believe in the unlimited should raise so many *aporiai*; but all of these are banished by Aristotelian exactitude, which, notwithstanding occasional digressions (403,22), never fails to keep the path (405,33). So attuned to nature is the thought of Aristotle that we who follow him can be said to share the perceptions of the Demiurge, 'looking on' (*apoblêpsantes*) the proto-typical, while others were misled by 'looking on' phenomena (403,13; 407,13). This juxtaposition of looking up with looking down is common in the Platonists (cf. Plotinus, *Enn.* III.9), whose thought Philoponus often labours to reconcile with Aristotle's text.

I have used the text of H. Vitelli (Berlin 1887) with little alteration. In order to make it possible to read Philoponus' commentary without a copy of the *Physics* close at hand, I have occasionally supplemented the text of the lemmata. In some places more of Aristotle's text has been included to provide a context. In this case, the addition to the lemma is enclosed in square [ ] brackets. At other points, I have provided a summary of the context in which the lemma occurs. Such summaries are enclosed in curly {} brackets. Within the text of Philoponus' commentary, square brackets are used to indicate words which the sense requires that we understand. I am glad to acknowledge my debts to those who read parts of the draft: Dr I. Bodnar, Dr G. Clark, Mr D.B. Fleet, Professor D. Furley, Dr A.R. Lacey, Professor D. Russell, Professor A. Rijksbaron and Professor G. Watson. The editing and preparation of the final draft have been supervised by Dr Dirk Baltzly, and Professor Richard Sorabji has filled the lacunae in my knowledge of Aristotelian physics. I owe my support for the last four years to New College, Oxford, and also to the Post-Doctoral Fellowship awarded to me in 1992 by the British Academy. Christ Church and the Faculty of Theology at Oxford University have recently supplied me with a secure environment for the completion of this task.

Philoponus

On Aristotle Physics 3

Translation

The Commentary of Philoponus on Book 3 of the *Physics* of Aristotle

200b12. Since nature is an origin[1] of change and of alteration. {At 200b12-15 Aristotle infers that as students of nature (physicists) we must study change/motion and the 'subjects next in order', which are the unlimited, place, void and time. Only change and the unlimited are treated in Book 3. Philoponus in this first comment anticipates the definition of change as 'the *entelechy* of that which is potentially, in so far as it is such', at 201a11.}

There are five things, incidental to the subject-matter of physics[2] with which we have said that Aristotle is concerned in this book. These are matter,[3] form,[4] change,[5] place[6] and time.[7] Aristotle has discussed matter and form in the books before this one (but speaking chiefly of matter in the first and of form in the second),[8] and so it remains for him to discuss the remaining three. And to begin with he undertakes the examination of change, and reasons that it is necessary for the physicist to give an account of change.

[This he does] in the following manner: since, he says, we have defined nature as the origin of change, it is altogether necessary, for one who wishes to know what nature is and the definition of it, to know also, long in advance, what change is. For what we adduce for the definition of something must be clear. For if a man does not know what change is, he will not know the definition of nature either, since change is included in the definition of nature. Therefore an account of change is necessary for the physicist.

Next:[9] since (a) all change is continuous, as is shown in the final books of this work[10] (for all change is in magnitude, and all magnitude is continuous, hence all change is continuous); and (b) the unlimited[11] is sometimes contained in the account of the continuous (for those who define the continous define it as unlimited in so far as that is continuous which is divisible without limit), therefore (c) it is necessary that one who is to know what change is should know what the unlimited is. And therefore an account of the unlimited is also necessary to the physicist.

Again: all change is in place or also in time; for everything that undergoes a change is a body, and all body is in place, and therefore

5

10

15

20

5   change also is in place. Moreover it is shown in the final books that all change is in time, since nothing undergoes change timelessly.[12] Therefore the account of place and time is also necessary. But, since certain physicists[13] thought that motion[14] occurs through the void – on the grounds that nothing could undergo change in a plenum, as
10   this would entail the presence of two bodies in the same place – for this reason, the account of the void is also necessary to the physicist. For either motion does occur through the void, so an account of the void is necessary; or it does not, and so an account of it is necessary for the refutation [of the false position]. And alternatively [they maintain it] because they define place as void and empty of body.

   The aim of both this book and the following one, then, is to examine
15   change, the unlimited, place, time and void, and in this book he discusses change and the unlimited, while in the following one he discusses place, time and the void. He discusses them not only because they conduce to the account of change, but also because they belong essentially to the whole subject-matter of physics. This was after all the object proposed from the beginning, to speak about those
20   things that are generally incidental to the whole subject-matter of physics.

   Now first he discusses change, and inquires what change is; secondly, in what media change occurs, and thirdly, how many forms of change there are. Before [the discussion of] these he assumes four axioms, which conduce to his elucidation of them. The first is that, among existent things, some exist in actuality alone, some in poten-
25   tiality and actuality (it is impossible that any subsistent thing should exist in potentiality alone, for matter never becomes devoid of form).[15] Things divine and incorporeal, then, exist in actuality alone,[16] and he has said of them in his work *On Interpretation*: 'they are actualities without potentiality.'[17] All things that exist in nature, on the other hand, exist in potentiality and actuality, for they exist in *entelechy*[18] in so far as they possess a certain shape, and in potentiality in so far
30   as they have the capacity to receive also a different one.

   This is true of things that come to be and are destroyed, but the ethereal body,[19] while existing only in *entelechy* in respect of its
341,1   essence (for it could never change in essence), partakes of potentiality also in some way, because of motion in place. For it is not everywhere at once. Perhaps indeed it is not free of potentiality even in essence; for if they are composed of matter and form, and matter is that which has potentiality, it is clear that the heavenly bodies are not entirely
5   free of potentiality even in their essence. For even if it is not the case that their matter has the form potentially, yet since matter by its nature is wholly potential, the consequence of this is that [things in the heavens] are not wholly free of potentiality like things that are immaterial, which have potentiality in no way whatsoever. For

this reason, at any rate, Plato too says that the latter exist in reality, while all the objects of perception do not exist, but are always coming to be.[20]

This, then, is his first assumption, that, of things that are,[21] some are in actuality alone, others in actuality and in potentiality. The second is that of related terms some are in respect of excess and defect, others in respect of change caused and suffered. Examples of those that are in respect of excess and defect are the greater and the smaller, for the greater is greater than something smaller, and of these terms the greater is the excess, the other the defect. The cause of a change acts on that which suffers it, and that which suffers it is changed by the cause of change. He does not set out other forms of relation, such as those with respect to equality, likeness or cause and effect, since the only ones that he requires are: (a) the relation of excess and defect, regarding which he wished to prove, against those who thought that change occurred in them, that change could not occur in them; and (b) the relation of the cause and the subject of a change, regarding which he wished to show that change occurred only in respect of these.

His third assumption is that there is no such thing as change in itself, independent of things undergoing the change. The things undergoing the change are either essences or quantities or some other of the things in the other categories,[22] and there is nothing that is in itself the subject of a change, if it is neither an essence[23] nor a quantity nor one of the other categorial predications. For this reason, neither is change another thing alongside these, but it takes place with respect to essence or to quantity or to quality or to place. Hence as these things change with regard to each category, e.g. to essence, to quantity and to the rest, the change is observed to be of two kinds, one from an inferior to a superior state, the other from a superior to an inferior. Thus with regard to essence it can be from not-being to being or from being to not-being; with regard to quantity, it can be from the complete to the incomplete, or *simpliciter* from the greater to the smaller or vice versa. With regard to quality it can be from white to black or black to white, and so with the other contraries. With regard to place it can be from higher to lower or conversely. Now in all contraries there is one superior and one inferior; for what is is superior to what is not, the complete to the incomplete, the white to the black, the higher to the lower, and likewise by analogy in the other cases. These remarks not only contribute to Aristotle's definition of change, but also towards his showing which of the things causing change also suffer it in return, and which cause change without undergoing change. For he will proceed to discuss these topics in due course.

Having assumed these [axioms], he next says what change is,

10

15

20

25

30

342,1

5

10

defining it as follows: 'change is the *entelechy* of that which is potentially, in so far as it is such.' The word '*entelechy*' in Aristotle signifies actuality and completion,[24] for it is a compound of the words *hen* ('one'), *teleion* ('complete') and *ekhein* ('have a certain state').

15   When any particular thing possesses its own completion, it is said to exist in *entelechy*. The added words 'in so far as it is such' stand for 'in so far as it is potentially that thing in particular', in order that the *entelechy* may come into being while the potentiality, whose *entelechy* it was, persists. For the *entelechy* in the case of any thing is of two kinds, one when the thing is already in its completed state, and has rid itself of all potentiality, one of the thing when, having changed from its potential state, it undergoes mutation according to its poten-
20   tiality, and is being turned into its form.

An example is the bronze which is potentially a statue. For its *entelechy* may consist (a) in its becoming a statue, being shaped in a certain way by the statue-maker, or (b) in its having already become a statue and having received the completed form of the statue. This [second] *entelechy* comes without preserving the potentiality which
25   made it possible for the statue to come into being; for it is already a statue and no longer retains the potential, so that this completion is not that of the potentiality (how so, when it destroys it?) but of the thing in which the potentiality existed. But the *entelechy* first spoken of, by which the statue was coming into being, still conserves the potentiality.

Entelechy of this kind, then, he calls change and the completion of potentiality, since all completion preserves what it completes. For as
30   long as the potentiality is preserved, so also is the change which
343,1   completes the potentiality; but when the potentiality ceases, so also does the change. The potentiality ceases when form and shape supervene. This, then, is change, the completion of that which has being potentially in so far as it has being potentially.

That this is indeed change he also shows by an example. The
5   buildable,[25] he says, when it is a thing of such a kind in actuality (I mean when it is being built) is at that time subject to change (for it is being turned into the form of a house, and building is a process of this kind), but that which is being built still contains potentiality (for it is still buildable); as, once it is completely built, it no longer preserves the potential nor is undergoing change. If, now, building is
10   a change, and the building is still in potential, it is right to say that the *entelechy* of that which has potential being, in so far as it has it, is change, since the first *entelechy* is a change and the completion of potentiality.

The first assumption also contributed to his giving a definition of change: this is the one which says of things that are that some are in actuality alone, others in potentiality and actuality. For he finds from

this that change occurs in those things that are potentially, and not 15
in those that are in actuality. The second axiom, the one that states
that of relations some are in respect of excess and defect, some in
respect of the cause and subject of change, contributes to his refuting
the view which some held,[26] that change is in those relations that are
with respect to excess and defect, but with respect to the cause and
subject of a change. The change, he says, has its origin in the cause
of change, but exists in the subject of the change. For he will show 20
this in what follows, that the change is not in the cause but in the
subject of the change.

The third axiom, which states that there is no change independent
of things, but that all change occurs in essence, in quantity, in quality
or in location, contributes to his showing how many forms of change
there are, and even more to his showing that there is no common 25
genus of change,[27] but that changes have the same name through
being derived from or related to one thing. For he will show that
change of place [viz. motion] is primary and the others secondary, and
that when it is eliminated it eliminates the others with it, whereas
their elimination does not eliminate it, so that it is primary in
nature.[28] For where there is a prior and a posterior, even what is
predicated in common of these is not a genus. His intent, then, is not 30
strictly to give a definition of change, but to sketch[29] an account which 344,1
will square with every change by analogy, just as he has done in the
case of the soul. Here, even though he has shown that there was no
common genus of souls, since there is in this case also a prior and a
posterior, nevertheless, he says, let us give a sort of common account
of the soul, 'if indeed there is anything that can be said of all soul in 5
common'.[30] So therefore he has done this also with respect to change.
The rest contributes to showing that change is of two kinds with
respect to the things that suffer it.

200b12 But, since nature is an origin of change and alteration.[31]

Nature is the origin of change and rest, but since he needs only change
now, it is this that he has mentioned. 10

200b16 [and] to go along the same route with regard to the
subsequent terms.

By 'the subsequent terms' he means 'unlimited', 'place', 'time' and
'void'. When he said 'subsequent', he was speaking either (a) of
whatever is seen to come in order after the account of change (for
since the account is of change, and the unlimited, place, time and the
void come after the account of change, it is necessary to speak about 15
these also), or (b) of those things that, coming in series after change,

have it in common that they follow the subject-matter of physics. By '[going] along the same route' he means inquiring by the same method what each is, and whether or not it is at all, and in what way it is or is not.

200b16 Now change seems to be one of the things that are continuous.

20   'Seems' means either (a) that it seems so to the multitude, or (b) that it seems so generally speaking to everyone and to him, [in which case] it stands for 'is seen'.[32] For it will 'seem' because of the fact that Aristotle does not bring change under the continuous, since he does not put it into the category of quantity, nor as a whole into any of the others. So that if there are two forms of quantity, the continuous and the discrete, and change is not brought under quantity, much less [is

25   it brought] under the continuous. For the categories were said of forms that have been completed[33] and of things that have acquired their complete forms, whereas change is an uncompleted activity. Thus, so far as [can be inferred] from what was said in the *Categories*, the statement 'seems to belong to the things that are continuous' must be understood as referring to the multitude; but since Aristotle here frequently urges that change is continuous, we are clearly to

345,1   take 'change seems' as meaning that it is seen to be so and he agrees. For in the *Categories*, even if he has not brought change under the forms of the continuous, that is not because it is not continuous, but, as I have said, because it is an incomplete activity, and in that work he is giving an account of complete forms.

5   **200b17** and the unlimited is seen primarily in continuity.

By 'primarily' he perhaps means 'in itself', according to the primary signification of 'in itself',[34] (for this is what is assumed in the account of the subject,[35] as also is the unlimited; for it is assumed in the account of the continuous, which is its subject; for we call that

10   continuous which is unlimitedly divisible). Or else 'the first' stands for '*par excellence*' and 'according to the primary account'. For the unlimited is present also in that which is divided, as for example in number (for number can be increased without limit), but primarily in the continuous, and, since in the continuous therefore also in the discrete. For it is by virtue of the fact that the continuous is divisible

15   without limit that number can be increased without limit. For the division of the continuous without limit produces the increase of number without limit. Thus the unlimited is primarily involved in the continuous, and, since in the continuous, also in the discrete.

200b18 Therefore those who are defining the continuous must often make use in addition of the account of the unlimited.

He was right to say 'often'. For it is not always the case that in defining 20 the continuous we adduce the unlimited in the definition of the continuous. For it is possible to give more than one definition of the same thing. At any rate, when he himself in the *Categories* defines the continuous he says, 'the continuous is that whose portions join to make some common boundary'.[36] And in this definition he does not make additional use of the unlimited.

200b20 In addition to this, change cannot occur without place, 25 void and time.

That change cannot occur without place and time agrees both with his own opinion and with the truth. For if: (a) change occurs in 346,1 something that is the subject of a change; (b) body is the only thing that undergoes a change; and (c) all body exists in place: therefore there cannot be any change without place. And that there could not be any change of place without place is clear immediately, since this is called change of place. Later, however, he shows that there can be no other change without change of place, by which he shows that the 5 change of place is the first of all. Yet change could not occur without time either, as is shown in the final books, for every change has a whence and whither. But it was not as his own opinion that he said that there is no change without a void, but as the opinion of the physicists.[37]

200b21 It is clear then that, on account of these facts, and 10 because these are common to everything and generally in every-thing, we must begin our inquiry by considering each of these. [For the study of specifics is posterior to the study of common [terms].]

For two reasons, he says, an account of these terms is necessary. First, the account of change is necessary for the physicist, since nature is an origin of change and these appear along with change; 15 secondly, our present task is to examine those common terms which are generally incidental to the whole subject-matter of physics. For this is what we advertised at the beginning. And this is well said, as the study of common [terms] always precedes that of specific ones. For it is impossible for someone to learn what a demonstrative syllogism is if he has not learned what a syllogism is *simpliciter*.[38] 20 And thus it is impossible for a man to know the nature of animals or plants if he does not know what nature is *simpliciter*.

Or perhaps then we are to understand in this way the words 'For the study of specifics is posterior to the study of common [terms]' in agreement with the prooemium of the work that lies before us (for at the outset he stated that we must begin from the more obvious, that
25   the more obvious is the more concrete, and that this is the more universal; and thus we must first say in this case also what change is *simpliciter*, and then subjoin the definition of change of place and the rest): either his words 'the study of common [terms]' mean this, as I have explained, or else, as is more probable, by 'common' he now means not those that are concrete and applicable to many things, but those that are incidental to many things.[39]
30   First, then, he says, one must speak of what are generally inciden-tal to the whole subject-matter of physics, and then of what is specific
347,1 to certain disciplines. That this is his meaning is clear from the words themselves; for having said 'it is clear then that, on account of these facts, and because these are common to everything and generally in everything' (clearly meaning by 'common' that they are incidental to everything), and having set forth the reason for his present discussion
5   of them, he added that 'the study of specifics is posterior to that of common [terms]'. Alternatively [we can argue] that he nowhere discusses time or place in particular applications. The words 'these are common to and generally in everything' stand for 'these things are common to and generally incidental to the whole subject-matter of physics'. For all body is continuous and exists in every case in place and time. And also the void, in the judgment of the physicists, is
10   incidental to everything, since they consider the void to be nothing but place deprived of body.

200b26 Some things are only actually, and some actually and potentially. {Aristotle adds that there is also 'this in particular', 'this much' and 'this kind'.}

15   From this point he begins to lay down his axioms, and the first is that, of things that are, some are in actuality alone, and some in actuality and in potentiality, and this not only with regard to essence, but in all the other categories as well. But to have only actual being belongs only to essence, for as we said before, nothing is completely free of potentiality except for the divine and immaterial essences. For every
20   body, in every case and in every way, contains the potential in one of our aforesaid senses. And if anyone shall assert that the essence of heavenly bodies exists in actuality alone, since they have no natural tendency to alter into anything else, he will by taking this way, assign those things that exist in actuality alone not only to essence, but also to quantity and the rest. For the number of heavenly bodies and the

qualities that naturally inhere in them also have only actual being, since in this very respect they admit of no alteration.[40]   25

200b28 As for the relative, some have respect to excess and defect. {Aristotle adds that some have respect to activity and affection, and that in general they have respect to the cause and subject of change.}

This is the second axiom.

200b31 For the cause of a change is a cause of change in the   348,1
subject of change.

Since he has said that the cause and subject of a change belong to the class of relatives, he also wished to establish this by these arguments. For the cause of a change, he says, causes it in the subject of the change, and conversely that which suffers it suffers it from the cause. Thus these things are related.   5

200b32 And there is no change apart from things.

This is the third axiom, that change occurs in things that cause and suffer change, and is not a thing in itself or separable. So that the changes are as many as the things that undergo change. Things that undergo change are changed in four ways, viz. with respect to essence, quantity, quality and place. Therefore in these [categories] there is change too.   10

200b34 And, as we have said, it is not possible to reckon anything common with regard to these, if it is not this in particular or this much or this kind.

He is arguing that there is no change apart from things. For if (a) change occurs only in these categories, and (b) there is no subsistent thing common to the categories and apart from them, and as it were   15
a genus of them (as animal *simpliciter* includes the particular animals, being an ensouled and percipient essence other than each of the particular animals and discerned in each of them, since being is predicated homonymously of the categories):[41] then it is clear that there would not be change apart from these categories. Taking their starting-points from this, the commentators say that change is not a   20
genus, but a word used homonymously. For if there is no change apart from the categories, and there is no common genus of categories, it is clear from this that there could not be any genus of change. For if there were a common genus of the categories in which there is change,

change would necessarily belong primarily to that genus and would
not have a variety of senses, but just as there subsisted that genus of
categories in which change was predicated, so the change belonging
to that genus would be the genus of the changes in the categories
which fall under that genus. In fact, however, change exists in the
same way as the things in which it occurs.

Therefore, just as the accounts of the aforesaid genera differ, it is
clear that so do those of the changes in them. So that even if he
[Alexander] should give a single definition,[42] this too will be homonymous and one of those things which have a variety of senses. And this
is what Alexander frequently establishes, that change is not a genus,
but a homonymous term.

Perhaps, then, it is possible to say that this denial of change apart
from things does not refute the notion that change is a genus, just as
what is understandable, in so far as it is understandable, belongs to
the genus of quality, and yet is not only predicated in regard to
quality, but also in the other categories (for essence is also knowable
and so is each of the others) so it is, I say, with change. For it belongs
to the genus of quantity (since it is continuous and this position, that
change is one of the things that are continuous, is argued everywhere
by Aristotle), yet it also appears in the other categories. So if change
is brought under quantity, and quantity is a genus, change itself
would also be a subordinate genus.

And this is a reasonable conclusion, I mean that change is not in
a single category, and so too with the knowable, since categories are
not divided from one another, but are all interwoven.[43] For if they
were all separate from one another, then it would not be possible to
find change except in quantity; but, since they are interwoven, it is
reasonably not unaccountable that the same thing should be found
in different categories. One might, however, wonder why it is, if
change is one of the things that are continuous and therefore brought
under the category of quantity, that Aristotle in his *Categories* did
not bring it under the forms of the continuous. To this, then, we say
that categories are of completed forms and of things that have
attained their forms, and it has been said that change is an uncompleted activity and a route from potentiality to activity. For this
reason change could not be numbered with the forms of the continuous.

201a3 Now each is present in two ways to everything, as in the
case of [what is] this in particular; for the one is shape, the other
privation. {Aristotle adds that in 'this kind' there is white and
black, in 'this much' there is complete and incomplete, in locomotion there is above and below, heavy and light.}

The fourth assumption is that, in every category where change occurs, it is not a simple thing but a double one. For in every category, he says, it is observed that this is form and that privation, and the route [of change] is either from the form to the privation or from the privation to the form. And it has been said that he calls privation the inferior of the opposites, and form the superior.

201a9 Being in *entelechy* and in potential having been distinguished with regard to every genus ... {Aristotle goes on to define change as 'the *entelechy* of that which potentially is, in so far as it is such'}.

Having set out the aforesaid axioms, he wishes, as his remaining task, to give the definition of change. And, since it contributes to his giving of the definition, he resumes the first of the assumptions, viz. that each of the genera of things that are is distinguished with respect to the actual and the potential. So then, he says, 'change is the *entelechy* of that which is potentially, in so far as it is such'; that is, in as much as each possesses the potential and the actual, while the potential is still preserved.

201a11 [The *entelechy*] of that which is mutable, in so far as it is mutable, is mutation.

Having defined change in general, he applies the account to changes in a particular respect. He is right, therefore, to call change with regard to quality 'mutation'. For it is the completion of the mutable, in so far as it is mutable. For the mutable, before it begins to undergo mutation, such as a whitening or a blackening, possesses the potential in an uncompleted state; and the completion of the mutable occurs when it receives its potential change.

201a12 The *entelechy* of what can increase and of the destructible which is its opposite (for there is no common name to cover both) is increase and destruction.

It is not the case, he says, that just as we have a common name with regard to whitening and blackening, cooling and warming and every change that occurs with respect to contraries, so we have in the case of increase and destruction, i.e. of change in quantity; instead, the changes with respect to the contraries have been given specific names, one [being called] increase and the other destruction, while they have no common name.

351,1   **201a16** For when the buildable, in so far as we call it such, exists
in *entelechy*, it is being built, and this is building.

It is confirmed by an example that the definition of change has been
correctly given. Stones are potentially buildable; when, therefore,
5   they are being built, they acquire the completion which has respect
to their potential, their capacity for building being actuated, and this
kind of actuation of theirs is called building, and this building is a
change. Consequently, the actuation of what can increase, in so far
as it can increase, would be a change, called increase, so too that of
the mobile, in so far as it is mobile, and so in the other cases.

But Themistius explains change with a slight alteration,[44] viz. that
10   it is the initial *entelechy* of that which exists potentially, in so far as
it is such. For the final *entelechy*, he says, is the change to the form
in which it then remains at rest, while the first one is the approach
to this, which is change. And the previous *entelechy* is an incomplete
actuality (for it is *en route* to form and the absolute and simple
entelechy), while the later one is complete. For when the subject of
change attains this state it is at rest and is completely free of
15   potentiality.

201a19 But, since some of these are [the same][45] both potentially and in *entelechy* [but not at the same time or in the same
respect].

Having said what change is, he now wishes to show that there are
certain things which, apart from being changed, undergo change. At
the same time, he also resolves a difficulty which these things raise
20   for the account of change. For if there are things which at the same
time cause change and undergo it, and the cause of change in so far
as it causes change is actuated, then certain things which are changed
have actual being. Yet change was said to be the *entelechy* of that
which is potentially, in so far as it is such. Therefore, either the
definition of change is false, or it is false that there are certain things
which both cause and undergo change. Now the latter is true; therefore the definition of change is not true.

Such, then, is the difficulty, and he resolves it in the light of what
25   is said here. For he shows how certain causes of change also suffer it
reciprocally, and first that there are certain things which at the same
time cause change and undergo it. He shows this by using an axiom
352,1   already assumed, viz. that of things that are some have actual being
alone, some both actual and potential being. And all things of this
kind will necessarily also be subjects of change when they cause it,
though they will not cause and suffer change in the same respect, but

will suffer it in so far as they exist in potential, and cause it in so far as they exist in actuality.

For example: fire is warm actually but cool potentially, and there-fore it causes change in so far as it is actually heating water, but it suffers reciprocally in so far as it is potentially cool, when it is quenched and alters to earth or to air. And water, in the same way, cools in so far as it is actually cool, but is warmed in so far as it is potentially warm. So that the difficulty is dissolved in the light of these considerations. The difficulty was that, if (a) that which suffers change also causes it, and (b) that which causes change exists in actuality, therefore the subject of change exists in actuality; whereas we have said that the subject of change is still in potentiality. This difficulty, then, is resolved in the light of what has been said, viz. that if what is in every way a subject of change is also a cause of it, the respect in which it is changed is not the respect in which it causes change, but it suffers change in so far as it has potential being, I mean according to its matter, and causes change in so far as it has actual being, by which I mean according to its form. It does not therefore follow that, if the subject of change also causes change, the subject of change already exists in actuality, for the respect in which it is changed is not the respect in which it causes change.

Having said this, he resumes the definition regarding change, wishing to explain it more clearly, and finally to articulate it better. At the same time he shows once again that the potentiality is not identical with the substratum, but it is one thing for each thing according to which it is said to be this in particular, and another according to which it is potentially this in particular. For example, it is not the same for bronze to be bronze and to be potentially a statue. That the potential is therefore something beside the substratum, he also shows by many other examples: for instance, he says, it is not the same for colour to be a colour and to be potentially visible, but the colour exists in actuality even if it is not seen, as at night, but it is not visible except in potentiality; and, whereas the colour, whether it is seen or not, exists in actuality, what holds of the colour does not always hold of the visible. So the potentiality is not identical with the substratum, since [in that case] the same would always hold of both. And whereas bronze is always bronze in actuality, it is not always a statue, but sometimes in potentiality, sometimes in actuality.

In fact, it is chiefly from the cases of contrary potentialities that he shows the potentiality to be distinct from the substratum. For, seeing that an animal has the potential to be sick, and not only this but also to be healthy, if it were the case that the potentiality was identical with the substratum, then indeed not only one potentiality would be identical with the substratum, but all of them. So that if the potentiality of being sick is identical with the substratum, it is

353,1 presumably obvious that that of being healthy is too. But if both are identical with the substratum, they are presumably identical with each other. For things which are identical with the same thing are identical with each other. But if the potentiality of being sick were identical with that of being healthy, then presumably sickness and health would also be identical, so that contraries would be identical. Therefore the potentiality is not identical with the substratum.

5 Now if the potentiality is not identical with the substratum, we see therefore that the definition of change has been well stated, viz. that [it is] 'the *entelechy* of that which is potentially, in so far as it is such'. This, therefore, is the accurate [definition of] change, when we have added the words 'in so far as it is such'. For the subject of change must have actual being in one respect, but potential in another. For nothing 10 is changed that has only potential being, since there is nothing that has only potential being. Hence matter does not even undergo change in respect of itself, since in respect of itself it does not so much as exist. The subject of change must therefore have both actual and potential being, but is changed, not in so far as it is actual, but only in so far as it is potential. For example, bronze is both actually this very bronze, and is potentially a statue. When, therefore, what is potentially this is turned into actuality by the maker of the statue, 15 we say then that the bronze is being changed. But it is changed, not in respect of its actual being, that is, in respect of its being bronze (for in this respect it is unchangeable, since it does not alter its essence of bronze in becoming a statue), but in respect of its potential being when what is potentially this receives its own actuality and is brought to its complete actuality, on arriving at which the potential hence- 20 forth disappears. Change, then, is the actuation of the potentiality, which is still preserved.

Thus, having explained and proved the definition of change, he proceeds to establish by many arguments that it is not even possible to give another definition of change. And the first of these is that the object in which the change is observed exists at different times. For 25 the bronze which is a statue in potential has three temporal phases. For at one point it is a statue only in potential, when it is not yet shaped by the artisan; at another it exists in actuality alone and is in no way potential, when it has already received the form of the statue; at another it is in the intermediate phase, when it is being turned from potentiality into the form and the potentiality is still present. These temporal phases therefore being three, in which phase 30 should the change be located? For it is not being changed when it exists in potentiality alone, the formative art not yet having actual- ised the bronze, nor when it has received the form of the statue; for 354,1 the formative art no longer works upon it when it has once received the form. Therefore it remains [to conclude] that the change took place in the intermediate phase, when the formative art was changing the bronze and was turning it from potentiality into form, the potentiality in the bronze still being preserved.

In the same way, we say with regard to the potential of a house, that the house is changed, not when the buildable has only the potential [to be a house] (as when the stones and the wood lie around and the builder has not done anything to them), nor when the house has completely come to be and has received its proper form; for then it is not being built but has already been built. For building takes place while the buildable is still preserved, so that only in the intermediate phase would the change occur, when the building also [is in progress]. For the building is nothing but a change from the first potentiality to complete actuality; but so long as the building still goes on, the buildable has not yet been made free of potentiality, since [in that case] it would no longer suffer change either.

'Since some things are the same in potentiality and in *entelechy*.' We find this to be presumed in the axioms already set out. Of this kind are all things in the realm of generation and destruction. For they are one thing in actuality, another in potential, since everything has a natural capacity for alteration into everything.

201a20 but not at the same time or not in the same respect. {Aristotle adds the example of what is actually warm but potentially cold, and concludes that many things have reciprocal action and affection.}

If something is at the same time in actual and potential, it is not possible for it to be actual and potential with respect to the same form (for it is impossible to be the same thing at the same time actually and potentially, e.g. to be warm both in potential and in actuality, but at the same time [the subject] will be warm in potentiality, yet cool in actuality), but if something is in one and the same respect actual and potential, it is impossible for it to be both at the same time; rather it will at some time be warm or cool potentially, at another the same thing actually.

201a23 For everything will be able both to act and to be affected.

Everything, he says, which possesses both the potential and the actual, will be able both to act and to be affected: to act in respect of actuality (for it is the forms that are agents), to be affected in respect of potentiality. For it is matter that can be affected, and the potential is matter.

355,1   **201a23** Hence also is the cause of change by nature changeable.

The words 'by nature' should not be taken to apply to the subject of change,[46] [meaning] that what is changed by the cause of change is changed by it naturally and not with force. For it is not necessary that everything which causes change in this way should itself undergo change. For it is true of the soul as well – I mean the rational soul –

5   that it changes bodies not by force but naturally, yet nevertheless is not changed itself. So it is with the power that causes change [of position] in things in the heavens, according to what he himself has said in the previous discussions, namely 'there are two principles that cause change naturally, of which one is not natural'.[47]

But 'by nature' should be taken instead with 'the cause of change', [meaning] that what causes change in such a way as natural objects

10   do by nature is in every case itself changeable. For none of those things which naturally cause change is unchangeable. For even nature herself, when she causes change in bodies, is herself subject to a concomitant change as she undergoes mutation and becomes weaker, and the potential for increase, mutation, generation and all the rest grow weak. If, therefore, it is only of those things that belong to the realm of generation and destruction that he says that the cause

15   of change by nature is changeable, we shall take 'changeable' to stand for 'reciprocally changeable', [meaning] that everything that causes change is changed reciprocally. If, on the other hand, he says it of all the natural things *simpliciter* and also of things in the heavens, we shall take 'changeable' to stand only for the subject of change. For it is also true of things in heaven that they cause [change] without being changeable but are themselves changed, though not reciprocally. For things celestial change things here while suffering change, but are not, however, affected by these reciprocally.

20   **201a25** So it seems to some that everything that causes change
        is changed; but in fact it will be obvious how these matters are
        from other considerations.

Since he has shown that certain things which suffer change also cause it, he says that certain people thought that whatever caused change was itself in every case changed. That it is not so, he says, will be

25   obvious elsewhere, and he communicates this account in the eighth book of this work,[48] in which he shows that not everything which causes change is also changed. And meanwhile [it suffices to say that] the desirable causes change though it is not changed itself, the image causes change in the lover though it itself is not changed, and bread causes change in the starving though it is not changed itself, and straw causes change in the ass.

201a27 And [the actuation] of what potentially is, when   356,1
<either> this itself or another thing is an actuant as being in
entelechy, is change, in so far as the thing is changeable.

He resumes the definition of change. Now the text is found in two
forms, one of which is as follows: '[the actuation] of what potentially
is, whenever it is an actuant as being in *entelechy*, and not as [being]   5
itself but as [being] another thing, is change.' That is, the actuation
of what potentially is – whenever this thing in potential is an actuant
through existing as something else in *entelechy* – is change, not in so
far as the thing is in *entelechy*, but in so far as it is in potential. But
Alexander transcribes another text which is found in the more ancient of the copies,[49] viz.: '[the actuation] of what potentially is, when
this itself or another thing is an actuant as being in *entelechy*, is   10
change, in so far as the thing is changeable.' We should read this as
a hyperbaton,[50] i.e.: 'the actuation of what potentially is, when it is
an actuant as being another thing in *entelechy*, is change in so far as
the thing is changeable.' He says 'this itself or another thing', because   15
among the causes of change there are some, like the natural ones,
that have the origin of change within themselves (e.g. those that
increase and mutate) and others that [receive it] extraneously, like
the products of art. This was the reason for his adding 'either this
itself or another thing', as if he were to say, 'I mean by actuality the
potentiality, whether the actuation is its own (i.e. it has the potential
to cause change within itself), or extraneous, i.e. from without.'

201a29 Now I mean 'in so far as' thus: [the bronze is a statue
potentially, but nevertheless the *entelechy* of bronze, in so far as
it is bronze, is not change].

He is explaining why in his definition he added 'in so far as it is
changeable', that is, 'in that respect in which it is changeable'. For,   20
he says, 'the bronze is a statue potentially', but also bronze in
actuality. Therefore it is not the actuality of the bronze in so far as it
is bronze that I call change but the actuation of the potentiality by
which it is potentially a statue, this is what I call change. Then, in
order that no one may ask, 'What is the difference between being
bronze and being potentially a statue? For it is the one and the same
to be bronze and to be potentially a statue', it is reasonable that he   25
next proceeds to show that for each thing it is one thing to be this in
particular, and another to be potentially changeable.

201a32 Since, if it were the same *simpliciter* and by definition,   357,1
the *entelechy* of bronze, in so far as it is bronze, would be change.

What he means is as follows. If to be bronze were identical with being potentially changeable, then since it has its being bronze in *entelechy*,
5   it would also have its being changeable in *entelechy*. But what is changeable in its *entelechy* undergoes change, so bronze, in so far as it is bronze, would undergo change. It would thus all be one to say 'bronze' and to say 'change in *entelechy*', which is manifestly false. For the tripod which is standing is bronze in actuality, yet there is no change in actuality; on the contrary, it is not even changed in any
10   way, but stands and is at rest. The phrase '*simpliciter* and by defini-tion' means if it were the same in general so as not only to be the same as regards the substratum, but also as regards the account of it. For, as to the substratum, the bronze and the potential subject of change are identical, but as to the account they are not identical, for each has a distinct definition. And he proceeds to show in the case of contrary potentialities – I mean those of being sick and being healthy or being warmed and cooled – that it is impossible for the potentiality to be
15   identical with the substratum, since then even contraries would be identical with each other, as things that are identical with the same are identical with each other.

{At 201a34 Aristotle declares that he will illustrate by contrar-ies: the potential to be healthy or to be ill is not the same.}

201b21 For [in that case] even being sick and being healthy would be identical.

If, he says, the potentialities of contrary things were identical, then presumably the actuations of the potentialities would be identical;
20   but, as it is, to be sick and to be healthy are not only not identical, but even contrary.

201b2 But the substratum, that which is healthy and sick, whether moisture or blood, is one and the same.

The substratum, he says, which is healthy or sick in part, is one and the same. So that if the potentialities – I mean those of being sick and
25   being healthy – are not one thing but even contrary, while their substratum is one and the same, therefore the potentialities are not identical with the substratum.

358,1   **201b3** But, since they are not identical, as colour and the visible are not identical [it is manifest that change is the *entelechy* of the potential in so far as it is potential].

He has used a different example. For colour is not in the same respect both colour and visible. For, while they are the same as concerns the substratum, the account of each is different. For colour is the source 5 of change in that which is actually transparent,[51] while being visible belongs to it as an accident. For colour is not a relation, but rather a quality, while visibility is a relation, since the visible is visible to an observer, and there is colour even if it is not seen but this is not true of the visible if it is not seen. If, now, it has been shown that potentialities are different [from the substratum], we have correctly given the definition of change, viz. that it is 'the *entelechy* of the 10 potentially existent, as potential, not as actual'.

> **201b5** That, then, it is this [and that change is suffered at the time when it itself is the *entelechy*, and neither before nor after, is clear] ...

That is, that change is what we have said, the *entelechy* of the potential in so far as it is such. And when he says that 'change is suffered at the time when it itself is the *entelechy*' he means that the 15 change occurs at this time only, when the potential, in so far as it is potential, acquires its own actuation, and neither before acquiring it, when it is only potential, nor after, when there is only the actuality.

> **201b7** For it is possible for each thing at times to be actual and at others not. {Aristole gives the example of the buildable, and concludes that the same account will apply 'in the case of other changes'.}

Since he has said that only an *entelechy* of this kind is change – I 20 mean that of the potential in so far as it is such – and neither prior nor posterior to this, what he wishes to demonstrate is that it is not possible for the condition prior to this to be a change, nor the posterior one. For the potential, he says, can be actual at times and at others not: for stones and wood, being buildable, lack this actuality at times, 359,1 as when they lie around by themselves and the builder does no work upon them, and possess it at others, at which times it is also said that building is [in progress]. That it suffers no change before it has actuality is, then, patently obvious, for change is actuation of a kind. The remaining possibilities are that change occurs when being built or after having been built. But having been built it is at rest, whereas 5 what is being built undergoes change when there is still also something buildable. So that change occurs only during the time when building occurs, the buildable being still conserved. For we said that change was the *entelechy* of the potential, in so far as it is such. What we have said in the case of the buildable, he says, we shall say 'also

10   in the case of the other changes', such as whitening, warming and the
      rest.

> **201b16** And that the matter has been stated correctly is obvious
> from what others say about [change], and from the difficulty of
> defining it otherwise. {Philoponus in this comment defines the
> opponents whom Aristotle leaves unnamed, and anticipates the
> conclusion at 201b35 that only the 'aforesaid way is left'.}

      As a token that he has given a correct definition of change, he says
15   that all who have spoken about it have not spoken correctly and that
      no other definition of it could even have been given. We have said
      before that he was not content merely to establish the definition of
      change, but he shows that it is impossible even to give another
      account of it. And therefore he now says both that those who have
      spoken otherwise about it do not speak correctly, and that it is not
20   possible to speak otherwise about it.
      Now the Pythagoreans said that change is difference, inequality
      and not-being.[52] Aristotle says therefore that those who hold that
      change is difference, inequality and not-being call it these things
      either (a) in order to say that change is identical with difference and
      inequality or with not-being, or (b) because change arises from these,
25   in that all that undergoes change is changed either from what is not
      or from inequality or from difference. It is obvious, then, (a) that
      change cannot be said to be identical with inequality, difference or
      not-being, for in many things there is difference whereas there is no
      change. For in almost all that is there is difference, but it does not
      follow that all that is is undergoing change. There is difference in
      earth, at any rate, with regard to the other elements, and yet the
30   earth does not undergo change for this reason (at least immediately);
      there is difference in Socrates[53] with regard to a horse, and yet
      Socrates does not undergo change for this reason at any rate, that he
      is different from a horse. No less is there inequality in five with regard
360,1 to ten, and in the side with regard to the diagonal, yet even so it is
      not necessary that these things which possess the inequality undergo
      change. And the parts of animals differ from one another, and the
      number of one's fingers is unequal to the number of one's hairs, but
      the parts do not immediately undergo change through being different,
      nor does number undergo change by being unequal. And likewise
5   change is not not-being either. For if anyone were to say that change
      is what a thing is not, [we answer that] for everything there is
      something that it is not, but there is not change in everything. And
      if not-being *simpliciter* is [supposed to be] identical with change, the
      account is still more false. For change belongs to things that are
      whereas that-which-is-not *simpliciter* is not in any way whatsoever.

Yet neither (b) does change arise from these, nor is it possible that change occurs with respect to these. For things that undergo change are not changed only from difference and inequality, but also from sameness; for not only are things that differ changed from being different and unequal, but it is certainly no less true that things which are the same and equal are changed from sameness and equality. So that change is no less identical with inequality, difference and not-being than with being, equality and sameness; for change arises both from this and from those.

Having said this, he proceeds to explain on what consideration the Pythagoreans said that these things are change. It is, he says, because change is indefinite and the indefinite is privation. For if the form is defined and is the definition, it is presumably obvious that the indefinite is privation. Since, therefore, (a) change is privation (for when a thing is defined and attains a form, it is no longer a subject of change), and (b) the aforesaid things are all indefinite and cause privation, since that is also true of every other principle in this column,[54] then it was reasonable for them to say that change is identical with these. For it must be understood that the Pythagoreans divided the principles of all that is into two columns, marking out each column with some ten principles, calling one the column of the goods and the other one the column of the evils. For the sake of information, let the two columns, as he himself informs us elsewhere,[55] be set out as follows: good/evil, limit/the unlimited, odd/even, one/many, right/left, light/darkness, male/female, resting/changing, straight/curved, square/oblong. Such, then, was the way in which the Pythagoreans divided the principles of what is into two columns, apportioning one to the superior contraries, the other to the inferior ones, and into these they brought all that is.

Aristotle says, therefore, that because the column of the inferiors was the privative one, and, being privative, indefinite – for this reason, they brought change, as a thing indefinite, under this. Aristotle, however, did not mean that the Pythagoreans divided the two columns between the formative and privative principles when he said that the principles in the second column were privative (for this division of principles into form and privation is his), but since he was accustomed to call the superior contraries forms and the inferiors privations, this was his reason for saying that the column of the inferiors was the privative one.

He has said, then, whence they derived the belief that change is difference, inequality and not-being: it is, he says, because change seems to be a thing indefinite. But the principles of the second column are also privative, and for this reason indefinite. Reasonably, then, they brought change under the indefinite principles. For not-being, inequality and difference they brought into the column of the inferi-

ors, and these are in themselves so many principles of change. And that change is indefinite he proceeds to show. For the syllogism is
15 that:[56] (a) change is indefinite; (b) what is indefinite is privation; therefore (c) change is privation. The second premiss, by which I mean the major one, we have constructed by negation and inversion;[57] for if it is the form that is defined, the indefinite will be privation. The minor premiss he himself constructs, I mean that change is indefinite. For since of things that are some are potential and others actual,
20 change is not brought under either, because it is neither what is only potential nor what is only actual that undergoes change, but change is strictly neither of these, while partaking of both, and is indefinite for this reason, that it cannot be posited definitely in any of the existents.

Having therefore explained the reason why they bring change into the class of privative principles, he goes on to establish that it is not
25 even possible to define it otherwise. For even if we agree, he says, that what is is divided into not only the potential and the actual, but also privation, it is not possible to bring change under any of these. And, while it has been said that it is impossible to bring it under the potential or the actual, it is obviously impossible to bring it under privation. For what partakes of privation will not already by virtue
30 of this fact partake of change, but it is possible, while being deprived of form, not to change but to be at rest. Alternatively: if we were correct to say that change is the *entelechy* of the potentiality, and privation is not a sort of actuation, then change is not privation. So
362,1 that, if it is impossible to posit change in any of these, 'the aforesaid way is left' to us as the only true one, and this is that change is a sort of actuation, though not the complete actuation which has acquired the form, but that which still conserves the potentiality. And for this reason it is incomplete in so far as it retains the potentiality, but an
5 *entelechy* because overall the change is from potentiality to complete actuality.

Having said this, before he concludes his discussion of change (he will conclude it when he finally shows that change is not in the cause but in the subject of the change), he resumes the discussion of the
10 causes and subjects of change, and inquires which of the causes of change it is that, while they cause change, also suffer one reciprocally. And this inquiry he pursues more completely than he does here both in the work *On Generation*[58] and in that *On the Soul*;[59] here, though, he says that those things cause change and suffer it reciprocally which are apt not only to cause change but to suffer it. And what, he asks, are these? They are, he answers, those whose changeless state
15 is one of rest. For things which admit change are said, when they are not being changed, to be resting, since when things are not by nature subject to change, their changeless state is not called rest but by this

very term changelessness, and also stability. It is therefore reasonable that such things [as admit change] should both cause and suffer
change, as they have potential being; for they must at some time have
become actual from rest and undergone change.

But in what way do such things both cause and undergo change?
To this he says that the cause and the subject of change must be in   20
contact with one another, and when they are in contact, each will act
on the other in so far as it is actual and be affected in so far as it is
potential. And the heavenly bodies, then, change things here by
contact, yet are not affected by them reciprocally, since they are not
potentially subject to change, but are in actuality both subjects and
causes of change; and this is change in place, but with regard to the
other changes the heavenly bodies are neither potentially nor actu-   25
ally subject to change. And to put it concisely, as he himself does in
his *On Generation*,[60] the things that are affected reciprocally in the
course of causing change are those that have the same matter. For,
since the common matter of generation is all things in potentiality,
it follows that when what acts is in contact with what is affected, it
works upon it according to its own actuality and the other's potentiality, and is affected itself by the other on the same principle.   30

For example, when a warm thing is adjacent to a cool one, it warms
it in so far as it itself is actually warm, the other being warm
potentially, but it suffers reciprocally from the other, in so far as it
itself is potentially cool, while the other is actually so. After this, he
gives a more complete definition of change, viz. that 'change is the
entelechy of the changeable in so far as it is changeable'. For the
previous definition, which said that it is 'the *entelechy* of what   35
potentially is, in so far as it is such', would also include the completed
actuality. For potentiality is spoken of in two senses,[61] with respect   363,1
to either a thing's receptiveness or its place in the scheme of things.
The actuation of the latter is not a change, but a complete acquisition
of the form, while change is the alteration from the former kind of
potential being to the former kind of actual being. So that the
definition of change that has now been given is the more proper one,   5
viz. that 'it is the *entelechy* of the changeable, in so far as it is
changeable'. For this definition no longer subsumes the second kind
of potential.

201b18 For neither would anyone be able to assign change and
alteration to another genus.

Since the genus under which he has brought change is *entelechy*, he   10
says that it is not possible for anyone to bring it under any other genus
than the one under which we have brought it.

201b19 as is obvious when we consider how others have assigned it, saying that change is difference, inequality and not-
being.

This has been said elliptically. For he has advanced two theses – first,
that the others have not spoken well concerning change, and second,
that it would not be possible to give another account of it – and, having
responded to the former position in the introduction to his demonstration, has said 'neither would anyone be able to assign change and
alteration to another genus', but he has not responded to the second
problem; now he has carried on the demonstration as though he had
given it. 'It is obvious,' he says, 'when we consider how others have
stated it, saying that change is difference, inequality and not-being.'
Something must therefore be added from without, in order that we
may remove the ellipticality from the account. For after the words
'neither would anyone be able to assign change and alteration to
another genus' one must add 'nor do those who have spoken otherwise
about change speak correctly', and then subjoin this argument: 'It is
obvious when we consider how others have stated it', and so on.

364,1   **201b21** There is none of these that undergoes change necessarily, whether there be different things or unequal or non-existent.

In this passage he posits and refutes the former proposition, which
propounded the identity of change with difference, inequality[62] and
not-being.

5   **201b22** Nor even would alteration seem to have to be towards
these, nor from them [any more than from their opposites].

The remaining two propositions are (a) that these are not the origins
of change (for it would no more be from these than from their
contraries), and (b) that it does not take place toward them any more
than toward their contraries. Now it is possible to say this in defence
of the men, that when they made change identical with difference,
inequality and not-being, it was not in the sense in which Aristotle
has understood it here, viz. that it is either identical with them or
has them as origins or ends (for that would be easy to refute, and
intelligent men would not be likely to maintain this proposition), but,
seeing that every change is a departure from the state whence change
occurs, it is obvious that every subject of change, departing from itself
in a certain sense when it departs from the form that it previously
had, becomes different with respect to itself through alteration in
either quality or place; and it becomes unequal with respect to itself
through alteration in quantity, and indeed becomes in a certain sense

non-existent, because the form that it previously had is not there. Thus change is inequality and difference, not in that the subject of it becomes unequal or different with respect to other things, but that it does so with respect to itself. And so too it becomes non-existent, since all that is changed is not what it was before, in so far as it is said to have been changed.

201b24 Now the reason for their positing it among these is that change seems to be an indefinite thing {and, Aristotle continues, the origins or principles in the left-hand column are indefinite because privative}.

Here he explains by what consideration they were moved[63] when they said that change was identical with these things. It was, he says, that change is an indefinite thing, and that the second column into which they brought difference, inequality and not-being, into which they brought change also, was itself indefinite through being the source of privation. Quite reasonably, then, since change is indefinite, they brought it under the yoke of the indefinite. But it is possible that in saying that change is not-being, they would come nearer to reaching it if their meaning in calling it not-being were not that it does not exist in any way whatsoever, but that the subject of change is not yet actually what it is being changed into, but still incomplete. For such we also mean by the potential.

201b26 For it is neither this in particular nor this much [nor any of the other categories].

Here the commentators inquire how it is that Aristotle calls privation indefinite because it is brought under none of the categories, and yet the genera of contraries are the same.[64] And they say that the privation of each thing which in reality is specifically opposed to it, from which also comes the alteration to the state of possessing, is indeed brought under the same genus as the state of possessing; but, seeing that such expressions as 'not-man', 'not-horse' and all the privatives (for now I employ the negation instead of the privation,[65] since in these cases we do not have a privative name for the opposite of the form) destroy a single form, yet fail to introduce, not only a definite form, but even a definite privation – for this reason, he says that the privation cannot be brought under any of the categories, not that it is not brought, but that it cannot be brought into any definite class. For what is 'not-man' can also be another essence apart from man, and another quality, quantity and any of the other [categories]. Thus he says that it cannot be brought definitely under any category.

201b27 The reason why change appears to be indefinite {is, Aristotle continues, that it is neither the potentiality nor the actuality of what exists, and appears to be an actuality of a kind, but incomplete}.

Accepting that change is indefinite, and having said that here was
25   the reason for the error in the Pythagoreans' account of change, now he establishes this very point, that change is indefinite, from the division of things that are into the potential and the actual, and having proved that change will properly be brought under neither. For what is actually an essence, a quantity or one of the others is not *ipso facto* changed as well, nor indeed is what is potentially so. For
30   neither is it necessary that what is potentially white should be *ipso facto* changed. Change, then, is none of these, neither actuality *simpliciter* nor potentiality, but a certain mean between them, a sort
366,1   of actuality, but incomplete and not free from potentiality. This is the reason for its being indefinite, that it cannot be accurately assigned to any class of existents – I mean of what is potential and actual, since what is is divided into these two.

201b33 And for this reason indeed it is hard to grasp what it is.
5   For it is necessary to posit it either as privation or as potentiality or as actuality {and neither, says Aristotle, is possible}.

Having shown that the account which the ancients gave of change was not a sound one, and from what consideration they arrived at it, now he addresses the remaining thesis, that it is not even possible to
10   define it otherwise. For if someone were to admit that existent things are divided between potentiality, actuality and privation, it would not be possible to posit change as any of these. And that it cannot be posited as potentiality and actuality is obvious; that it cannot be posited as privation either would seem to be obvious in the same way, for there are many things partaking of privation but not of change.

15   **202a1** It is a sort of actuality, but an actuality of such a kind as we have stated.

Having destroyed the opinions concerning change which either were entertained or could be entertained, he contrives, by this destruction of all, to leave as the truth the one that he expressed. Actuality is of
20   two kinds: (a) that with respect to the acquisition of the completed form (as seeing is the actuation of the eye, according to which it has already acquired vision and actuality) and (b) that of what is potential in the object, which preserves the object's potential (such as when fire changes its position to a higher one, for even as it rises it still retains

the potentiality to rise aloft). The former I do not call change (for it is rather compared with stability and rest), but the second I do. On 25 the one hand, it is an actuality because overall the potential has retired; on the other it is uncompleted, because it is not entirely free from potentiality, but continues to draw it along. For when the subject changes its position for a higher one, and still retains the potential for a change to a higher position, this is how it undergoes change.

202a3 And the cause of change is also changed, as has been said, 367,1
all that is potentially changeable and whose changeless state is
rest.

Here he takes up the account of the causes and subjects of change, and says that every cause of change, which apart from causing change is also potentially changeable, is in every case a cause of change while 5 suffering change itself. By these I mean such causes of change as are potentially changeable, whose changeless state is rest. For when things have a capacity for change but are not yet changed, the changeless state of these is rest. He shows this in the later books of this work.

202a5 For actuation with respect to this [viz. the changeable],
in so far as it is such, is essentially what it is to cause change.
And this it does by contact, so that at the same time it also is 10
affected.

Having said what sort of things are causes and subjects of change, i.e. that those things which are changeable as well as sources of change are things of the kind whose changeless state is rest, he explains in what way things of this kind, when they cause change, also suffer a reciprocal change. And first he says what change is, viz. that it is 'actuation with respect to this, in so far as it is such', that is, for example, actuation with regard to what can be warmed, in so 15 far as it can be warmed, which means the warming of it, and this 'actuation with respect to that' does not occur unless there is contact between the actuating and the affected bodies. Since, therefore, what is actual is not only that certain thing in actuality, but is also another in potentiality, it is necessary that what is potential in the cause of change should be affected when they are in contact with one another by what is actual in the subject of change. And this is what change 20 is. So that in every case it is changed reciprocally, but changed reciprocally by the affected subject, since each of the contraries works upon nothing except its contrary, yet in every case it is potentially what its contrary is. Since, then, the warm is potentially cool, but the warm acts on the cool by contact with it, and the potential when it

25   approaches the actual is brought into actuality, it is altogether
      necessary that what is potentially cool should be affected by the cool.
      And so it is necessary that when the warm acts it should be affected
      reciprocally.

      202a7 Therefore change is the *entelechy* of what is changeable,
      in so far as it is changeable.

      As I have said, he is giving the definition of change more accurately
      in the light of what has been said, saying that it is not the *entelechy*
368,1 of the potential *simpliciter*, but of the changeable. For one might say,
      as an objection to the previous definition, that what is potentially to
      my right, when it becomes this in actuality through my displacement
      (say) to the left, alters to *entelechy* from its potential being, yet is not
      changed. And this is well said, then, against those who find it difficult
5   that only what is potentially to the left has changed and not what is
      potentially to the right, and also that there is only one potentiality in
      related things. For their relation towards one another is either a
      potentiality or an actuality, the actuality being that of the present
      relation, the potentiality that of its opposite, at least in those cases
      where complete inversion is possible. Thus in the case of father and
10   son, since it is not possible for the son to become the father of his
      father, there is not even potentially the opposite relation for the same
      people, but in the case of the right and left and the like, one relation
      is the actuality of the current position and the potentiality of its
      opposite. If, however, there is one relation of related things, in which
      the right and the left, the before and the behind, are mutually related
15   and said to be so, then somehow it is altogether necessary that if
      either has changed the other has changed as well. For the right and
      the left subsist in a relation of this kind. So when the relation has
      changed, both those states which subsist in respect of it would
      undergo change as well.
          But Themistius[66] says flatly that actuality with regard to the
      relation does not preserve the potential in the way that actuality with
20   regard to mutation preserves what is potential in the alteration from
      potentiality to complete actuality; instead, he says, the alteration
      from potentiality to actuality happens all at once. There is at least a
      single actuality that is observed in them properly and *simpliciter*, but
      this is still incomplete. For what is to the left does not gradually come
      to be on the right by moving with regard to things on the left, but
25   without taking time, and I, when I move to the left, undergo a change
      of position, but not of relations. First, then, it is necessary to show
      the actuality of such things to be incomplete, and then to refute the
      definition [by showing] that it is not through change that the actual
      state is brought out of the potential one.

But, granted that this difficulty is to be dealt with in this way, Aristotle, in view of the fact that potential being belongs to every category but change does not belong to all, reasonably amends his definition; another reason is, as I have already said, that the passage from potentiality to actuality is predicated not only of incomplete actuation – by which I mean the actuation turning what is potential in the former sense to what is actual in the former sense – but also of the complete one which turns what is potential in the second sense into what is actual in the second sense.

And no one should attack this definition on the grounds that it tries to show what change is from the changeable; for it is not showing the same by the same. For it is particularly impossible, since change is a relation (this we have agreed in the foregoing discussion) and is related to the changeable (for change is the change of the changeable), to define it otherwise, without taking into account what it is related to, just as [it would be impossible] to define the father without the son or the double without the half. Moreover, the changeable is more knowable than change, since it is not the same thing to know that change is occurring and to know what it is. For the occurrence of it is knowable to everyone, but what it is even we are now inquiring. That change is occurring can indeed be known from the subjects of it, and these are the things that are changeable, so that one who uses the changeable for the definition of change has used the more knowable to explain the less known.

202a9 But the cause of change will always bring a form. {Aristotle adds that this, in whatever category, is the cause of the change, as an actual man will actualise a potential one.}

The cause of change, he says, will always have some form which is one of the ten categories; for this is the reason for change and its origin. For it is matter that can be affected, but what acts is the form. Therefore it is necessary that the cause of change should possess some form, which is the reason for its causing change.

202a13 And the [solution to the] difficulty is manifest, that change occurs in the changeable. {Aristotle's continuation is discussed in detail below; Philoponus in this comment anticipates the example of the road between Thebes and Athens at 202b13.}

The subject of the inquiry in this passage is as follows: since there is a cause of change, a subject of it and a change, is the change in the cause of change or in the subject of it? ...[67] And he establishes this from the definition of change. For change, he says, is the *entelechy* which the changeable receives from the source of change. If, now, change is the *entelechy* of the changeable, and the *entelechy* of each thing is in that thing whose *entelechy* it is, therefore the change will occur in the changeable. And as it is the changeable that is changed, the change will occur in the subject of change, and it is there that on the whole we find potential being of which change is an actuation. But if there is also a certain actuality of the cause of change, he says, this is nevertheless nothing other than the actuation of the subject and is not in isolation from it, but has its being in it: it comes to be from the cause of change, but is there [already] in the subject of change. For there is not one actuation that comes into being from the cause of change and another that is present in the subject of change, but being one it simultaneously makes the source of change a cause of it, and the changeable a subject of change. There is thus a single actuation of both, but it is single as to the substratum, not in the account. Just as the upward and the downward are one and the same interval, but it is uphill for those beginning at one point, downhill for those beginning at another: so in the case of change, it is single as to the substratum yet not as to relation, but beginning from the cause of change is called agency, and beginning from the affected subject affection. But if it is called agency, it is obviously still observed in the affected subject (for the agent acts upon an affected subject), and all the more when it is called affection.

   Having said this, he raises a difficulty with regard to the account, and says that perhaps there is not a single actuation of both, but two. For the actuation of the agent is one thing and that of the affected thing another. And this is obvious both from their names and from their ends; for in the agent actuation is called agency, but in the affected subject it is called affection, and the function and end of agency is the action, that of affection is the affect. But when the ends of things are different, their origins also are different. So that the actuations are two and so are the changes. If, therefore, they are two, then either one will be in the cause of change and one in the subject, or else both will be in the subject. The other segment of this division he does not propose, viz. that both are in the cause of change, since the absurdity of this proposition is patent. For if both should be in the cause of change, it will follow that the cause of change possesses two changes while the subject would possess none; which is illogical. If then one is to be in each, for example the agency in the agent and the affection in the affected subject (for the converse cannot hold – I mean the affection in the agent and the agency in the affected subject – since in that case the affected subject would not be affected but act, and the agent would not act but be affected) – if, now, the agency is to be in the agent, the affection in the affected subject, it is altogether necessary that, just as the affected subject, possessing its own actua-

tion, has the change in itself, so the agent, possessing its own
actuation, should have change in itself.

If, now, the cause of change has change in itself, it will either 30
undergo change or will not undergo change. If, then, it is to undergo
change, it will follow that whatever causes change is also changed, 371,1
for every one will have its own actuation in itself (but this is patently
false; for the image works a change in the lover, bread in the starving
man and straw in the ass, and remain themselves unchanging); but
if it is not to undergo change, there will be something possessing
change that is not changed, and that is unreasonable. If, on the other 5
hand, both the actuations were in what suffers change and is affected,
first it is absurd that the actuation of one thing should be in another,
then (he says) it will follow that two actuations differing in form will
lead to one and the same end, which is impossible. For there is no
impossibility in the occurrence of two changes which are different in
form and lead to different forms (for the same thing may undergo
change of position and mutation, or increase or learning), but it is 10
impossible for two changes differing with respect to form to lead to
one and the same form. For either (a) the two changes, proceeding
from different origins, will lead to one and the same termination or
(b) they will proceed to the same termination from the same origin.
If, then, (a) they proceed from different principles, since these will be
contrary (all alteration being from one contrary to another), it will
follow that two things are contrary to the same, which is absurd, since 15
one thing always has one contrary. And if (b) they proceed from the
same principle, alterations from the same origin to the same end
always take place through the same intermediaries (as the alteration
from blackness to white always takes place through the medium of
grey, and the alteration from water to air through the medium of
steam, and so in every case), so that it is impossible for two different
changes to lead from the same origin to the same end. It is therefore 20
impossible to posit two actuations, either where one is in one and one
in the other, or where both are in one.

Perhaps, then, he says, a single actuation comes from both – I mean
from the cause of change and from the subject of change – but certain
absurdities follow on this proposition too. For first, he says, the very
notion that two things which differ in form should have the same
actuation is an absurd one (for just as there is not one and the same 25
actuation of what is whitened and what is warmed, so it is plausible
that there should not be the same actuation of the agent and the
affected subject); then, he says, if there is to be a single actuation of
both, then also learning will be the same thing as teaching and still
more generally agency will be the same thing as affection, for these
too are actuations. If this is so, then also agency is the same thing as 30
affection, and this is to become actual in respect of the actuation (for

whenever I say 'whitening' or 'teaching', I speak of the actuation itself,
while whenever I say 'to whiten' or 'to teach', I mean strictly 'to be
372,1 changed' and 'to be actual' with respect to the actuation or the
change); then since the actuation is one and the same, it will also be
one and the same thing to be actual in respect of it. But if this is so,
then the actuating subject will also be one and the same; therefore
the one who teaches will be the same as the one who learns, and
5   therefore it will follow that the teacher learns in so far as he teaches,
and the agent is affected [in so far as he acts], which is absurd.

And there is something else which he himself does not add in
[discussion of] this difficulty, as having already posited it in [discus-
sion of] the former proposition which suggested that there were two
actuations; none the less, as though he had also posited this absurdity, he dissolves it in giving his solution. For in which one will this
single actuation occur, since it must occur in the cause of change or
10   in the subject of change? But it is unreasonable that it should occur
in the cause of change (for then the subject of change will not possess
change, and how can it be changed if it does not possess change?); if,
on the other hand, it is in the subject of change, it is again absurd
that the actuation of one thing should be in another, rather than that
the actuation of each should be in each.

Having thus expressed a difficulty with regard to the account, he
15   proceeds to dissolve it, and with regard to the proposition that there
are two actualities and the absurdities that follow from this, he says
nothing, since the proposition is not true, and the absurdities that
follow are a refutation and not a difficulty; but the absurdities that
follow from the other proposition, which states that there is one
actuation of both, he dissolves, because this proposition also appears
20   to him to be true. In the first place, he dissolves the objection that the
actuation of the one occurs in the other, which he posited in the
[discussion of] the difficulty as following on the former proposition –
the one stating that there were two actuations and these in the
subject of change – though in the solution he dissolves it as though it
followed on the one which states that there is one actuation occurring
in the subject of change. For, as I have said, he says nothing with
25   regard to the objection refuting the proposition that there are two
actuations, since the proposition does not seem true to him.

He says, then that it is no absurdity that the actuation of the one
should occur in the other, that indeed this is necessary in the case of
related terms. And we have it as an initial proposition that the cause
of change and the subject of change are related terms. At any rate,
30   the actuality of the father is nowhere else than in the son; for the
actuality of the father is not in isolation from the son, but has its
existence in him, beginning from the father but taking shape in the
son.[68] In the same way, the actuality of what whitens is nowhere else

than in what is whitened, and that of him who teaches is in him who learns, and generally that of the agent is in the affected subject. For there is no other affection of the affected subject than the action of the agent. For when the agent actuates, the affected subject is simultaneously affected. If, now, the action of the agent is the affection of the affected subject, and the affection of the affected subject is in the affected subject (for the affect is in the affected), then the action of the agent is in the affected subject. This is a syllogism of the first figure.[69] So that if agency is the actuation of the agent, and is itself in the affected subject, it is necessary in the case of related terms that the actuation of each occurs in the other.

And regarding the second absurdity, which says that it will follow that there will be a single actuation of two things which are different in form, he says that in some cases even this is not absurd; I mean in the case of relations when one exists potentially and the other actually with respect to this potentiality, but their actuation is one in the substratum though not in the account. For it is a single whitening process which the source of whiteness effects and the whitened object suffers, and it is a single theorem that the teacher teaches and the learner learns. And it is a single teaching of the theorem that the teacher imparts and the learner receives. For teaching is nothing else than learning from the teacher. And likewise it is with learning.

But, while they are identical as to the substratum, they are not so as to the account, just as with the upward and downward journey and 'the road from Thebes to Athens and the road from Athens to Thebes'.[70] For in these cases there is a single distance, up from below and down from above, but the accounts are not alike. For if one begins in one place it is an upward, if in another place a downward [journey]. And so then in the case of the agent and the affected subject, there is one actuation of both, but beginning from one place it is called agency, and beginning from the other affection; beginning from one place, teaching, and beginning from the other, learning. And this is a reasonable consequence, since the agent's act has no other result than what the affected subject is potentially. Therefore the actuation of the agent is itself the actuation of the potentiality of the affected subject. Therefore the actuation of both with respect to the substratum is single, differing only in relation.

And with regard to the final absurdity, which states that if there is a single actuation of both, then also teaching is the same as learning, and if this is so, then also the one who teaches is the same as the one who learns – in response to this he says that it is not necessarily true that, if learning were the same as teaching, to teach and to learn would *ipso facto* be the same thing and the teacher the same as the learner. For if teaching and learning were the same in

373,1

5

10

15

20

25

30

374,1

every respect, like a cape and a cloak,[71] what has been said would
necessarily follow in fact; but since they are not the same in all
respects, but the same as to the substratum and different as to the
account, it is not necessary that the teacher be the same as the learner
or teaching the same as learning.

While the upward and downward journeys are the same as to their
substratum, to go up and to go down are not the same, nor is the one
who goes up the same as the one who comes down; nor, because there
is a single distance from Athens to Thebes and from Thebes to Athens,
does it by any means follow immediately that to go from Athens to
Thebes is the same as to go from Thebes to Athens, or that the one
who comes from Thebes to Athens is the same as the one who goes
from Thebes to Athens. Just so, then, even if teaching is the same as
learning, it is necessary neither that to learn should be the same as
to teach nor that the one who teaches should be the same as the one
who learns. For it is not at all properly and in all respects that
teaching is the same as learning, but only as to the substratum. So
that, if teaching and learning are not the same in all respects, neither
is to teach the same as to learn, nor the one who teaches the same as
the one who learns.

For first he conceded that teaching is the same as learning, and
then he showed the inference to be false – I mean that to teach is the
same as to learn and the one who teaches the same as the one who
learns – and finally he has not conceded even the original [postulate],
saying that even teaching and learning are not the same. For they
are not the same in definition, but only as to the substratum. So that
there is no absurdity in there being a single actuation of both,
proceeding from the agent but subsisting in the affected subject; so
that if (a) the actuation of the changeable is a change, being identical
with that of the source of change; (b) this actuation is engendered in
the changeable by the source of change; and (c) the changeable is the
subject of change: then change is in the subject of change and not in
the cause of change.

'And the [solution to the] difficulty is manifest.' For the difficulty
was whether change is in the cause of change or in the subject or in
both.

202a14 For it is the *entelechy* of this from the cause of change.

Because it is shown in the definition of change that the change is in
the subject of change and not in the cause of change: for, he says, the
change is an *entelechy* of the changeable from the source of change.
And now he gives the definition of change more completely; for he
brings in also the cause of the actuation. For, he says, 'it is the
entelechy of this from the cause of change'. For the previous definition,

which said that 'it is the *entelechy* of the changeable, in so far as it changeable', does not say what gives rise to the *entelechy*, but the present one makes this apparent also. 'And the actuation of the source of change is nothing else.' For if change is the *entelechy* of the changeable proceeding from the source of change, the actuation of the source of change is not a different one from that of the changeable, but is one and the same, completing the substratum – I mean the subject of change – but proceeding from the cause of change. For this is the actuation of the source of change, to change the changeable, and to change the changeable is the same thing as it is for the subject to be changed. 10

202a15 For there has to be an *entelechy* of both [for it is the source of change through having the potential, the cause by actuation].

Since he has said that 'the actuation of the source of change is nothing else', for this reason he has said that his meaning is not that each of them does not have a certain actuation, for they must. And that the subject of change has an actuation is thoroughly obvious; that the cause of change also has a certain actuation, however, he establishes. 'For it is,' he says, 'the source of change through having the potential, the cause by actuation.' If the cause of change, he says, at times only has the potential to cause a change, but at others is actual in respect of this, it is obvious that the cause of change also has a certain actuation, in respect of which, from being potentially a source of change, it becomes a cause of change in actuality. 15 20

202a17 But it is the actuating principle of the changeable, so that likewise there is a single actuation of both [just as there is the same interval between one and two as between two and one, and so too with the uphill and the downhill].

If the cause of change too is actual, he says, yet it is actual in no other way whatsoever than in the changeable thing itself, in as much as the changeable also is changed in actuality. So that if (a) it is actual in the changeable, and (b) the actuation of the source of change is what the change of the changeable is, then there will be a single actuation of both. And that it is not surprising for there to be one and the same actuation of two things which differ only in relation he confirms by the examples. 'Just as,' he says, 'there is the same interval between one and two as between two and one.' For this is one and the same thing in respect of the substratum. For what is the difference between a change from two to one and a change from one to two? That is, to say what ratio two has to one does not differ from 25 30

376,1   saying what ratio one has to two, excepting only in the relation, while
        as to the substratum they are one and the same. But if there is one
        interval, it is the relations then that differ. For two has to one the
        ratio of being double, while one has to two the ratio of being half.
        Likewise, the upward and downward are different relations, while
  5   the distance is single.

> **202a21** But it involves a logical difficulty [for there will be two
> actualities, action and affection, producing an act and an affect].

        By 'logical' he means one worthy of logical scrutiny, as being persua-
        sive and worthy to receive a logical scrutiny and a solution.[72] What
        then is the difficulty? That perhaps it was not correct for him to say
        that there is one actuation of both, but there has to be a specific
  10   actuation of each, which is something different from the actuation of
        the other, as is obvious from the fact that different names are
        assigned to the actuation of each (for one is agency, the other affec-
        tion), and the results also are diffferent. For the end of agency is an
        action, that of affection is an affect. If, now, both the names and the
        ends of the actuations differ, they themselves also presumably differ
  15   from one another.

> **202a25** So then if both are changes, if they are different, in what
> do they occur? {Either, says Aristotle, they are both in the same
> thing, or the activity is in the agent and the affection in the
> affected. Philoponus in this comment anticipates the assertion
> at 202a36 that there will be a single actuation.}

        If there are two actuations, he says, either both are changes or one
        change comes from both. Now if they are both changes, either one is
  20   in the cause of change and one in the subject of change, or both are
        in the subject of change. For, as I have said, he does not even propose
        that both are in the cause of change. It was possible for him to make
        the following division: if there are two actuations, then either both
        are changes and differ from one another, or one change comes from
        both, or one actuation is change but the other is not change. Yet he
        does not even propose the third, I mean that one is change and one
  25   is not. I say then that in no way does the [statement of the] difficulty
        posit actuation as anything other than change, but it says that
        actuation and change are the same thing, so that in this way the
        difficulty may be more persuasive. His division, then, proceeds in the
        following manner: there being both a cause and a subject of change,
        either there are two actuations of these and two changes (for actua-
  30   tion and change are the same), or the actuation and change of both
377,1   is one thing. And that the [statement of the] difficulty makes actua-

tion and change identical is obvious from the fact that here, having said 'if then both are changes', he says in the remaining limb of the division 'but there will be a single actuation', taking actuation as identical with change.

202a27 But if this [sc. affection] also should be called agency, then it would be a homonym.

Since he has established from the difference of names that there are   5
two actuations, as one is called agency and one affection, he does not wish anyone to say: 'I do not give different names to the actuation of the agent and the affected subject, so that I should be forced to call the actuations also by two names; for it makes no difference to me if I also call the actuation of the affected subject agency, since it is one and the same as the actuation of the agent.' In order to prevent this,   10
and because the word *pathêsis* (affection) is not found at all in the usage of the Greeks, he therefore replies to this point that even if one calls the actuations of both things by the same names, they will obviously not be synonymous but homonymous.[73] For the actuation of the affected subject would certainly not receive the definition of the agent's actuation, since that will also make the agent an affected   15
subject and the affected subject an agent. So that along with these the natures of the actuations are also distinguished, even if you should call the actuations of both by one and the same name.

202a28 And yet, if this is so, the change will be in the cause of change. {Aristotle here draws an inference from his supposition of two actuations, arguing further that the same account applies to cause and subject of change, and concluding that either the cause will be changed or will possess change without being changed.}

If, he says, there are two changes, one of which will be in the cause and one in the subject of change, just as change occurs in the subject,   20
so there will also be a change in the cause. For just as the subject of change has a change in itself, viz. its own actuation, so will the cause of change also have a change in itself, viz. its own actuation; for the same account applies to each. But if there is a change in the cause of change, then either it will undergo change or it will not undergo change. If then it undergoes change, it is necessary that all that causes change should *ipso facto* suffer change, which is false (for the   25
object of desire does not suffer change when it works a change, nor does the Prime Mover[74] suffer change, as he will show in the eighth book); if, on the other hand, it does not undergo change, it is absurd that something should possess change without undergoing change.

378,1 **202a31** But if both are in what suffers change and is affected {then, Aristotle continues, both the agent and the affected subject will undergo two changes, which is absurd}.

Having proposed that there is one change in the cause of change and one in the subject of it, he now proposes that both the changes are in the subject of change. It will therefore follow, he says, that teaching

5 and learning, and agency and affection, will be in one and the same, the subject of change. But if this is so, then (a) it will be absurd that the actuation of one should be in the other; and (b) it will follow that two actuations differing in form lead to one and the same end, which is impossible. For two mutations would never be able to lead to one and the same form, as for example that both whitening and warming

10 [should lead] to whiteness. For if different changes led from different origins to the same end, then: (a) it is absurd that one thing should have two opposites (for alteration is never from a casual origin, but always from the contrary), and (b) change from the same origin to the same end always takes place through the same intermediaries; for motion from Thebes to Athens is always through the same intermediaries, such as mountains, inns and the like.

Yet someone might raise the following difficulties with regard to the discussion: (a) a person might move between the same places

15 without going through the same intermediaries; (b) it is not impossible for changes of different origins to have the same end. For there are two ends to the diameter of the circle, and a person might move from one end to the other either by way of the diameter or by way of the semi-circle. So that there has been movement from the same point to the same point by different motions, I mean the circular and the

20 straight. And a person might move in the middle of the air and reach the same point in the air either from the ground or from the heavens.

My reply to the first difficulty is that, in the first place, the discussion is now of natural changes, not of those that are from the soul,[75] and it is impossible in the case of natural motions for what moves by the straight way also to move by the circular one. And if the

25 fiery sphere and the continuum of air are moved together with the universe, yet this is not natural but preternatural,[76] just as also the bodies of animals, being heavy by nature, are moved sideways by a change coming not from nature, but from the soul. It is therefore impossible for one and the same subject of a natural movement to suffer it both by the straight and the circular route. For it is impos-

30 sible for fire to reach the upper place otherwise than by the straight way, and even then the origin and end of its motion must be perpendicular or parallel. And if the ant can move between the same points by way of both the diameter and the circumference, this would not

379,1 entail two different forms of change, but only a longer and a shorter route. Just as, if a person changes from black to white, the mutation is now in a longer, now in a shorter time, either gradual and slow or swift and sudden: so here too, I say, if a circle is drawn on a plane and one moves to the same point by way of the diameter and another by way of the circumference, to arrive at the same point, they have not suffered two different forms of motion but both have suffered a sideways motion. It is also this way at least in the case of one who goes round the perimeter of the earth: he would not be said to suffer a rotatory motion, for then all creatures would be said to suffer a rotatory motion (for they move on the circumference of the earth's surface) and the soul would no longer be said to cause a sideways motion. And how would they differ, on this principle, from things that move in a circle? Thus these are not different forms of change, for they both arise from a single potentiality and they differ only in the magnitude of the distance travelled.

But neither does the conclusion of the syllogisms refute the account – I mean the fact that the same conclusion can be established in several ways (for the same thing is shown both directly and by means of an impossible instance, and by the direct method you are to gather the same conclusion through various premises, both true and false, as he himself has observed in his earlier remarks). On the contrary, it is obvious that syllogisms are not natural changes, but logical methods, and the discussion concerns natural changes. So much, then, regarding the first difficulty. As to the second, I say that it really is impossible to reach one and the same natural terminus from different origins. For the place between the earth and the heavens is not the terminus either of the light or of the heavy, but is the route which the light and heavy take, since the route is through the same intermediaries even when the origins and ends are contrary, as, for example, the alteration from white to black and that from black to white go through the same intermediaries, such as grey and other intermediate colours.

202a36 But [the objection is that] there will be one actuation, yet it is unreasonable that there should be the same actuation of things different in form.

He turns to the other proposition, which states that there is one and the same actuation of the cause and the subject of change. Must one not surely therefore, he says, propose a single actuation of the agent and the affected subject? But this is unreasonable, to propose a single actuation of two things that differ in form.

202b2 And if indeed teaching and learning are the same thing,
5   and so are action and affection, then it will be the same thing to
teach and to learn.

These four things are in order, 'the one who teaches', 'the teaching',
'to teach', 'the tuition'. And the tuition is the end to which the teaching
process leads (as with the building, that is the house, so the tuition
itself is the theorem which is implanted in the soul), while 'to teach'
10   and 'teaching' appear to be the same thing, yet are not properly the
same, but differ from one another. For the word 'teaching' indicates
the change – the actuation, in itself – whereas the term 'to teach'
indicates the relation of the teacher's actuation to the learner. As,
then, the terms 'change' and 'to change' stand to one another, so do
'to teach' and 'teaching', and so *simpliciter* do 'agency' and 'to act'.
15   He says, therefore, if there is a single actuation of the two – I mean
the one who teaches and the one who is taught, and *simpliciter* of the
agent and the affected subject – then obviously teaching would be the
same as learning and more generally agency would be the same as
affection. But if these are identical with one another, those next in
order after them will also be so, I mean to teach will be the same as
to learn and it will follow that the one who teaches will, in as much
20   as he teaches, be learning, and the agent, in as much as he acts, will
be affected. But this is absurd. Moreover, if this single actuation
should be in the cause of change, it will follow that the subject of
change possesses no change, while if it is in the subject of change, the
actuation of one thing will be in another.

202b5 Or else it is not absurd that the actuation of one should
be in the other.

25   Here he dissolves the difficulties, and, for the time being, the first,
which says that the actuation of one thing will be in another; and he
says that there is nothing absurd in this, that in certain cases the
actuation of one thing should be in another. For thus it is in the case
of all relations. And it will seem that he offers this solution with
381,1   regard to the former proposition, I mean the proposition that although there are two actuations they are both in the subject of change
(for it was from this proposition, he said, that it followed that the
actuation of one was in another), but it is more reasonable, as we said,
that it should be taken to follow it and the proposition that there is
5   a single actuation, and this in the subject of change. For he does not
think that there is any truth at all in the proposition that there are
two actuations, so as to answer the difficulties raised against this
also.

202b6-7 [for teaching is the actuation of the teacher] yet in someone, and not in isolation, but the actuation of the one in the other.

For the actuation of the teacher does not occur in isolation from the learner, but it proceeds from him while coming to be in the learner. The actuation of the teacher must not, however, be thought of as simply the application of the theorems (for even when he is not teaching but by himself he handles the theorems), but the change which occurs in the soul of the learner as a result of the theorems. It is granted that if the teacher speaks in the presence of the learner, but does not work upon the learner, he is not said to be teaching; teaching, therefore, is not simply the application of the theorems, but the persuasion which the words of the teacher bring about in the learner, which same thing in another relation is called learning whenever we start from the learner and progress to the teacher. And to put the case simply, whenever we go up from the caused to the cause, it is an affection, and whenever we do the converse, it is an action.

202b8 Nor does anything prevent there being one and the same [actuation] of two things [continued at 202b10].

He dissolves the second absurdity. Nothing, he says, prevents there being a single actuation of two things different in form, but it is one as to the substratum, two in the account.

202b9 [(not in the sense of being the same] but as what is in potentiality stands to what actuates)

Now what he means to say is this: nothing prevents there being one actuation of two things that differ in form, yet not in all respects, but just as the potential and actual are one thing (for the potential teacher of grammar, when he has become a teacher of grammar in actuality, is one and the same as to his substratum, but not one in his account and definition, for I define him in one way as a potential teacher of grammar and in another as an actual one; and thus I say that it is possible for there to be one actuation of two): either, then, he means this or, as we said before, he means by this that there can be one and the same actuation of those things that differ in form, as in the case of those with potential being and those which have actual being according to that potentiality and which lead it to actuality. And such things are, to speak generally, the active and the affected.

10   **202b10** Nor is it necessary that the one who teaches learns, even
        if to act and to be affected are the same thing. {Aristotle explains
        that they are the same thing, not as synonyms (the cloak and
        the cape), but as the road from Thebes to Athens is that from
        Athens to Thebes.}

He has turned to the other [charge of] absurdity. For this was as
follows: if there is one actuality of two things, since the actuation of
one party is called teaching and that of the other learning, then
teaching will be the same as learning. But if this is so, then the next
15   terms in the order are the same, viz. 'to teach' and 'to learn'. But if
this is so, then it will follow that everyone who teaches is learning.
Now Aristotle himself has used the analytic solution, beginning from
the posterior and reverting to the prior.[77] For it is not necessary, he
says, that if to teach were the same as to learn the one who teaches
would also be learning in the very act of teaching, so long as to teach
20   and to learn were not identical in such a way that the identity held
both of the substratum and of the account. And if they are not
identical in this way, but as the road from Athens to Thebes is with
that from Thebes to Athens, [the alleged result] is not necessary.

        202b14 For things are not all identical with whatever is identi-
        cal with them in any respect, but only with those whose being
        is identical.

25   It is not necessary, he says, that if certain things are said to be
identical in some respect, the identity holds of all properties and
consequences; but those things are in all respects identical whose
definition is the same. And at this point we say that to teach is the
same as to learn, not in definition (for in this respect they are
383,1 different), but in respect of the substratum. So that it is not necessary,
if they were identical in this way, that one who teaches should *ipso
facto* learn as well.

        202b16 But even if teaching and learning are the same, it does
        not follow that to learn and to teach are the same as well {just
        as, Aristotle adds, if two places are equidistant, the distance
        from one to the other is not the same as the converse}.

5   Retracing his steps, as I have said, he has first shown that it is not
necessary, if to teach is the same as to learn, that he who teaches
should *ipso facto* learn, and since the [charge of] difficulty inferred
that to teach was the same as to learn from the belief that teaching
is the same as learning, he now says that even this does not follow of
10   necessity. For consider that the distance from Thebes to Athens is

one and the same as that from Athens to Thebes, and yet it is not the same to travel thither from here and hither from there. Likewise, then, even when teaching is the same as learning, it is not *ipso facto* necessary that to learn is the same as to teach.

202b19 And to speak comprehensively, neither is it teaching and learning that are properly identical, nor is it agency and affection, but that in which these inhere, viz. the change.   15

Since what follows was deduced from the proposition that teaching is the same as learning, he has first agreed that teaching is the same as learning and shown that it is not necessary that to teach is the same as to learn, but that, even if these things are the same, it is not   20
necessary that he who teaches should *ipso facto* learn as well. Now, however, he says that teaching and learning are not on the whole identical, but what is the same is that in which teaching and learning inhere as a substratum. Just as it is not ascent and descent that are the same, but the ladder in which they inhere, or rather the change itself, I mean the very walking and translation of the feet (for that is   25
the same in the full sense, since it receives one and the same definition), but the ascent and the descent, which inhere in a change of this kind as in a substratum, are not the same in a full sense. For the definitions of these are different. '... but that in which these inhere, the change.' He says that change is the very alteration that occurs in the learner as a result of the teaching process; for this is one   384,1
and the same, and when referred to the teacher it is called teaching and, when referred to the learner, learning.

202b21 For the actuation of one thing in another, and the actuation of one thing by another, are different in account.

That learning is different from teaching he shows by the definition.   5
For we shall define in different ways, he says, the actuation of one thing in another, i.e. that of the agent in the affected subject, and that of one thing by another, i.e. that of the affected subject brought about by the agent. The former we shall perhaps define as 'the *entelechy* of the source of change which completes the changeable', the other in the same manner as 'the *entelechy* of the changeable caused by the   10
source of change'.

   This, then, is what is found in Aristotle, but someone may perhaps inquire if the account that locates change only in the subject of change and not at all in the cause of it is true of every cause and subject of change. And in the case of mutation or increase it really is the affected subject and not the agent that undergoes change (for what becomes white is not what whitens but what is whitened, and what increases   15 is not what causes increase but what suffers it, that is, not the agent but the affected subject), but in the case of change in place, where certain causes of change suffer change while causing it, the account will not seem to apply. For if the heavens move the fiery sphere by

20 being moved,[78] how could I deny that the cause of motion, in so far as it moves, is also moved itself, and that the changes also are two, one of the cause of motion and one of the subject? And there is one motion in the heavens, another according to which things here are moved when they suffer mutation of one sort or another as a result of the motion in the heavens. So that there are two actuations and two motions, not only in the definition but also as to the substratum. And

25 while the fiery sphere undergoes the same motion as the cause of its motion (just as when I move my cloak undergoes the same motion with me), not only do the neighbouring regions undergo this change when the heavens move, but all things in common undergo the commutative change. For the sun's change in place just in as much as it changes place, is the cause of one mutation or another in things here.

30 But regarding this difficulty, I briefly say here that Aristotle does not say that none of the causes of change cause change by undergoing it (he did at least say clearly that all things natural are such as not to be able to cause a change except by suffering change themselves); but that the power of change imparted by the cause to the subject of change,[79] I mean the force and actuation in respect of which it is

35 changed, as being changeable in potential and completed by an
385,1 actuation of this sort – this power, while being one and the same, proceeds originally from the cause of change, but has its end, its termination and (as it were) its permanence in the subject. For when it has occurred in what has potential being, it does not abandon it, but, as it were, remains in it and completes it, and the completion is the exercise of the power, and this is change.

5 For the man of understanding advances his theorems even if there is no one to learn, but when they are advanced within the learner and work upon him, I say that this working power by which he is affected is one and the same, having originated in the teacher but come to be in the learner, and having changed him and completed what is in him

10 potentially, which is obviously in the subject and not in the cause of change. For the cause of change did not suffer change in respect of it.

202b23 Thus what change is has been stated both in general and in particular. {It is not unclear, Aristotle continues, how each form will be defined; mutation is the *entelechy* of the mutable in so far as it is mutable.}

For first he defined change as 'the *entelechy* of what is potentially, in

so far as it is such'. Since potential being is also understood to belong   15
to the state of possession, he said, defining it more accurately, 'the
entelechy of what is changeable, in so far as it is changeable'. Speaking
generally, therefore, he says, this is the definition of change, and from
this it is obvious how each of the forms of change will be defined. For
we shall say that mutation is the *entelechy* of the mutable in so far
as it is mutable, and growth that of what can grow in so far as it can   20
grow, and locomotion that of the spatially movable in so far as it is
spatially movable.

But, when he said, 'we have said what change is both in general
and in particular', since he has in no wise stated the defining properties of particular changes, but has spoken as though it were in our
power to apply the general definition to particular cases, he therefore
added: 'For it is not unclear how each of the species of it will be
defined', because the conjunction 'for' is the giving of a reason. This   25
was the reason, he means, for my saying 'and in particular'; that from
the general definition of change which has been given it will be clear
to us also how each of the species of change will be defined.

202b26 Still more intelligibly, [change is the *entelechy*] of the   386,1
potentially active and the potential subject of affection, in so far
as they are such, both *simpliciter* and again in each case.
{Aristotle adds the examples of building and healing.}

It is possible, he says, to make the account of change still clearer and
more intelligible from what has been said: it is the *entelechy* of the
potentially active with regard to what can be affected (for this is
change, the *entelechy* of what can be active with regard to what can   5
be affected), or, as he has said a little earlier, the *entelechy* of the
changeable which comes from the source of change. This definition,
he says, will apply also to changes individually and not only formally.
For he says that building is the *entelechy* of the building capacity and
of the buildable, in so far as they are such, and so in the other cases.   10
And this definition also indicates that there is one actuation of the
cause and the subject of change, for it was on this account that he
also defined it thus. For if it is the *entelechy* of the potentially active
and the potential subject of affection, then there is a single actuation
of both.

202b30 But since the science of nature has to do with magnitudes and change and time {we must, says Aristotle, consider   15
the unlimited. He quotes the Pythagoreans, and at 203a15
Plato, with whom Philoponus ends this comment.}

We have said from the beginning of this book that the philosopher is discussing two terms, 'change' and 'unlimited', as he does in the next [book] with 'time', 'place' and 'void'. And therefore, having finished the account of change, and having said what it is and in what things

20   it is observed and how many forms of change there are, he proposes from this point on to discuss the unlimited. And the practice which he has followed regarding nearly every thesis he also follows here: first he shows that the discussion of the present problem is necessary to the study of the whole matter. And here (as he is about to discuss with regard to the unlimited whether or not it exists, and if it exists,

25   whether it is an essence or an accident and in what things it is observed and in what things it has its being) he first shows that an account of the unlimited is necessary to the physicist, in order to make those who desire proficiency in the study of nature more eager to acquire it.

That the account of the unlimited is necessary to the physicist he therefore shows in two ways: first, from the fact that all the objects

30   in the domain of the physicist are assigned by division either to the unlimited or to the limited, and then from the fact that all those who

387,1 have been in any way eminent in philosophy have not only formed opinions about the unlimited, but have proposed it as the origin of all existent things.

What then are the objects in the domain of the physicist of which he is giving his account? Magnitudes, he says, and change and time.

5   For it is these that all the physicists discuss. But it is altogether necessary that all these be either limited or unlimited, magnitudes in the same degree as change and time. For this inquiry is usually made in the case of each of these. So that if the physicist wishes to know these things, and these admit division into the unlimited and the limited, it is therefore impossible for a person to know these

10   accurately if he does not know generally speaking what the unlimited is, and first indeed whether generally speaking it exists or not. And a token that we are right to pursue the account of the unlimited in the study of physics is that all who have addressed the study of nature with any distinction not only say that the unlimited exists, but also propose it as the origin of all existent things.

15   Yet there is the greatest difference of opinion among them about the unlimited, both in common and specifically. For the physicists themselves all posit the unlimited as an origin, yet not as an origin in itself, but accidentally. For they say that some other thing is the origin in itself, such as air or fire or one of the other [elements], or all of these, or some, or their intermediate stuff, but that to be unlimited

20   belongs to this accidentally. So that water or air or their intermediate stuff happens to be an origin, but because it belongs accidentally to air or water to be unlimited in magnitude, for this reason the unlimited is described as an origin. But Plato and the Pythagoreans,

he says, propose that the origin in itself also is the unlimited, not
saying that some earth or air or fire or some other body is unlimited,   25
but that there is a certain peculiar essence of the unlimited which
essentially consists in the very fact of its being unlimited, and that
this is the origin and cause of all existent things.

But Plato and the Pythagoreans differ from one another; for while
the Pythagoreans say that the unlimited is a number,[80] and not a
separable or incorporeal number, but some object of perception and
an element and an origin of the objects of perception (for they derive   30
all the objects of perception from numbers as if these were their
origins, and proceed to say 'everything resembles number', and [the   388,1
Pythagoreans] say that the tetractys[81] is the source of nature); they
add that not only is the unlimited in the objects of perception, but
also what is outside the heavens is unlimited, yet they do not define
the quality of this or the purpose for which it is useful. Plato, on the
other hand, also states as his own view that the unlimited is an object 5
of perception and the origin of all the objects of perception, but states
that outside the heavens there is nothing whatsoever, whether a body
or an incorporeal thing,[82] while the unlimited, however, is not only
in the objects of perception but also in the Ideas, the Ideas being
neither within the heavens nor outside them.[83] And, whereas the
Pythagoreans say that the unlimited is the even, Plato says that the   10
unlimited is two, which he calls great and small.[84]

Thus Plato and the Pythagoreans differ from the physicists in that
the former propose the unlimited as an essence, the physicists as
something accidental to the essence, and for this reason they propose
the unlimited as an origin in itself, the physicists [as an origin]
accidentally. And it follows for the Pythagoreans and for Plato that   15
the part of the unlimited is also unlimited,[85] since they say that the
unlimited is a peculiar essence[86] (thus, just as the part of essence is
essence, so the part of the unlimited is unlimited), while for the
physicists the part of the unlimited is no longer unlimited. For it is
on the whole of either air or water that the unlimited supervenes as
an accident, and not on the part.[87]

There is also the greatest difference among the physicists themselves. For all the physicists in common posit the unlimited in   20
magnitude or in amount, and they all divide them into these two
classes (for some posit it in magnitude, some in amount); but how
they differ with regard to each other we shall see as we pursue the
text.

Now it must be understood that, as the Pythagoreans were accustomed to express their teachings symbolically using numbers, so it   25
was also symbolically that they put the unlimited among the origins.
And that this is the case it is possible to gather from the words of
Aristotle himself:[88] for, he says, they held the unlimited to be the

even, just as the odd was therefore the limit, and that all things were
thus composed from limit and limitlessness. Therefore, just as they
said that all the numbers up to the decad were each symbols of
30   different things (for they called five 'justice' because it divides halfway
389,1 the numbers up to ten, and six 'marriage' because it is arrived at by
multiplying two (the first even number) and three (the first odd one)
with each other, and the even is analogous to the female, the odd to
the male, six being therefore called 'marriage' because it is born of
the combination of these; and they made other numbers the symbols
5   of certain other things) – just as, then, they made each number a
symbol of different things, they did likewise with their functions and
they made the even a symbol of matter, the odd of form, from the
combination of which the things are born.[89]

And they likened the even to matter, because, just as the even
10   comes from division and the odd from the indivisible, in the same way
matter is the cause of division and indefiniteness, form of limit and
definition. It was for this reason, then, that they said that the even
was unlimited: that the even is the cause of division without limit.
For bisection causes the unlimited dissection of magnitudes. Matter
too is unlimited, since in magnitudes and in all things natural this is
15   the cause of separation and indefiniteness and of dissection without
limit and of multiplicity. And that Plato, as a Pythagorean,[90] said
that matter was unlimited, Aristotle says in the text itself: for he says,
'Plato says that the things unlimited are two, the great and the small.'
And that Plato declared matter to be the great and the small Aristotle
has clearly stated in many other places also, and especially in the
20   first book of this work,[91] and also that the monad is the form.

202b32 [These things must be either unlimited or limited] even
if not everything is either unlimited or limited.

Since he has divided the objects in the domain of the physicist into
the limited and the unlimited, but the division by privation and
possession is not universal (for only a division by contradictories
25   applies to all things existent and non-existent), for this reason he says
that all the objects in the domain of the physicist are divided into the
unlimited and the limited, even if not all that is is either unlimited
or limited. For in those things in which it is necessary that there
should be either possession or privation, the division by possession
and privation has the same scope as the division by contradictories.
390,1 [It is] just as if someone said that of men there are some who have
sight and others who are blind, he was subsuming all men, since
man's nature is such that *ipso facto* he has either sight or blindness,
and the division by privation and possession in these cases has the
same scope as that by contradictories; if, however, he said that of dogs

there are some who have sight and others who are blind, the division
has not now subsumed all dogs because of puppies. In the same way,   5
I say, since all the objects in the domain of the physicist are of such
a nature that they are *ipso facto* either unlimited or limited, he
therefore said that all the objects in the domain of the physicist are
necessarily either limited or unlimited, even if this division does not
subsume all that exists.

202b33 such as an affect or a spot; for of such things it is perhaps   10
not necessary that any should be one or other of these.

By an 'affect' he means whiteness or blackness, indeed quality simpliciter. These things, then, are neither unlimited nor limited, since
they do not even have any magnitude at all. But he added the word
'perhaps', because it is sometimes said of whiteness that it is much
or little, as has been said also in the *Categories*,[92] not in itself but   15
accidentally, because it is in a large surface. Just so, a quality might
be said to be either unlimited or limited, because the surface in which
it inheres is either limited or unlimited. And the point might be said
to be unlimited, not because it cannot be traversed, but because it has
no limit, being itself the limit, just as we also say that the circle is   20
unlimited because it has no limits, and they speak of 'a coat without
limits' when it has no seam to divide it, or:

In skein unlimited they wrap their feet[93]

The words 'one or other of these' mean 'unlimited or limited'.

202b35-6 [the physicist must ask whether, and in what sense,
the unlimited exists.] And a sign that the study is germane to
this science {is, says Aristotle, that all philosophies of nature
have made it an origin, the Pythagreans and Plato saying that
it is not an accident but an essence}.

Obviously, he means physical science. For having shown from the   25
things themselves that the discussion of the unlimited is germane to
the physicist, he now shows it also from the usage of the ancient and
distinguished philosophers.

203a6 [The Pythagoreans, on the one hand, posited it among
the perceptibles,] for they do not say that number is separable,   391,1
{and they stated, Aristotle adds, that what is outside the heavens is unlimited, whereas Plato, denying such an external body

and the locality of the Ideas, says that the unlimited, or unlimitedness, also exists in both of these}.

It was not number *simpliciter* that they stated to be unlimited, but
even number. This number, therefore, they pronounce not separable,
that is, not incorporeal or completely separated from the objects of
5 sense, but contained in them as some element. '… and that there is
something unlimited outside the heavens.' [He says this] because
they affirm that there is something unlimited outside the heavens,
either void or perhaps rather body, which they say we live by inhaling,
as Aristotle himself is also going to say.[94] By this it is obvious that
once again these statements of theirs are symbolic; for they did not
10 believe that the heavens were perforated, and that thus the unlimited, which we live by inhaling, entered into the universe from
without; but perhaps they were speaking enigmatically of the unlimited power of the demiurge, from which all things derive their being
and duration.[95] And this phrase 'outside the heavens' is to be understood as referring not to place, but to essence; that is, it signifies that
it is divorced from every corporeal substance. And Plato too, when he
15 ascribed the unlimited to the Ideas, will presumably have meant the
unlimited in respect of potentiality, in so far as they have an unlimited potential to generate things here.[96]

203a10 And the former [sc. the Pythagoreans] say that the
unlimited is the even, for this, when enclosed and limited by the
odd, imparts unlimitedness to what exists.

20 The Pythagoreans, he says, declared the unlimited to be the even.
For they declared this to be the cause of unlimitedness in what exists.
For the odd is the source of limit and definition in things (for it does
not admit division), while the even is unlimited. Therefore he says
that the even, when enclosed by the odd, is for existents the cause of
the unlimited dissection of the forms and the individuals, and of the
25 unlimited division of objects. For the odd limits and defines, while the
even is the cause of dissection without limit, as it always admits
bisection. It is therefore clear from these considerations also that by
way of the even they were speaking enigmatically of matter, by way
of the odd of form.

Seeing, then, that every form is in itself without parts and indivis-
30 ible, whenever this comes to be matter and, as it were, defines it by
392,1 enclosure: it follows that it has been partitioned into many individuals, not through itself (for the account of a man is simple, uniform
and inseparable from the essence), but on that of the matter in which
it has come to be. For this is the cause of the unlimited increase in
amount of the individuals while the form remains one and the same,

just as when a ring makes seals at different times in different wax.[97]   5
Here too, then, the cause of the unlimitedness is not the form of the
ring (for this is one and the same), but the matter, that is the wax,
which is defined by being enclosed by it, though it is itself indefinite.

203a12 And a sign of this is what occurs in the case of numbers.   10
For when the 'set-square' is added to the one one form arises,
but without it always a different one.

Here too it must be noted that Aristotle himself knew that they said
this symbolically. For as by the even, which he has stated to be limited
by the odd, they did not mean the numerically even and odd, but used
them to signify certain other things, he has added that, as a sign of   15
the aforesaid, they alleged what occurs in the case of numbers,
implying that those things of which they said that the numbers are
symbols are not numbers, even granting that the terms used were
'the odd' and 'the even', the former of which they equated with limit,
the latter with the unlimited. But they were therefore expressing
certain things enigmatically by these terms.

So much, then, on this point; but in order that we may understand   20
what is said, let us first say what the arithmeticians and geometers
call a 'set-square'. If you take a square area and divide it into four
squares, then the three squares which make a figure like the letter
gamma are called a 'set-square' by the geometers, and this 'set-
square', when added to the remaining square, increases it, as is said
in the *Categories*,[98] but does not make it into any other kind of figure.   25
For this was the reason for giving it the name 'set-square', that when
added to the square it conserves the same form. But it is not only with   393,1
the square that the set-square conserves the same form, but also with
every parallelogram. For a set-square, as the geometer defines it, is
formed in every parallelogram by any one of the parallelograms about
the diameter when added to the two complementary ones, and this   5
when added to the same form always conserves the same one.

And the arithmeticians give the name 'set-square' to all the odd
numbers for the same reason. For if, starting from the monad, you
add consecutively all the odd numbers, such as 1, 3, 5, 7, 9, 11, 13 and
so on without limit, and then make a new beginning by adding 3 to
the monad, you make a square number, viz. 4 (and the monad is also   10
a square; for one multiplied by itself makes one again); and having
then added 5 you make 9, another square; and adding 7 to this you
make 16; and adding 9 to this you make 25; and adding 11 to this you
make 36; and in this way adding the odd numbers consecutively to
those you have made, you conserve the same form, that of the square.

And they also hand down another means of generating squares –   15
even if we now digress a little from the present topic – which is called

the method by duplication, and reveals to us, not only the generation
of square numbers, but also the side on which each is constructed.
For if you pour out the whole series of numbers from the monad and
without limit, and then starting from the monad and having added
20   it to those that follow, you retrace your steps to the monad, you will
find that all the squares are generated – such as 1, 2, 3, 4, 5, 6, 7, 8,
9, 10, 11 – and so without limit. Add the monad to the dyad, and
returning add the monad, and you make the square 4; count again
from the beginning up to 3 and go all the way back to the monad, and
25   you make 9, and the number up to which you make the addition is
the one that you will find to be the side of the generated square. For
2 forms the side of 4, and likewise 3 of 9 (for we retraced our steps
after adding up to 3), and so it goes on without limit.

394,1   This then, is outside the present question, but what he says here
is as follows. The even, being unlimited, when interwoven with the
odd, becomes the cause of unlimitedness also in those things which
are generated from them, whereas the odd, because it is the source
of limit, becomes both the limit of definition and the cause of sameness in what arises from it, and a sign is what occurs in the case of
5   these countable numbers.[99] For if you start from the monad and add
all the odd numbers (which he also calls the 'set-squares') to one
another consecutively, you will always find that it is squares that are
generated (thus the odd is the cause of a certain definition and unity,
for which reason they also called it limit), but if you add the even to
the monad and in order to all, whether even or odd, you will never
10   make the same form, but you will go on generating numbers in
unlimited variety. For add the monad to the the dyad and you will
make the triangle; then add 4 to this and you will make the heptagon;
add to this 6 and you will make another form again.[100] And it is not
only when they are added to one another that the even numbers
generate indefinite and unlimited quantities, but also when added to
15   the odd ones. So it is, therefore, that the even is from unlimitedness
and the indefinite, while the odd is from definition and limit. They
were right, then, to call the even unlimited, but the text has a certain
obscurity because of its conciseness.

        'For when the set-square is added to the one one form arises, but
20   without it always a different one.' He means that when the 'set-
squares' are either added repeatedly to the one, <or else>, in the
manner which we have explained, are added to one another, it is
always one and the same form that is generated; but if they are added
'without it', i.e. are not added to one another but to the even numbers,
the same form will never be generated, as we have said. Add 2 to the
monad, then to 3, then to 5, or if you will add one of the 'set-squares'
25   repeatedly to the even numbers in order, as 3 to 2 then 4 then 6; for
by no method will any defined form be generated, but the variation

goes on without limit. We were therefore right to say that the even, when enclosed by the odd and limited, imparts unlimitedness to what exists. For it requires the interweaving to produce the form; but of unlimitedness the only cause is the even, as has been shown. 30

203a15 But Plato says that the unlimited is two, the great and the small. 395,1

The reason why there are two unlimited things, the great and the small, is that in the bisection of magnitudes one of the parts is increased without limit, while the other is diminished without limit. And the cause of this in magnitudes he declared to be matter, which 5 he called the great and small for this very reason, that it was the cause of these. For when first the form has come to be in it, it *ipso facto* possesses the difference with respect to the great and small.

203a16 But all who wrote about nature have proposed another nature for the unlimited than the aforesaid elements.

He sets the physicists against the Pythagoreans and Plato, whose 10 interest was more theological. All the physicists, then, he says, did not propose that the unlimited was an essence, but said that the unlimited was an accident and another essence underlay it, though each proposed a different one which he believed to be the origin of what exists. They therefore had it in common that they declared the unlimited to be an accident, not an essence, and for this reason said 15 that it was an origin, not in itself, but accidentally. For each alleged an origin that was different in itself, either air or water or something else, but they proposed the unlimited as an accident of the origin because of the perpetuity of generation.[101] This, then, was the common opinion of the physicists concerning the unlimited, but what their difference was with regard to one another, he proceeds to show, and to begin with [he states that] each proposed a different underlying essence for the unlimited. 20

203a18 And of those who make the elements limited none makes them unlimited.

None, he says, of those who proposed that the elements were many but limited in number, as Empedocles proposed the four elements,[102] makes either one or many unlimited in magnitude; for that would be 25 foolish and impossible. For if one should be unlimited, it will occupy the whole of space and give no room for the others to exist; while the proposition that many were unlimited would be still more absurd. For if one cannot be unlimited when the elements are many, all the more, presumably, is it impossible that many should be unlimited.

396,1   **203a19** And all who make the elements unlimited, like Anaxagoras [and Democritus].

Those, he says, who make the elements unlimited in number (now these were both Anaxagoras[103] and the followers of Democritus,[104]
5   the former saying that the [number of] homoeomeries is unlimited, and the latter the same of atoms), differ from those who proposed one element, but of unlimited magnitude (and these were those who proposed either air or water or the intermediate stuff), in that the latter made the unlimited continuous, since body is one thing, whereas the former made the unlimited consist in contact. For, letting the homoeomeries be unlimited in number, it follows that when they are in contact a body comes into being which is a single
10   thing and unlimited in extent. And he speaks of 'a seminal mixture of all the figures', because the followers of Democritus said that the atoms were unlimited, not only in number, but also in their figures.[105]

203a23 And some [sc. Anaxagoras] held that any portion was a mixture, like the all, because they saw that anything comes from anything. {Hence, says Aristotle, his belief that all things were together, since the origin of secretion was not in one but in all.}

15   Democritus and Anaxagoras differ from the other physicists in that the latter hold the unlimited to be continuous, while these men say that it consists in the contact of bodies unlimited in number, so that it followed that they begin from the numerically unlimited and end with the unlimited in magnitude; while sharing this common ground, they differ in that Anaxagoras says that things are born from one
20   another by secretion from the homoeomeries,[106] while Democritus denies that the atoms are born from one another.[107]

'And some held that any portion was a mixture, like the all, because they saw that anything comes from anything.' Now according to Aristotle, Anaxagoras, just as he said that everything was originally commingled in the whole and that there was, as it were, a single great homoeomery containing all within itself, so he also said that every-
25   thing is in each of the particulars. To this opinion, says Aristotle, he was led by seeing that everything comes from everything, and that nothing comes from what is not, nor from what is but of a different form, but like from like. So that everything was present in this flesh in actuality, and from it is secreted whatever first happens to be ready for secretion.
30   For it was from this case, he says, that he seems also to have

demonstrated that everything is in everything. For if this flesh, he   397,1
says, and this bone might come from anything and all from them,
then also anything might come from anything. So that all things come
from all, and if all comes from all, and not only is there an origin of
the separation of this bone and this flesh, but there is also an origin
of the separation of all things, therefore it seems that everything is   5
in everything before it begins to undergo separation. For if there is
an origin of the separation of all things, and everything is naturally
liable to separation from everything, therefore before the original
separation of objects, all were together. For all separation has begun
at a certain time.

And that there is an origin of all separation, he goes on to establish
as if speaking in the character of Anaxagoras, taking certain things
from his doctrine as agreed, and deducing certain others as corollaries   10
from what was implicit in them. But Aristotle would appear to be
saying something contrary here to what was said in his first account
of Anaxagoras; for there he said that mind wished to separate the
homoeomeries, but was unable to do so (whence he also said that mind
acted mindlessly in trying to do the impossible),[108] whereas here he   15
says that mind began at a certain time to separate the homoeomeries.
We say, then, that these are not contrary; for there he said with
regard to each of the particular homoeomeries that [mind] is unable
to separate each homoeomery discretely, such as that of flesh, containing nothing of any other essence in itself, whereas here he says
that the single homoeomery – unlimited in magnitude, in which all
the existents were contained and on account of which he affirmed that   20
'all were together' – was separated by mind into particular homoeomeries, not discrete, but themselves also possessing everything,
yet receiving their appearance and their name from the dominant
stuff.

203a28 For since what comes to be comes from a body of such a
kind, and there is a generation of all things [and there is one
origin of all things, but not simultaneously, this must be mind,
which moved all things from their initial state through intellec-
tion].

He wishes to establish that there is also an origin of the separation   25
of all things, and that before they were separated, all things were in
all. He therefore accepts that all that comes to be comes from its like
(for that is what he means by 'from [a body of] such a kind'), and that
there is a generation, though not at one time, but of one before
another, whichever happened to be ready for secretion. And there
must, he says, be a certain principle as the agent of generation, and   30
this, in Anaxagoras' view, is mind.[109] If, then, there is nothing

ungenerated, and mind, as the cause of generation began to separate objects from a certain origin, there is therefore an origin of the separation of all things. But indeed it is also true that everything comes from everything, and it is impossible that what comes to be

398,1 should not come from its like. Therefore it is necessary that everything should be in everything, in order that in this way everything may be secreted from everything. And before mind began the separation, nothing was separated; for there is no other cause of separation than mind. Therefore it is necessary that all were together. For if mind were the cause of the separation of the objects, but not

5 everything was naturally liable to come from everything, then there was not a time when everything was together; and if everything was naturally liable to come from everything, but mind was not the only cause of the separation, not even so was it necessary that everything should be in everything, but it was possible that the all might be divided in another way into little homoeomeries, as happens now.[110]

203a33 [Democritus denies that any primary body is from another,] but none the less, even for him, the common body is

10 one thing differing from all with respect to its parts and in figure.

Democritus, he says, affirms that the primary bodies (I mean the atoms) are ungenerated (for none comes from another, as if the spherical were to come from the pyramidal),[111] yet he proposes one common nature of body for all figures, and the indivisible particles as

15 portions of these, differing from one another in magnitude and in figure.[112] For not only does one have one figure, one another, but among them there are some that are larger and some that are smaller.

203b4 And it is with reason that they all posit it also as an origin[113] {for it could not exist pointlessly, but must have an originative potential. It could not itself have an origin, as it would then have a limit; yet eveything is either an origin or from one. Philoponus anticipates the statement at 203b8 that it will be ungenerated and indestructible.}

Having shown that the account of the unlimited is necessary for the physicist – both because the objects in the domain of the physicist are

20 divided between the unlimited and the limited, and because all the more ancient physicists proposed not only that the unlimited exists, but also that it is an origin of what exists – he now wishes to show that it was reasonable that, when proposing the existence of the unlimited, they also proposed that it is an origin. The reason is that,

if it exists at all, it is impossible for it not to be an origin. For it is
necessary, if it exists, that it should exist either pointlessly or for the
sake of something. It does not, therefore, exist pointlessly; for things
that exist pointlessly are ephemeral, whereas the unlimited is one of   25
those things that always remain the same (for it is both indestructible
and ungenerated). It exists, therefore, not pointlessly, but for the sake
of something.

But if it exists for the sake of something, then it will either be an
origin or from an origin; for each of the existents is either an origin   399,1
or from an origin. If therefore I show that it is impossible for it to be
from an origin, what is left is to propose it as an origin. Now the term
'origin' is used in many senses; for an origin is spoken of with regard
to a magnitude, as the origin of a ship is its prow or its keel and that
of a house its foundation; and an origin is spoken of with regard to   5
time, as the origin of a war is some particular day; or an origin is
predicated of objects, both those that serve as elements, I mean the
matter and the form, and the other two, the active and the completive
[i.e. the efficient and final causes].[114] I say, then, that there is none
of the significations of the term 'origin' according to which the unlimited can have an origin.

And let us first consider the origin in respect of magnitude. For if
the unlimited has the origin in respect of magnitude, then *ipso facto*   10
it will also have a limit (for the origin is also a limit), so that it would
no longer be unlimited; for we call that unlimited which is deprived
of limit, since it is predicated in respect of the privation of limit.
Though I think it is completely obvious that it is not the same to speak
of a limit as to speak of an origin or end; for the origin [is defined] in
relation to the end, the limit not in relation to either the origin or the
end, but to that which is limited. For the limits of planes are lines,   15
and the limits of lines are points, and whereas these are limits by
nature, an origin and end do not exist by nature but by convention in
every case; for, while it is possible for me to set the origin of a line at
whatever limit I like, and the origin is as much a limit as the end, the
limit is not in the full sense, however, an origin or an end.

That, therefore, the unlimited does not have the origin in respect
of magnitude, is patently obvious; and it will be shown that it does   20
not have the origin in respect of time either, since it does not even
have that which belongs to objects. In order, then, that we may show
this, let us make this assumption: 'it is altogether necessary that
whatever is generated in substance, if it has the temporal origin, will
also have the origin that belongs to objects.' Thus, by negation with
inversion, 'all that lacks the origin which belongs to objects will
necessarily also lack the temporal origin'. If therefore we show that   25
the unlimited cannot have the origin that belongs to objects, it will
obviously not have the temporal origin either. And it has been shown

that it cannot have that which is in respect of magnitude either. In no way, therefore, will the unlimited have an origin. But it was necessary that it should either be an origin or from an origin; the unlimited can therefore only be an origin.

30　　I have used the phrase 'in substance', because things that do not come into being as substance, but in a mutating form, do not fully possess the origin that objects have, at least if alteration also happens all at once; but those which come into being in substance, if they are to possess a temporal origin, also possess that which belongs to objects. For no substance has its generation all at once, but in every case one comes before another in the stages of generation according to the substance. For first the sperm comes into being, which is the

400,1　matter of the whole creature, then the flesh from this and one stage from another consecutively; and the matter must first be worked upon and rendered workable and ready. So that it was right to say that those things which come into being in substance, if they should come into being in time, should in every case possess also the origin

5　　that belongs to objects; but it does not follow that if it possesses that which objects have, it also possesses the origin in time, as is obvious from the heavens, if indeed they are eternal. On this principle, if it does not possess the origin in time, it follows that it does not have that which belongs to objects either.

Whence, then, [comes the premiss] that the unlimited does not possess the origin that belongs to objects? For when this has been shown we have [the result] that it does not have temporal origin either. For since there are four kinds of origin, if I show that the

10　　unlimited cannot have the material or the formal one, we also have therewith a demonstration that it cannot have the final and efficient ones either. That the unlimited, then, does not have the material origin, let us show as follows: if the unlimited is to have matter, this will necessarily be either limited or unlimited. If, then, it is limited, then things composed of it will also be limited (for nothing whose

15　　matter is limited is unlimited), but if the matter is unlimited, we have [the result] that the unlimited is an origin, and that the other things come from it, not it from the others. And if anything should possess the unlimited, it will have it not in itself, but through the fact that the origin from which it has taken shape is unlimited. Therefore it is not possible that the unlimited should have a material origin; for if this should be unlimited, we have the result we are seeking, viz. that

20　　the unlimited is an origin; and if it should be limited, then what comes from it will also be limited.

But neither can it have a formal origin. For, in the first place, form is always what limits and defines objects, whereas the unlimited is indefinite; and, in the second, the form will be either unlimited or limited, and again the same results will follow. The unlimited therefore cannot possess a formal origin either. But if it is not to have these, neither will it have the efficient and final ones. For the former, if it effects anything, effects it on matter and some form. If, now, it does not possess a form or matter, neither will it have an efficient cause (and now it obvious that we are discussing the case of natural bodies, which are in all cases made from matter), and for this very reason it will not possess the final one either, because the form is [defined] in relation to the end, and the end is the same as the form with regard to the substratum, as has been said earlier. So that if it is impossible for the unlimited to have the origin that belongs to objects, neither will it have the temporal origin; it will therefore not possess any kind of origin. The remaining possibility is therefore that it is an origin.

These, then, are the facts which show that the unlimited is an origin and that it is impossible for it to have an origin. But the discussion involves a difficulty: first, what did he mean by saying that the matter of the unlimited is necessarily either limited or unlimited? For if matter must be entirely formless and without magnitude or quantity, it will obviously be neither limited nor unlimited, but will escape the division, just as it is not necessary for the point to be either limited or unlimited. For the division is not by contradictories. And how, even if matter is at all limited, will what is made from all also be limited? For it is not the case that, since matter is incorporeal and without magnitude and the forms are in themselves incorporeal and without magnitude, what is composed of them will *ipso facto* be incorporeal and without magnitude. And just as, if this perceptible body should come into being, it will come into being from what is not a body, since also everything that comes into being comes into being out of the privation of itself (for it comes from what is not such [as itself]), then in the same way also, if the unlimited is generated, whether in time or in respect of a cause, it will obviously come into being from what is not such [as itself]. So that it will come into being from what is not unlimited. But it comes into being from matter and form, since all other things do also. It is therefore not necessary that these things should be unlimited; but neither will they be limited, for the aforesaid reason.

And this difficulty [our opponents] dissolve in the following manner. There is nothing, they say, in compounds which is not also in simple entities. For even if matter is not a magnitude, at all events the form of the body, which supervenes on the matter timelessly, is such as to be the source of the presence of magnitude in the compound. And my meaning is not that the form of the body is a perceptible magnitude, but that by its proper formula magnitude is separable from matter, and the formula, when it supervenes on the matter, produces the perceptible magnitude. In the same way also, if there is some unlimited thing composed of matter and form, this unlimited-

25

30

401,1

5

10

15

20

25   ness must be in its origins; for if the origins did not contain it, that
which comes from them would not contain it either. So that even if
the proposition that the unlimited and the limited are in matter is an
impossibility, it is still necessary that they are at least in the form.

Someone will reply to this in turn that if it is necessary that all
that is in the compound should also be in the simple entities, but body
30   is divisible without limit, then either matter or the form will contain
what is divisible without limit. But the form is not divisible (at any
rate we say that the form is indivisible by its proper formula, but that
it is partitioned and separated when it comes to be in matter),[115] yet
we also say that matter itself is without magnitude and inseparable.
The divisible is therefore not in the simple entities, unless indeed
potentially. But this has nothing to do with the discussion, for the
35   discussion is now of what is actually unlimited. Again, whiteness – I
402,1   mean the whiteness in the body – divides the sight,[116] and nevertheless the form of the whiteness in itself is not like this, neither the
elemental which is not yet interwoven in matter,[117] nor that in the
demiurge. Again, man is a rational mortal animal, yet nevertheless
5   neither is the idea of man mortal, nor is his matter. And in general
we say that the forms in the demiurge are not of such a kind,[118] as
for instance that the form of the body is extended in three dimensions,
or that the form of quantity is continuous or definite, or that of man
a rational mortal creature, but [we call] them the formulae and causes
of these properties.[119]

To this they reply that in all things there is a certain essential
10   likeness both in the forms in the demiurge and in the things that
proceed from them down to matter (for the former and the latter are
not called man by simple homonymy, but as being from one origin
and related to one thing), in which there is also a certain essential
community with regard to things from which they also differ, as
healthy food differs from health. For if the demiurge is looking on
that [the form] when he produces the effects here, and yet presumably
15   the community in essence must be great (for whereas the painter,
looking on the man, does not produce the man in reality, but imitates
what is accidentally present in the body, such as the colour or
figure,[120] it is not at all the case that the demiurge likewise produces
effects here that are only simple imitations and have no community
with the forms there, but the forms are modelled essentially in these
20   effects, just as the seal also [impresses] the character which it bears
upon the wax)[121] – [if this is so] then, since the likeness between them
is according to their essence, if there is something present in the
compounds which helps to complete their essence and is so to speak
a constitutive element in the whole combination, it owes its presence
in every case to the simple entities; but, as the forms proceed from
there down to matter, since it is necessary that there should in every

case be a certain subordination of what is emitted to the source of the emission, certain things supervene upon the things that proceed that are not present in the source of emission.[122]   25

I mean something like this: the light in the air proceeds from the sun, and it is obvious that the likeness and essential community between this and the light in the sun is great (for these lights are not merely homonymous), but in the course of progression certain affections supervene upon the light that proceeds which are not in the sun,   30 such as to assume the same figure as the regions that it illuminates, to have the darkness set over against it, and innumerable others. Thus, just as here certain accidents necessarily supervene upon the light which proceeds from the sun, but this does not entail that the constitutive ingredients of its essence are not derived thence, from   403,1 the sun, so I say it is also in the case of the forms that are in matter: if the compounds possess any constitutive ingredient of their essence, they have it from the simple entities, but it is not at all impossible that certain accidents should supervene upon their progression in matter which are not present in the prototypes, such as divisibility, destructibility and all such things.

If, now, the unlimited, in so far as it is unlimited, comes to be from   5 certain origins (as, for example, the material and formal), it is altogether necessary that what is present in it essentially should be in one of the simple entities, either in matter or in the form. So that if the unlimited does not derive from matter this very property of being unlimited, it is altogether necessary that it should derive it from the form. For it [sc. being unlimited] is not simply an affect of it, but its being consists in this. But when we say that what comes   10 into being comes into being from what is not such, and that everything comes into being from its privation, the reason for our speaking thus is that what comes into being is matter and what it comes to be is the form. Now in that particular case, when we look to the separable form and its progression and the illumination that comes into being from it in matter, it is altogether necessary that like should come into being   15 from like. But when, as I have said, (a) what comes into being undergoes mutation (for generation is a sort of mutation and alteration); but (b) it is not the form that undergoes mutation but the matter that becomes ready for the reception of the form, and (c) matter is always in [the condition of] privation, for this reason it is true that what comes into being becomes such [as it is] from what is not such.

But again the argument is opposed by examples. For it is commonly agreed that the compounds arise from the commingling of the   20 four elements with each other, but it is impossible to ascribe the specific attributes which are naturally present in the compounds to the powers of the simple entities. For example, by what power of the simple entities is it that magnetic stone draws the iron, or the one

that is said to be antipathetic to this abhors and drives it away?[123]
25   And frequently both are in one part or another of the very same clod.
And there are the [numerically] unlimited powers of plants and
stones, and those of the parts of creatures too, and generally of those
things which through a certain antipathy work by contact alone. But
in reply to this again, one of the philosophers will say that not all the
powers of the compounds come, as the medical writers say, from the
30   simple entities;[124] but the mixture of the simple entities takes on the
formula of matter, and on this matter as it is mixed in one way or
another the forms supervene as a result of the whole workmanship.

So then, in saying this we have exceeded the bounds of the present
subject, and let us therefore return to the continuation of it. Aristotle,
having shown that when they proposed the existence of the unlimited
404,1   they also necessarily proposed it as an origin, asserts that it is also
ungenerated and indestructible, and this with good reason. For if it
should come into being, in every case it begins to come into being from
an origin (as flesh might chance to be first of the homoeomeries, or
the heart of the organs, or roots in the case of plants); but there is no
5   origin of the unlimited (for, as has already been said, the origin is a
limit), and if it should be destroyed, it will in every case be destroyed
up to some final point. For all things that are destroyed are destroyed
in this way, the most easily destructible undergoing destuction first,
then the less easily destructible, and finally the most difficult to
destroy, and so on until what is being destroyed arrives at some
extreme. So that it is necessary that the unlimited and indestructible
10   should also be ungenerated.

Having said this, he proceeds to state the causes which compelled
them to propose that the unlimited was in existent things, and these
are five. The first (a) is time, which increases without limit. The
second (b) results from the fact that the dissection of magnitudes has
no limit. For it has been shown that the geometers bisect every
straight line, and if this is so, it is possible to practise bisection
15   without limit. And that the dissection of magnitudes has no limit is
shown also from the fact that a [scalene] triangle has two sides
greater than the remaining one. For if you mark off from the two sides
a length equal to the [remaining] one, and from the point where you
marked off a section equal to the smaller measurement, you extend
a straight line parallel to the smaller measurement, whose equivalent
you have marked off from the [other] two, you produce a smaller
20   triangle.[125] Since the two sides of this in turn are greater than the
remaining one, if you do the same you will again produce a smaller
triangle, and this [goes on] without limit. So that the dissection of
magnitudes has no limit.

But obviously the triangle must be made a right-angled one, lest
in the other cases the marking off should produce an equilateral

triangle, and it should no longer be possible to mark off the length of one side from another. For the intersection will then no longer fall inside the triangle, and if it does not fall inside it will no longer be 25 possible to go on for ever drawing a triangle inside. But if we make the triangle right-angled, and mark off the length from the side that subtends the right angle, the division will always fall inside the triangle (for the line that subtends the right angle is always longer than either of the remaining ones), and in this way, since the triangle that is generated will always be right-angled, it is always possible to take from the hypotenuse a length equal to the smaller measurement, and thus to inscribe a triangle internally without limit. But if you 405,1 mark off from both sides together, the calculation will always be sound.

The third reason (c) for their belief in the existence of the unlimited was that there must be perpetual generation (for if there should be no unlimited stuff from which the things that come into being were taken away, then generation will cease); [they said this] because they 5 did not understand that nothing is reduced by destruction to what has no existence whatsoever, but the destruction of one thing is the generation of another and the resolution of the elements is into one another.

The fourth reason (d), he says, was their belief that whatever is limited is limited in relation to something, that is, that everything limited is limited by something; in which case what limits is also itself 10 either limited or unlimited. If, then, it is unlimited, there will be the unlimited; if, on the other hand, it is limited, it will be limited by something and so on without limit. For if what is taken is limited by something else, there will necessarily be no limit to the number of things taken, if what is taken is always limited. So that it is necessary that the unlimited be introduced in either case.

The fifth, which is the most proper reason and the one that gives the greatest plausibility to the foregoing statements, is, he says, that 15 thinking never ceases; that is, it never reaches a limit and an end, nor does it fail by virtue of the fact that there is always something imagined outside what has been apprehended. For because of this we also assume number to be unlimited, and the dissection of bodies without limit, and what is outside the heavens. For imagination has no point of rest, but when it passes beyond the heavens, it seeks 20 outside it an unlimited void or a body. If you conceive an unlimited body, there forthwith the unlimited has been proposed; and if you conceive an unlimited void, *ipso facto* it is necessary to bring in an unlimited body. For hence it was that Democritus proposed an unlimited number of universes, proposing that there is an unlimited void.[126] For by what dispensation is some particular part of the void to be filled by the universe, but others not? So that if a universe is in 25 any part of the void, therefore [this is true] also in the whole void. Since, therefore, the void is unlimited, the universes also will be unlimited [in number].

And it is not only the irrationality of the dispensation that proves the existence of the unlimited, but the argument itself. For they say that the void is nothing other than place deprived of body, and if this is so, yet every place is receptive of body, therefore the whole void also is naturally liable to receive. But if this is its natural liability, then it is altogether necessary that either it should already have received or should receive. The void being unlimited, then, the body in it will also be unlimited. For in the case of things eternal, he says, there is no difference between the potential and the actual. For in the case of what is generated and destroyed, he says, it is possible that the potential will not be brought to actuality, the object having forestalled by its destruction the completion of its potentiality through being made actual; but in the case of the eternals, if something exists at all in potentiality, it is altogether necessary that it should also come to be in actuality. For it will be pointless for it to have its potentiality if it should never be brought to actuality. So that if some one of the eternals exists in potentiality, then in every case it will also exist at some time in actuality, as if it were never to come into being, it would not have the capacity for coming into being. So it would not even exist potentially. For the potential is what has the capacity to come into being, for which reason there is also no capacity in the full sense in things eternal. For it does not have a tendency to both conditions, but by necessity always exists, since in the case of these things, to have a capacity to be does not differ from being. For they are not in different states at different times. So that, if there is an unlimited void, by necessity there will also be unlimited body. So it is, at any rate, that [Democritus] declares the universes to be unlimited, while others say this of air or water or the intermediate stuff.

Having said this, he proceeds to state that the discussion of the unlimited involves many difficulties, whether we posit it or not. For if it does not exist, we shall take away unlimited progression of time and the unlimited increase of number, and the dissection of magnitudes without limit; while if it exists, it is worthy of inquiry whether it is a substance or an accident, and if an accident, whether it is an accident in itself or not in itself but an accident *simpliciter*. And he defines what kind of unlimitedness is the subject of the account, that it is unlimitedness in magnitude. For this is the question that it is particularly the physicist's task to consider, whether body is or is not of unlimited extension.

203b6 For everything either is an origin or comes from an origin.

All existents, which have not taken shape pointlessly and accidentally, either have the status of an origin or come from an origin (for
things that exist pointlessly can be neither of these by virtue of the   407,1
very fact that they exist pointlessly); but the unlimited does not exist
pointlessly (for it is eternal), so that it either is an origin or comes
from an origin.

203b8 For it is necessary that what comes into being should
attain an end, and there is a terminal point of all destruction.

If it is necessary that what is generated must be destroyed, and the   5
things that suffer destruction have a certain limit with respect to
magnitude, at which the destruction leaves off, the more easily
destructible being always the first destroyed, therefore no generated
thing is unlimited. And nothing that is generated in substance is
projected into being all at once, like certain subjects of mutation, but
[the process occurs] in parts. So that if the unlimited exists, it is
necessary that it should be both ungenerated and indestructible.   10

203b10-11 [It has no origin, but seems itself to be the origin of
the rest] and to embrace all things and to govern all things, as
those say who do not reckon other causes apart from the unlimited, such as mind or love. {Anaximander, and most physical
theorists, adds Aristotle, call it the divine, since it is immortal
and imperishable.}

Whenever the ancient physical theorists, he says, did not look to the
agent cause – as Anaxagoras looked to mind, which he stated to be
an agent cause, and Empedocles to strife and love[127] – whatever these   15
men proposed as the matter of all things, they proposed that it was
unlimited in magnitude, ungenerated and indestructible, and they
proposed this as the divine, which also governed all things and stood
over the constitution of the sum of things, and indeed as the 'immortal
and imperishable', which Anaximenes stated to be air; Thales, water;
Anaximander, the intermediate [stuff]; and different thinkers, differ-   20
ent things.[128] And it is not at all surprising, he says, that the first
men in our era,[129] having failed to assign one of the elements to the
power which stands over the sum of things, believed that whichever
one each conjectured to be the cause of the others was *ipso facto* also
a god. Just as they, then, looking only to the material, conjectured
that this was the first cause of all that exists, clearly so it was that   25
Anaxagoras also proposed mind as the origin of all that exists and
Empedocles, love and strife.

203b15-17 [The first two of the five proofs for the unlimited are
time and magnitudes] for the mathematicians too make use of
the unlimited.

408,1

This is by the dissection of magnitudes without limit. For they are
able to bisect any given straight line, and to mark off from the given
straight line a shorter one. Since, therefore, the third side of the
triangle is shorter than the other two, it is always possible, by
5 marking off the shorter measurement from the longer, to produce by
this section a straight line parallel to the shorter one, and to produce
a triangle, and so on without limit.

{203b15-25 summarise the five proofs set out above by Philoponus. 203b25-7 argues that if there is unlimitedness outside
the universe, body and the universes too must be unlimited,
since there is no reason for them to occupy one part of the void
rather than another.}

203b27 So that if mass is in one place, it is also in every place.

What is the dispensation that causes a body to exist in one part of the
void, but not to exist also everywhere, if the void is place deprived of
body?

10 **203b28** And at the same time, if there is no limit to void and
place, necessarily there is also none to body.

Since previously he refuted the argument only by showing it to be
arbitrary, he now argues for this conclusion also, that there must be
something unlimited if there is an unlimited void as a substratum.
For they declare the void to be nothing but place deprived of body;
15 but every place is receptive of body. And if this place is eternal, it is
no more potentially than actually receptive of body.

203b32-4 [If the unlimited exists, we still must ask how it exists
whether as a *per se* accident of something with a nature or as
an essence or neither.] ... but there is none the less something
unlimited and things unlimited in multiplicity.

One does not, he says, eliminate the unlimited by proposing it either
as a substance or as an accident, in itself or *simpliciter*. For whatever
20 we propose it to be, nothing prevents there from being unlimitedness
in extension, which when divided also produces unlimitedness in
multiplicity.

204a1 But it is the particular task of the physicist to consider whether there is a perceptible magnitude that is unlimited.

Here you learn what kind of unlimitedness it is his object to discuss in the ensuing discourse, viz. that it is the perceptible kind, which is to say the natural one that is formed according to natural qualities. For whether there is anything else outside the heavens that is a non-natural body devoid of qualities, or something of that sort, he will inquire in his work *On the Heavens*[130] and will show that it is altogether impossible for there to be a body outside the heavens; but now he is inquiring whether it is possible for some natural body to be extended to an unlimited degree. And concerning what is unlimited in multiplicity, he has shown in the first book as well, in his arguments against Anaxagoras and Democritus,[131] that it is not possible, but he will also show it more accurately in his work *On Generation and Destruction.*[132]

409,1

5

204a2 First, then, one must determine in how many ways the unlimited is spoken of. {Aristotle explains that some things, such as a voice, are by definition untraversable; others are conceptually traversable, but in fact cannot be traversed to the end; others are barely traversable; others are naturally such as to have a limit but have none; and finally there is the unlimitedness in addition and division.}

Having shown that the discussion of the unlimited is necessary for the physicist, and that those who posited the unlimited had reason to propose it as an origin of the existents, he next proceeds to the consideration of it. And since the unlimited is spoken of in many senses, he first sets down the significations of the term 'unlimited', then shows by this means what sort of things are signified by the term 'unlimited', and what sort is not. For it is the mark of a well-informed man to determine the significations of homonymous terms, and to say what sort of thing they agree with and what sort they do not agree with.

10

15

Now the unlimited, he says, is spoken of in five ways. In one sense that is said to be unlimited which is not even such as naturally to have any limit at all, but is as it were impossible to cross or traverse completely, in consequence of there being no means whatsoever of passage, since it is not any sort of quantity; as, for example, we also say that a sound is invisible since it is not even such as naturally to fall into the field of vision. And such are the point and the qualities. For these are unlimited, the point because, being itself a limit, it does not have a limit, by virtue of being utterly without magnitude (for the reason is certainly not that its limits are inapprehensible on account

20

of its unlimited extension), and likewise whiteness and quality in general, by virtue of the fact that they admit of no transit at all.

25   Unlimited in the second sense is 'that which cannot be traversed to the end'. No limit of this can ever be found, in consequence, not of our lacking power to traverse it, but of the fact that it never comes to the end of its extension and its magnitude has no limits. Concerning this it lies with us also to consider whether there is such a magnitude or not in existent things.

    And thirdly we speak of that as unlimited which has a limit but
30 one that by reason of a difficulty is beyond our reach. And this occurs
410,1 in two ways, either through quantity or through quality. For if the road is rough and difficult of passage and has a tortuous shape, we say that such a road is 'unlimited' on account of our being unable to make a passage by way of it (thus, then, we say that the labyrinth was unlimited not because there was no limit to the path through it,[133] but because it was tortuous and for this reason difficult of
5 passage), and we also call the road unlimited because of its great extension, just as we say that the ocean is unlimited because we cannot traverse it completely on account of its great extension, even though it is in fact fully limited and surrounded by earth on every side.[134] Likewise the Red Sea also is said to be unlimited for the same reason.[135] We also say indeed, when we ourselves are going by a long
10 road without experience,[136] that the road is unlimited.

    And that is said to be unlimited in the fourth sense which is naturally such as to have a limit, but does not have one. And of such a kind is the circle; for it is possible to take some actual point on it and to fix the origin there, but it does not itself have any point defined in actuality. For I take whatever place I wish as an origin, since the
15 man who draws the circle with a centre and a radius also does not fix the origin at some definite point, but wherever he wishes and what moves in a circle can begin its motion from whatever point it will. Thus, the circle is unlimited, having no limit intrinsically, and for this reason is called unlimited, though it can receive one in relation to something else.

20   The fifth signification of the term 'unlimited', he says, is in respect (a) of addition, or (b) of division, or (c) of both. In respect (a) of division as in the case of number and time (for we say that number is unlimited through its capacity to be increased without limit; for it is always possible to take a number larger than the one that has been taken, and for this very reason it is also possible to increase time); in respect (b) of division by virtue of the fact that magnitudes can be bisected
25 without limit; and (c) in both respects as in the case where you think of a single straight line, and then of this bisected, and again of the one part bisected, and of the [resulting] part being added to the one

part [from the first bisection] and taken from the other; for in this way one will be increased and one diminished without limit.[137]

The unlimited being spoken of in so many different senses, the argument now inquires concerning the second signification, the un- 30 limited in extension, whether or not there is any such unlimitedness in things that are, such as that whose existence the physicists propose. For if someone should say that there is unlimitedness in any of the remaining significations, we shall not differ (for we too grant the existence of such things which are signified by the term 'unlimited'), but the unlimitedness in extension is what it now lies with him to refute.

And first he refutes those who say that the unlimited itself is a 411,1 substance (not something else, then unlimited, but essentially unlimited), and that the substance of the unlimited is of the same kind as that of air and fire.[138] This then, he says, will be either divisible or indivisible. If then it is divisible, it will be divisible either in magnitude or in multiplicity (for all that is divided is divided in respect of one of these forms), but if this is so, it will be a quantity, not an essence 5 (for it is of quantity that these are both forms, the continuous and the discrete), so that the unlimited will not be a substance in itself. If, on the other hand, it is indivisible, it would not be an unlimited thing such as we are seeking, and such as all the physicists meant when proposing the existence of the unlimited with respect to extension. For this, being a magnitude, is in every case divisible, unless indeed 10 we are to say that it is unlimited in the way that points and qualities are. But no argument of ours is about [unlimitedness] of this kind, but only whether there is something unlimited in extension that cannot be traversed or completed. It is, then, not possible for unlimitedness of such a kind to be an essence.

Having said this, he turns in mid-argument to those who say that the unlimited is present as an accident in another thing, and then 15 returns straightway to the matter in hand. For if, he says, the unlimited were present as an accident in another thing, it would not be the unlimited that is an origin of existents, but that to which the unlimited belongs as an accident. For we say that the sound is an element of speech, and we say that the sound is invisible, but we are not yet forced to say that invisibility too is an element of speech, since invisibility belongs to speech, not in itself, but as an accident. And so 20 I say it is in the case of the unlimited. The fact that it was an accident of something else, such as air or water, that was in itself an origin of things, would not lead me to say that the unlimited was also an origin of things that are. For no more would anyone prove it to be an origin even if he should say that it is an origin accidentally; for things that are causes of something accidentally are not causes *tout court*. So 25 baldness is also said to be the cause of a house, not being a cause by any means, as it was not in so far as he was bald that the builder built it, and therefore even had he not been bald, he would no less have built it. Neither, then, is the unlimited an origin. But yet it has been proved that, granting its existence, it is impossible for it not to be an

30   origin; therefore the unlimited cannot exist as an accident either.

But, though he will show this more fully as he proceeds, he returns to the present thesis, which is that it is impossible for the unlimited in itself to be an essence. And he handles this as an argument *a*

412,1 *fortiori*. The unlimited, he says, has its existence in magnitude and in number ... .[139] If, now, those things, viz. number and magnitude, which ought *a fortiori* to have existence in themselves, as the sub-strata of the unlimited, nevertheless in themselves subsist in other things (for magnitude and number supervene as accidents on other things, since they supervene on essence), being unable to subsist in

5   themselves, then much more should it be true, presumably, that the unlimited cannot subsist in itself. For the unlimited is an accident of magnitude and number, which are themselves accidents of sub-stance. The syllogism is therefore hypothetical:[140] if the unlimited subsists in itself and is a substance, then much more will this be true of number and magnitude. If, however, those things which ought *a fortiori* to subsist in themselves, i.e. number and magnitude, never-

10   theless do not exist, then presumably will this be true all the more of the unlimited.

Moreover, he says, if the unlimited, existing in actuality, is a substance, again it will be either divisible or indivisible. But if it is divisible, it will suffer division in every case, as also the homoeomer-ies do. Therefore, just as air is divided into airs, and water is divided into waters, so the unlimited, if its essence consists in this fact of being unlimited, will suffer division into parts that are unlimited, so

15   that it will follow that each part of it is also unlimited.[141] Thus the same thing will be many unlimited entities, or rather will be <un-limitedly> unlimited entities (at least if each of its parts is divisible too), which is impossible. But if, when it suffers division, it should not suffer it without limit, the unlimited will not be homoeomerous. But if this is so, [the unlimited] will be neither simple nor an origin (for its origin will be the non-homoeomerous things); yet the unlimited

20   must be simple, since it is also an origin, and what is an origin is simple. For if it be compounded, it is not itself the origin, but those things in which it consists.

But those who propose the unlimited as origin say that it ...[142] nor will it be unlimited. For the unlimitedness which is the subject of our present inquiry is either in magnitude or in multiplicity, but if it is indivisible it will be neither of these, since each of these is divisible. It is impossible therefore that what is unlimited in this way should

25   be indivisible. If, however, granted that the unlimited is a substance,

it is impossible for it to be either limited or unlimited, it seems that the unlimited is not in any sense a substance. But if it is not a substance, it will be an accident; and if it is an accident, the unlimited will not be an origin in the sense that the Pythagoreans proposed.[143] But, he says, this inquiry as to whether there is some common nature 30 of the unlimited which is the one present in mathematics and in the perceptibles and in the separable incorporeals, and whether this is an intelligible essence or some other thing, appears to be of the most common application, and not to touch [only] the present issue. Let us therefore postpone this subject of inquiry, but let us turn back to the 413,1 present one which is of greater relevance to us, viz. whether there is a perceptible body which is unlimited in magnitude and untraversable. For it was the existence of such a body that the physicists too proposed.

204a5 ... or what is barely so[144] [or what is by nature such as to admit of a passage or limit but does not].

[This is] the third signification. 'Or what is by nature such as to admit 5 a passage or limit, but does not' is the fourth signification, by which I mean the circular. And the words 'by nature such as to admit a passage or limit' stand for the possibility of traversing, or also that of limiting, the whole circle, but, since there is no actual point implicit in it, the circle is not traversable for this reason: that what moves on it does not have any limit at which it can stop. 10

204a8 It is, then, impossible that the unlimited should be separable from the perceptibles, being unlimited in itself.

Obviously the term 'unlimited' means the kind that is also the subject of the argument, the unlimited in extension. That this should exist in itself and be a substance is impossible. For in every case such an unlimited thing is nothing apart from the perceptibles, but it is either 15 water or air or one of such things, just as the physicists proposed that it is.

204a9 For if it is neither magnitude nor multiplicity {but is still an essence, says Aristotle, it will be indivisible, and hence not really unlimited, except in the sense that we predicate invisibility of voice}.

This is the first demonstration that the unlimited is not an essence. For if, he says, the unlimited should be neither magnitude nor multiplicity, which are forms of quantity, but is an essence in itself, 20 it will not admit division (for division is of quantity), so that it is indivisible. But if it is indivisible, it is not an unlimited like the unlimited that we are seeking and that which the physicists used to discuss, unless it is unlimited in the sense that a point or quality is unlimited, through not being such by nature as to have dimension.

204a14 And if the unlimited exists as an accident, it would not
25   be an element of what exists, in so far as it is unlimited {just as, says Aristotle, invisibility is not an element of speech, though voice is invisible}.

Since he has shown that it is not possible for the unlimited to be an essence, he therefore in mid-argument throws in a certain refutation of the other proposition, which states that the unlimited is an acci-
414,1 dent. For if the unlimited exists, but is not an essence, what is left is that it is an accident. But if it is an accident, it would not be the unlimited that is an element, but that to which it belongs as an accident, just as it not invisibility that is an element of speech, but the sound of which this is an accident.

204a17 Moreover, how is it possible anything can itself be
5   unlimited when it is not even possible for number and magni-
       tude?

He turns again to showing that the unlimited is not an essence. And he handles this *a fortiori*. Since it is more true that the substratum of something subsists in itself than that the thing which is an accident to that substratum [exists in itself], and since number (which is a substratum to the unlimited) does not subsist in itself, it is all the more true that the unlimited (which is an accident to number) would
10   not subsist in itself. But if it is not one of those things that subsist in themselves, it could not be an essence either.

204a20 And it is manifest that it is not possible for the unlimited to be an essence as a thing that exists in *entelechy* and as an essence and an origin.

[This is] a different proof that it is impossible for the unlimited to be
15   an essence and origin of what exists. For it is altogether necessary, if the unlimited is an origin, that it should be simple and have nothing as its substratum. For if it were compounded or had any sort of substratum, it would no longer be an origin, but [the origin would be] either the substratum or those ingredients of which it consists; for the origin is a simple thing. If then the unlimited is such a thing, a simple entity and one that has no substratum, like the soul or the
20   mind, then in this case to be the unlimited will be the same as to be

unlimited.[145] For in the compounds it is one thing for each to be 'this' substantively and another to be it adjectivally, as has been said also in the *Categories*[146] (for 'to be this in particular' signifies the compound, as when I say 'to be an animal', but 'to be animal' signifies the form whereby there is also being for the animal); but in the case of simple entities it is the same thing to say 'to be a soul' and 'to be soul' (for not even in the account of it can it be divided into more), and to say 'to be mind' and 'to be a mind'. If, however, the nature of the unlimited is such that to be the unlimited is for it the same as to be unlimited, every part of it will be unlimited. For if the part receives the same account as the whole, the part also will presumably be unlimited; while if it receives another, it could not be a simple entity, being compounded of unequal, or rather unlike, parts, just as man too is not a simple entity, being compounded of animal, rational and mortal.

If, then, someone makes a number or a magnitude unlimited, it will not follow that he also makes the parts of the unlimited unlimited.[147] For he proposes another nature for the unlimited, such as number or magnitude, and there is nothing at any rate that prevents the part of number from being a number, yet not an unlimited one. For it is not the same to be number and to be unlimited, since number is a multiplicity composed of monads, while the unlimited is an untraversable quantity. And it is likewise in the case of magnitude. But when someone says that the unlimited is a substance in this way, that [the essence] has its being in the account of the unlimited, how would this man not find that also every part of the unlimited is unlimited? For just as the part of water is water, having the same account, so is the part of the unlimited unlimited since, as we said previously, there is the same account of the whole as of the part. The one unlimited will thus be many unlimited entities, since its parts are also many, or rather, since each of its parts is divisible, it will be necessary for the same thing to be unlimitedly unlimited, which is absurd.

{204a22 Aristotle argues that the part of the unlimited must be unlimited, hence either indivisible or divisible without limit. He explains the first clause parenthetically.}

204a23 [For the unlimited and being unlimited are the same thing] if indeed the unlimited is an essence and not predicated of a substratum.

The phrase 'predicated of a substratum' stands for 'in a substratum'; the meaning is 'if it is an essence and not an accident'.

20 **204a26** For just as a part of air is air, so also a part of the unlimited is unlimited [if indeed it is an essence and an origin. Therefore it is without parts and indivisible.]

This is continuous with the words above. This then is the full construction of his words: after the phrase 'if indeed the unlimited is a substance and not predicated of a substratum', add next 'for just as a part of air is air, so also is a part of the unlimited unlimited, at least if it is some essence and an origin'; then add 'so that it is either

25 indivisible or divisible without limit; but it is impossible for the same thing to be many unlimited entities'; and then again add 'therefore it is without parts and indivisible'.

416,1 **204a33** [Hence the Pythagoreans are absurd,] for at the same time they make the unlimited an essence and divide it.

Those men speak incorrectly, he says, who maintain that the unlimited is a substance in itself. For it follows from their argument that they make the same thing both capable and incapable of division into parts, both substance and accident. For while they say that it is a

5 substance, in saying that it is unlimited they *ipso facto* also make it a quantity, since the unlimited is divisible. And yet, even supposing that the unlimited is a substance, it has been shown that it will be indivisible. So that they make the indivisible divisible, and the substance an accident.

204a34 But perhaps this inquiry should rather be a general one. {Aristotle proceeds to suggest that it might be extended to mathematical and intelligible entities.}

Since he has shown that it is not possible for the unlimited to be a

10 substance (meaning the unlimited in respect of extension), yet it was not an unlimitedness of this kind that they assigned to the Ideas – to inquire about this, he says, whether there is any substance of the unlimited and whether this is in mathematics or in the forms, would be to inquire about a matter of more common scope which has to do with the origins of all that is in so far as it is; whereas the inquiry specific to the present method, which is that of physics, is that as to

15 whether there is a body unlimited in extension, having neither origin nor limit in respect of magnitude. That there is, then, no body of this kind, such as the physicists too proposed, he undertakes to show next.

204b1-4 [But we are concerned with the existence of the unlimited among perceptibles ... .] When, therefore, one reflects logically in the light of these considerations, it would seem that it does not exist. {Philoponus then goes on to summarise the subsequent argument in Aristotle.}

Having shown that the unlimited is not in itself substantially consti- 20
tuted, like a substance, by its being unlimited, as the Pythagoreans claimed, he now undertakes to show that the unlimited is not such as the physicists said: [they affirmed that it is] not something whose substance consists in being unlimited, but, while the substance is something else, like water, air or the intermediate stuff, this is unlimited in respect of magnitude. That therefore the unlimited does 25
not exist even in this way he shows first, as he says, 'logically' (that is, persuasively, and from what is generally admitted; or else 'logically' stands for 'more broadly', for this proof will be relevant not only to natural bodies, but also to the mathematicals. For this reason, therefore, he says 'logically'). Then he shows it in a still more coercive way from the very nature of things. 417,1

The logical handling of the argument is as follows. The geometers define body by saying that body is what is determined by a plane. If, however, body is what is determined by a plane, but the unlimited is not determined by a plane, there is therefore no unlimited body. And this is an argument in the second figure.[148] And not only, he says, is 5
there no unlimited body, but it is not possible even for number to be unlimited. For no number, he says, is separable in itself, but every number is numerable, and what is numerable can be traversed. The unlimited, however, cannot be traversed, therefore no number is 10
unlimited. And there are two syllogisms in this argument, of which the first is in the first figure, the second in the second. (1) Number is in the numerable, the numerable can be traversed, therefore number also can be traversed. (2) [All number can be traversed], but the unlimited cannot be traversed, therefore number is not unlimited.

Such then, are the logical demonstrations, and he called them logical because, as I have said, they are not coercive, but derive from admitted premisses. For even those who propose the existence of the unlimited would not grant that the general definition of body is that 15
it is what is defined by a plane, as if it might have neither length and breadth and depth nor that which is apprehensible by sight. For definition in these terms does not subsume all bodies; neither, therefore, does the definition that it is what is defined by a plane. For, they say, an unlimited body is that which is not defined by a plane, such as the heavens; for the outer surface of this is not defined. But neither would they grant that all number is numerable; for they would say 20
that there is also an unlimited number.[149]

From this he turns to the demonstrations that are more coercive and more concerned with natural phenomena. And he shows that an

unlimited body is impossible both from the natural potentialities, I
25   mean those of affection and action, warmth and coolness, and dryness
and dampness; and secondly from the places of bodies, the higher and
the lower; and moreover from their tendencies, I mean heaviness and
lightness; and finally also from certain other concepts. First, then, he
refutes the [existence of] the unlimited from the natural potentialities, and he carries on the argument by division. For if there is an
unlimited body, it is altogether necessary that this be simple or
30   compounded; but whether it be simple or compounded, it is impossible
for it to be unlimited; therefore there is in no case an unlimited body.

And first he shows that it is not possible for a compound body to
be unlimited. For if it should be compounded, it will either be
composed of unlimited elements or from limited ones. Now that it
should be composed of unlimited ones is impossible; for it has been
shown in the first argument that it is impossible for the elements to
35   be unlimited, and he will also show this in his work *On the Heavens*,[150]
418,1   and particularly in his work *On Generation and Corruption*.[151] For if
the elements are unlimited, he says, it is altogether necessary that
their contrarieties also should be unlimited (for if the contrarieties
which give birth to the elements are not unlimited, but limited, it is
altogether necessary that the things composed from them should also
be limited; for a limited number of combinations occurs also); but if
5   the contrarieties are to be unlimited, since each contrariety embraces
two qualities (for the contraries are two at the very least), it follows
that the unlimited has been duplicated, which is absurd.[152] It is
therefore impossible for the elements to be unlimited; so that the
unlimited cannot be composed of unlimited elements.

But if it is composed of elements that are limited in multiplicity,
either one of these is unlimited in magnitude, or more, or all, or none.
10   If, then, none of them should be unlimited, but all limited, then what
is composed of them will also be limited. So that it is necessary that
one or more or all should be unlimited. And first he shows that it is
impossible for any one of them to be unlimited, and once this has been
shown, it will at the same time have been proved that it is not possible
either for more to be unlimited (and if not more, then much less all),
15   yet he will still show specifically that it is not possible for more [to be
unlimited] either.

That it is not possible, then, for any one of the elements which
compose the unlimited to be unlimited, he shows as follows. Every
natural body, which bodies are also the subject of our present account,
has a certain innate potentiality in itself, either warmth or coolness
or dryness or dampness. It is therefore altogether necessary, if there
is any compound body, that the things which compose it should be
20   equal in their potentialities, so that thus some one mixture may arise
with none becoming more dominant, the disproportionality of each

being on the contrary restrained by the contrary potentiality of the other. For if any one of them is more dominant, it destroys the others and alters them into itself. If, however, the unlimited is a compound and one of its elements is unlimited, since it is altogether necessary that the unlimited in bulk should have an unlimited body and potentiality, the potentiality being unlimited in the unlimited, this will consume the others and alter them into itself, and thus again the whole will be simple and not compound. For even if, in an equal bulk, the unlimited has a weaker potentiality, and not one so intense as the limited has, even so, since it is in an unlimited magnitude, it will exceed by virtue of this every limited [element] and will destroy the potentiality in the limited, even if this is more intense.

For let it be proposed that in the unlimited there is some one of its components, e.g. water, which is itself unlimited in magnitude, and another, e.g. fire, which is limited in magnitude. And let there be one potentiality in the water (such as the cool) which is much weaker than that in the fire (I mean the warm) [when they are taken] in equal bulk. If, then, from the two I take two bodies of equal bulk, such as a pint from each, since in the pint of fire the intensity of the warmth is greater than the coolness of the cool in the pint of water, obviously the warmth will consume the cool. For where there are two contraries the lesser is overcome by the greater one. And let the warmth in a body of fire of equal bulk be ten times as warm as the coolness is cool in an equal amount of water. Yet even if the warmth in the fire of equal bulk is more effective in such measures, if I increase tenfold the bulk of the water, taking ten pints of water, the coolness in the ten pints of water will be made equal to the warmth in the pint of fire. Since, therefore, the proposition is that the fire, though it has the more intense potentiality, is limited in bulk, and everything that is limited is in a ratio to what is limited, obviously even the whole of fire will have a certain ratio to the given part of it. Let this then be ten-thousandfold. Since, then, the pint of fire has a potentiality equal to ten pints of water, it is presumably possible for the whole of fire to receive from the unlimited water [an equivalent] on the same principle as with the part. If I take ten times ten thousand pints of water, the coolness in these will be made equal to the warmth in the ten thousand pints of fire. Since, therefore, the proposition is that water is unlimited, and there is no ratio of the unlimited to the limited, the coolness in the whole of water will obviously be greater in an unlimited degree than the coolness in the given part of it, which has also been equated with the warmth in the whole of fire. And if this is so, then the coolness in the whole of water will be greater in potential to an unlimited degree than the warmth in the whole of fire. It will therefore consume and alter it, and thus the whole will be simple and

25

30

419,1

5

10

15

20

25

not compounded. It is therefore impossible for any of them to be unlimited.

And this is also obvious from patent fact. A small amount of water 30 thrown on to a large lamp is destroyed and alters to the essence of the fire; but if that lamp is thrown into a receptacle of water, it suffers the opposite affection (for it is destroyed and alters), though the warmth of the fire is at any rate intenser than the coolness of the 420,1 water (if indeed the coolness of the water is that of an element), while the warmth of the domestic fire is an excess of the warmth in the element. Likewise the coolness of ice is an excess of the coolness in the element. But nevertheless, although the potentiality of the fire is more intense, the fact that the quantity of the water is great, even 5 though the quality of the water is less intense, entails that the coolness of the water still gets the better of the warmth of the fire, because of the quantitative amount. For qualities become more powerful when those of like form occur together.

And this is clear and can be seen more plainly too from weights. For if you combine two pound weights, the composite of both will be 10 heavier than either. For it will not only have a weight of two pounds, but more. In the same way, if you divide a two-pound weight into two equal parts, each of the parts will not have the weight of a pound, but less.[153] Thus it is that in coming together things of like form become more powerful, but when divided, weaker. And likewise in motions, the more heavy things you combine, the faster they move, and if 15 bodies that happen to weigh five pounds are divided, even if they are in contact with one another, they will not describe such a fast motion, but if brought together in one they will move much faster. It is the same with light things.

Just as in the case of these things, then so it will be with the warm, the cool and the rest of the contraries. At any rate, if you throw the same piece of wood on to a small fire and a large one, it will be consumed more rapidly when thrown on to the large one than when 20 thrown on to the small. So that even if the unlimited is less in quality, even so, by magnitude and the unlimited compounding of ho-moeomerous entities, the quality will also be increased without limit. For if it is generally true that the parts when compounded strengthen and increase the quality, presumably when they are compounded without limit they will increase it without limit. So that necessarily the potentiality in the unlimited will be unlimited, and being unlim-25 ited it necessarily destroys the rest. It is not possible, therefore, for any one unlimited thing to exist.

But against this argument an objection of the following kind is brought, that it is not necessary that quality should increase with quantity. For neither is it the case that if I take a pound weight of white lead, possessing such-and-such a degree of whiteness, and then

multiply this by adding many other equal magnitudes, I thereby 30
make the whole whiter. Nor yet if I take a large mass and cut it into
parts does the whiteness in the parts become less intense than the
whiteness in the whole. Nor yet if I pour many similar measures of
water into the same receptacle does the whole become cooler than
each of the parts. Nor, by the same token, if many warmed-up 421,1
measures are thrown in at the same time, does the whole become
warmer than each of the parts.

If it is observed, however, that the same wood is burned by a
smaller flame in a longer time, and by a greater one in a shorter time,
this does not result from an increase in the intensity of the caustic
quality; but the reason is that whatever is affected by something, 5
where things are of the same material, in every case works upon it in
return, but the affection of the smaller by the larger is greater than
the one's [reciprocal] action upon the other. This is not because the
quality of the greater is more intense, but because each thing is less
liable to affection in combination than when separate from the
entirety. Just as, then, it becomes more liable to affection when
separated, so it becomes less liable to affection when it enters into
conjunction. And this follows according to reason. For in the large 10
magnitude there are many similar parts,[154] and each obviously has
an operative power; thus, whenever the contrary, being small, is
juxtaposed and works upon some portion, straightway the adjacent
portions that are similar to the affected one, touching the affected
portion itself, also work on it and do not allow it to be altered, but
together restore it from the state of affection to its original nature.[155] 15
And in this way it follows that as the juxtaposed contrary is affected,
and is not strong enough to work reciprocally upon the portions that
are acting on it (which entails a weakening in their operative power),
it is altered more rapidly.

I mean something of this kind. Let a large bonfire be posited with
a height of ten cubits. When, therefore, a small amount of wood is
thrown on to this, the wood also undoubtedly works on certain 20
portions of the bonfire adjacent to it, say on one cubit; but since there
are certain other similar cubits of like nature with the affected one,
which are not at all affected and obviously also have an operative
power themselves, they immediately exert it on the part that is
beginning to be affected and restore it to its own nature. And, while
the fire in contact with the wood is not affected by the wood because
it is helped by the adjacent similar parts, the wood, by contrast, being 25
small and affected in every part but unable to act reciprocally,
undergoes a more rapid alteration. But certainly if a large amount of
wood has been thrown on to a small bonfire, then, because it acts more
than it is affected, it undergoes a more gradual alteration; for the

30   affected part of the fire has no adjacent similar one to help it and
     bring back the affected power.

     For this reason, then, quantity seems more potent when increased,
     and not because quality is increased with quantity. For in other ways
     too it is completely unreasonable and a mere postulate that we should
     have to say that quality was increased with quantity; for then in
35   similar things what has greater bulk ought to have a greater intensity
422,1   of power, whereas in fact this is not necessary. At any rate, pepper
     has greater power in respect of the quality of warmth than a large
     radish. And in case anyone should say that there are various forms
     of warmth, this at least needs to be shown: since warmth, in so far as
     it is warmth, does not vary, it follows that it is raised or relaxed in
5   intensity, not according to the magnitude of the bulks, but to the
     receptiveness of the receiving parties. Quality is not, therefore, liable
     to be increased with quantity.

     But if quality is not increased with quantity, it is not necessary, if
     one of the elements that compose the unlimited is unlimited in
     magnitude but is inferior to the others in its quality in respect of
     operative power, that the quality should be increased with the unlim-
10   ited extension of the magnitude; instead, just as it is possible for the
     bulk to be greatly increased without a concomitant increase in power,
     so, presumably, even if it has been increased without limit, it will be
     no more intense. And this is confirmed by patent fact. For let it be
     posited that the air around the whole city has been made extremely
     cool,[156] and that the flame of a lamp is kindled. Now if quality is
     increased with quantity, the flame of the lamp should have been
15   extinguished by the air. For presumably the excess of the one quality
     over the other is not so great as that of the one quantity over the other,
     but the excess in quality is far smaller. Yet nevertheless, since quality
     is not increased with quantity, the effect produced by the lamp's flame
     on the air, because of its superior intensity, is greater than the
     affection that it receives from it. But even if I do not confine the cold
20   air within the limits of the city, but extend it over the whole universe
     so that the air is cooled likewise throughout the whole universe, the
     flame of the lamp will suffer nothing more, if at any rate even in this
     case of the whole inhabited area around us having been cooled, the
     enclosed flame of the lamp does not suffer anything. So that even if
     I increase the cool air without limit, the same result will follow.

     But let it not be the case that the air that is taken be so cooled and
25   compressed as to be already drizzle and water (since we are not taking
     any lesser degree of coolness, but one that is equal or scarcely
     differing) and hence it acts more than it is affected, in the way
     described, through the help of the numerous similar parts. So that if
     it is even weaker, there will be no affection even if the air is unlimited,
     since even when the flame of the lamp is adjacent to the earth, it

works on it but is not at all affected. Yet certainly if quality became   30
more intense with the increase of quantity, then since the flame of
the lamp is nothing in comparison with the whole earth, the coolness
of the earth would be many times more intense than the warmth of
the lamp, which we do not see to be the case. And this is reasonable;
for neither the air nor the earth acts with its whole self on what is
adjacent to it, but only in those portions which are in contact with the
adjacent things, and hence, since their quality is less intense, their
affection from the lamp is greater than their action upon it.   35

How then is it absurd that even if one of the elements that compose   423,1
the unlimited is unlimited in magnitude, but falls short of the others
in intensity, the affection which it suffers from the limited thing that
exceeds it in intensity of power will be greater than its action upon
that thing? For the unlimited does not work with its whole self on the   5
limited, but through the portion adjacent to it, just as the air which
contains the flame of the lamp does not work on it with its whole self
either, since in fact it extinguished it by virtue of its amount and the
continuity of the affect. For when many things are working continuously to one effect, it follows that, since the power in the agent is
always at its highest, even though it is weak, and that in the affected   10
party is always failing, even though intense, the affection of the more
intense by the weaker will be greater than its action upon the weaker.
At any rate, in the case of the flame in the lamp, olive oil poured on
it continuously would extinguish the flame. If, now, the unlimited
does not work as a whole, but through the portion that lies adjacent
to the limited, while the power in it is weaker, it will produce no effect
upon the limited, but on the contrary will be affected by it. And the   15
limited will always be increased, yet neither will the unlimited come
to an end nor the limited become unlimited.

Thus far, then, the objection to the argument, and they try to
resolve it in this way. First they say it is false that natural powers do
not act with the whole of themselves, even if they are in an extensive
substratum; weight, at least, they say, is manifestly a power of this
kind. If, therefore, a ten-pound weight is applied to something, the   20
bulk is not in contact as a whole with the object to which it is applied,
but is so partially, or rather at the surface; yet it works with the whole
of the power that is in the total bulk. For it causes compression in the
measure of its whole weight. At any rate, if you cut off a portion of
the bulk in the part which is not in contact with the vehicle, say two   25
pounds, then although the same surface is in contact with the vehicle,
the compression is not the same; this implies that the weight in the
portion cut off, even if it was not touching that part of the vehicle,   424,1
was working to some effect along with the whole. Thus, therefore, the
whole power in the body is liable to act as a whole, even if the agent
is not in contact as a whole with the thing affected.

Likewise, with things that are driving or drawing, a portion of the thing that drives or draws is in contact with the thing that is drawn or driven, as with the hand. Yet it is not just the power in the hand that draws but the whole power as of the whole creature; for there are many things that are also affected as a whole when their parts are working. For we walk with our feet as the whole of us moves, and we build with our hands while the whole of us is active, and so it is in many other cases. If, now, these things are so, then things that warm and cool, or dampen and dry, even if only a part of the agent is in contact, are nevertheless active with the whole of the power that is in them;[157] and so it is with the other qualitative affections. But if they are active as a whole, then where the substratum is unlimited it is necessary that the the operative power is also increased. For we have said that whenever something works with many parts on one and the same object which is much smaller in magnitude, then even if the agent is much inferior in power, yet it will overcome the other because its parts are more numerous. And if the case is so, then the larger will always have the greater effect. Therefore the unlimited will possess unlimited operative power.

But again someone will say against this, that what happens in the case of weights will not necessarily happen also in the case of the qualitative affections. For warmth and heaviness are not the same form of quality (for warmth and coolness and qualities of this kind are operative and commutative, while lightness and heaviness are causes of change in place), and it is not necessary for the same properties to inhere in powers that differ in form. Consider at least the case of figure, which is a quality, but in no way subject to affection. We certainly see patently that the air does not work upon us as a whole, but only in the part that immediately surrounds us, since [otherwise] those in Scythia and in Ethiopia ought to suffer the same affects as one another.[158] And why do I mention those who are as distant as possible from one another? We see indeed that even those who are in the same place are differently affected, whenever some stand in the full glare of the sun and others in the shade, a mere line often dividing the one party from the other. If, however, the whole air produces its effect as a whole, then everyone should suffer the same affects, since the air in its entirety is a single thing; and this we see patently does not happen.

That (a) when the power in the unlimited is supposed to be less, it is not in every case necessary for it to destroy the rest, and certainly not if it is much inferior, since quality does not increase with quantity – this has been said at a moderate length according to the needs of the present case. That (b) it is in fact impossible for there to be a composite body one of whose elements is unlimited in extension, you will prove as follows. Let us make this assumption, that if the powers

of agents equal those of the affected subjects while their magnitudes 15
also are equal, they will either fail to work on one another or will be
affected equally by one another, but if the powers are not equal and
one is larger in magnitude and the other smaller, the smaller magnitude will be affected by the larger, for the reason that we have stated.
For if the one that is smaller in magnitude also works, yet it will be
affected more than it will act.

This, then, being the case, I say that it is not possible for a natural 20
body which is unlimited in magnitude to be composite. For it is
altogether necessary that the elements which compose it should be
equal in some way in respect of the powers. For if they should not be
equal, there will be no mixture from them, but the dominant one will
transform the rest into itself. And this is patent from all natural
bodies, and particularly from living creatures; so that it is necessary
also for the elements that compose the unlimited to be equal in their 25
powers. If then, its components are limited in magnitude, the whole
will also be limited. Suppose, on the other hand, that some one of the
components is unlimited in magnitude. Now, composition in natural
bodies is by mixture and not by juxtaposition (for it is products of art
that are compounded by juxtaposition), and in things compounded by 426,1
mixture the elements as wholes pervade the whole (for a part differs
from an element in this way, that the element pervades the whole of
which it is an element,[159] while the part does not), and therefore it is
necessary that this should be so in the present case. But it is
impossible for the limited to be extended as far as the unlimited, since 5
it is first exhausted and destroyed. It is just as if you should wish to
extend a pint-measure of air or fire through a hundred pints of water,
or a pitcher of wine through the whole sea. For the whole of it is first
destroyed before any mixture can occur.

And why do I say 'if the powers are equal'? For even if that of the
limited is greatly superior, the limited has no ratio to the unlimited,
and therefore it is altogether necessary that when it is extended 10
throughout the unlimited it is destroyed more rapidly than it is
mixed. For if it were extended throughout the unlimited it too would
be unlimited. Therefore it is impossible for there to be a composite
natural body if one of its components is unlimited in magnitude. But
if someone should say that the composition is by juxtaposition, then:
(a), most seriously, he has not conserved the original proposition (for
the argument concerns a natural body), and (b) furthermore, we have
shown that if a thing whose power is of equal strength is juxtaposed 15
with something larger in magnitude, it is completely destroyed. And
we have given the argument, in as much as even a piece of ice thrown
on to a large bonfire is first destroyed before it can produce any visible
effect upon the fire.

That it is impossible for one of the elements composing an unlimited body to be unlimited has therefore been sufficiently proved; that it is not possible either for many or all of them to be so, he proves thus. If, he says, a body means what is produced on every side (by 'on every side' he means in the three dimensions, since it is impossible for there to be any other dimension), the body produced without limit on every side would also be unlimited, that is the one that was extended without a limit in every dimension. But if it has occupied all the dimensions, it will not leave space for another to exist, so that it will be impossible for there to be two or more unlimited things.

This same thing, indeed, applied also to the first proposition; for if there is one unlimited thing at all, and the unlimited occupies the whole of place, it is impossible for there to be any other, even if it were of the shortest. And it is possible to use the refutations advanced there for the present case, by which I mean that if only some and not all the components should be unlimited, it will therefore be impossible for an unlimited natural body to exist. And this was a plausible consequence of what had been proved already. For if it has been proved that, (a) if the unlimited exists, it is in every case an origin not from an origin, but (b) no origin is in its true and primary sense composite, it follows reasonably that the unlimited cannot be composite either. Perhaps then it is simple; but this too is impossible. For if the unlimited is simple, then it is either one of these elements (such as air or water or some one of the others) or it is something different from them, as Anaximander, for example, declared it to be an intermediary.[160] That an unlimited body, therefore, can be neither one of the elements, nor something else apart from these, he proves by a common argument, but what he shows first is that it is completely impossible for there to be a certain body which is different from the elements, being their intermediary and the origin of the rest. For if there were, he says, some body mediating between the elements, whether limited or unlimited, from which the others received their origin, then, since the source from which anything begins is that into which it is dissolved, the elements also when they are destroyed should be resolved into it, and if they were resolved into it, then it would become apparent what sort of thing it was. For just as air arising from fire or water is in every case dissolved back into these and they appear patently, in the same way this too would have to appear. But there does not appear any element apart from the four. Therefore it does not exist.

...[161] For matter exists potentially and the things that arise from matter arise as from matter that exists potentially (for matter does not exist in actuality, but it has always had form imposed upon it), and on this account the things which are dissolved into it are also potentially dissolved into matter, and quite reasonably it is not apparent, since it does not exist in actuality; for it is never separated

from form. But these men say that the intermediary exists in actuality, so that it ought also to be apparent. Now when he says this he does not mean that there is no intermediary between contraries. For it is wholly necessary that the alteration to the contrary properties should take place through certain media (as the alteration to contraries is not immediate), but this intermediary is not anything defined, 30
nor an element of the others, but a sort of route to the contrary. 428,1

And that there is not even any possibility of there being a single simple element he shows by an argument common to air or fire or anything else, and this too whether it be limited or unlimited. For if the element is one, it will not possess powers that are contrary (since [then] the contraries would be in the same thing, and it is impossible for contraries to be in the same thing), and if it should not possess 5
powers that are contrary, then generation will be eliminated, and destruction, and generally all alteration. For all alteration is from a contrary to its contrary, such as that from warmth to coolness and from not-being to being. So that if it is in any case impossible for there to be a single and simple element as an origin, it is obviously not possible for this to be unlimited either. For the same argument 10
applies equally to both the unlimited and the limited.

204b7 Nor indeed is number such as to be separate and unlimited; for number or what has number is numerable.

Either he says this, that number, taken both as that [reckoned] on the fingers (which I myself call the numerator[162]) and as that of things 15
themselves (or as I say of numerables) is at all events limited, because each is a numerable thing, and the numerable can be traversed completely. And number therefore can undoubtedly be traversed, whereas the unlimited cannot be traversed. Therefore no number is unlimited (the words 'or what has number' mean 'and what has number' for the purpose of this exegesis) – he either, then, says this, 20
or, what is more likely, that no number is separable from the numerables, but every number has its being in the numerables. But the numerable can be traversed, and therefore number can be traversed also, so that it is not unlimited.

Now if this is so, it is therefore impossible that time should not have begun from some origin, nor is it possible that the universe should be in any sense eternal.[163] For if the universe is eternal, it is 25
obvious that the number of men who come into being will be unlimited, and unlimited in actuality (since, obviously, all have come into being in actuality), so that it is possible for number to be unlimited. And not only this, but the unlimited will be traversable in its actuality. For if all the single instances of mankind have come into being in 429,1
actuality up to now, and we are, as it were, the limit of that unlimited

number of men who came into being before us, it is obvious that the
unlimited has become traversable in actuality. Nor will this be the
5   only absurdity to follow on this proposition, but there will also be
something greater than the unlimited, or rather what is actually
unlimited will be increased without limit, at least if taking the
forefathers for every generation I find that the number of their
predecessors is unlimited in actuality, and yet that in every case the
successors of these when added to them make the number larger. And
10   the addition goes on without limit, at least if the universe is indestructible; and therefore the unlimited will be increased without
limit.

Moreover, it will also follow that the unlimited exists an unlimited
number of times. For every generation of men will have an unlimited
number of human predecessors; you may take my own for example.
The same will also happen in the case of all men. If we add to these
15   also the multiplicity of horses and of other creatures and plants and
the motions of every sphere, it will undoubtedly follow that in some
way the unlimited exists an unlimited number of times, or a great
many. So that if this is impossible – I mean that the unlimited should
have come to exist in actuality, that there should be something
greater and more unlimited than the unlimited, and that this should
not come to an end as it is increased and should be always becoming
20   greater than itself – therefore it is impossible that time should be
eternal, or that this should be at all true of the universe.[164]

But against this someone has raised the most thoughtless objection that nothing prevents their being unlimited on each side;[165] he
failed to see that one cannot speak of unlimitedness on each side in
relation to number, but we propose this only of the continuous
[magnitude] as a geometrical method. For the unlimited in the case
25   of number is nothing other than the unlimitedness of the monads.
And in any case it is true of the continuous also that if the unlimited
can be traversed on one side, then undoubtedly in some way it will
be traversable on the other. For what is the dispensation whereby
one of its parts is traversable and the other not? He said that it is not
possible for the unlimited to subsist in its entirety all at once at the
430,1   same time, but that it is not impossible for it to come to be in actuality
by parts. However, it is not at any rate to what is unlimited in this
way that Aristotle addresses his refutation, understanding it as one
simultaneous whole, but simply to what is unlimited in actuality. And
what difference does it make, if the unlimited is by nature entirely
untraversable, whether it is impossible for it to have come to be all
at once, or to be coming to be in parts? But I say that existence is
5   possible for the numerically unlimited rather as presently existing
than as past, for what presently exists need not be completely
traversable, but what is past is necessarily traversable – which is

impossible. And the unlimited that presently exists need neither increase nor exist an unlimited number of times, but the same thing follows for what is past, as we have said. But let us consider specifically the more complete argument concerning this. 10

> **204b11** The unlimited body, then, is not composite if its elements should be limited in multiplicity; for it is necessary that there should be more than one and that the contraries should be always equal, and that no one should be unlimited.

If the unlimited is composite, he says, it is composed either from 15 things that are limited in multiplicity or from things unlimited. That it should be composed of things unlimited, then, is impossible, for it has been shown to be impossible for the elements to be unlimited. But neither is it possible for the unlimited to be composed of things that are limited in multiplicity; for it is necessary that the things composing it should be contraries, but the contraries must somehow be equal in the composition, at least if it is not going to be destroyed by the dominant one. If, now, the unlimited should be composed of things 20 that are limited in multiplicity, and if they are also all limited in magnitude, then what is composed from them will be limited too. It is therefore necessary that one or more should be unlimited in magnitude. If, then, one should be unlimited, then, since the unlim- , ited also has unlimited power, it presumably destroys the rest, and the components must be equal in some way in order that they may 25 also be preserved. It is therefore impossible that any one of them should be unlimited.

> **204b14** For if the power in one body falls in any way short of 431,1 the other, as in the case of the fire being limited, but the air unlimited {then, Aristotle continues, the unlimited will overcome the limited, whatever the ratio of power in equal quantities}.

His expression is disjointed, but the sense is as follows. If, he says, one is unlimited, such as the air, and the other limited, such as the fire, even supposing the power in the unlimited one to be far weaker 5 than that in the other, [nevertheless] if I take from them two portions equal in magnitude, one of air and the other of fire, then even if the intensity of the power in the portion of fire far exceeds that of the power in the portion of air that has been taken, yet still, since there is a certain ratio between every two limited things, the intensity of the power in the portion of fire that has been taken will undoubtedly 10 have a ratio to [that in] the portion of air, for example ten or a hundred to one. If, now, we find that in an equal bulk the power of the fire

happens to be in the ratio ten to one, then if I take a bulk of air a hundred times greater, I shall equalise the powers. Since, then, the proposition is that the air is unlimited and the fire limited, and there
15 is not any ratio between the unlimited and the limited, neither will the power in the unlimited have a ratio to that in the limited. For as bulks stand to one another, so do their powers. If, then, the bulks have no ratio to one another, neither will the powers have any ratio to one another. The power in the unlimited will therefore have no
20 ratio to that in the limited, but it will exceed all, and in its excess will destroy the rest.

> **204b19** And that each should be unlimited is impossible {for, Aristotle argues, an unlimited body would have to be 'extended without limit' in all dimensions}.

He has turned to the other proposition, that it is also impossible for all the components of the unlimited to be unlimited. For if body, he says, is that which is extended on every side, i.e. has all the dimen-
25 sions, then that body would be unlimited which is 'extended without limit' on every side. Consequently, it will, through occupying the whole place, leave no room for the existence of any other body – I do not say, an unlimited one, but even a limited one, even if it be of the shortest. And what prevents the unlimited from being unlimited not
432,1 in every dimension, but only in length, so as to leave room for others? But this is a factitious case; for why, granting at all that it is unlimited, is it not unlimited on every side?

And alternatively: no one has ever proposed the existence of such an unlimited thing, but always of that which was unlimited on every side. For if, generally speaking, the unlimited is naturally liable to
5 exist, it is not naturally liable to exist here or here, but on every side.

> **204b22** Yet it is no more possible that the unlimited body should be a single simple entity. {Aristotle adds that some held simply this, while 'others' posited an unlimited entity beside the elements.}

Having shown that it is impossible for the unlimited to be composite, he now shows that it is also impossible for it to be simple (for this was the what remained from the whole division), either as one of the
10 elements or as an intermediary between these, as Anaximander held.

> **204b24** For there are many who make the unlimited a thing of this kind, but not air or water, so that the other elements will not be destroyed by the unlimited one.

Anaximander thought that the origin must be unlimited in order that   15
perpetual generation may not cease; he gave no attention at all to the
fact that that there is vicissitude in things, that everything is resolved
into the source from which it arises. He noticed at the same time that,
as in the four elements there was a certain contrariety [of each]
toward the rest, if he proposed one of them as the origin,[166] then, since
this is necessarily unlimited, being unlimited it destroys the rest   20
because the power in it is unlimited. So he did not propose any of
these as the origin, but said that the origin was something else apart
from these, from which both the elements and the other things derive
their generation.[167] This he proposed as a sort of intermediary between them, so that the rest might be preserved by its participation
in all the contraries, rather than destroyed by the unlimited power
that it contained. On this account also, all of the rest who proposed   25
that either air or water was unlimited, proposed this one through   433,1
observing that the power in it lacked intensity, and through thinking
that the rest would not be destroyed even if it were unlimited in
magnitude. Heraclitus, however, proposing fire as the origin, because
the power in it was more intense, did not propose that this was
unlimited in magnitude (for then none of the others would have
subsisted for any period of time), as even in proposing that it is limited   5
he says that all things will at some time suffer combustion, being
resolved into fire.[168]

204b26-7 [For the elements have a contrariety toward one
another,] as, for example, air is cool [and water wet and fire
warm].

He said that air is cool by way of proposition; for he himself shows in
the work *On Generation* that it is warm.[169]

204b29 [Now they say there is another unlimited body, the   10
source of the elements.] But it is impossible for there to be such
a thing, and not because it is unlimited. For a certain common
argument is required in this case and likewise in all others. {The
disproof of this, says Aristotle, is that no such body beside the
elements is known to perception.}

The present question is a double one: (a) whether it is possible for
there to be some other body apart from the four; and (b) whether any
of the simple entities is in any sense unlimited, whatever its description. That (b) it is not possible for one of the simple bodies – either   15
those that are known to us or any whatever – to be unlimited, we
shall show he says, by a common argument; that (a) neither is there
any perceptible body, which is also the subject of our argument, which

is other than the elements and their origin and substratum, we shall
show first and specifically. And he shows that perception knows
nothing of this kind, either as the substratum of things that are
20   coming to be or as the extreme of those that are being destroyed.

> **204b35** But neither fire nor any other of the elements can be
> unlimited. {Aristotle argues further that, even apart from the
> question of unlimitedness, the elements could not all become
> one element, since mutual change is perpetual.}

Having shown that the existence of the intermediary is impossible he
434,1   goes on to show that it is wholly impossible for any other simple body
to be an origin and unlimited, then, having laid this down, he brings
the argument to a somewhat more general level. For why, he asks,
do I say 'for any one of the simple entities to be unlimited'? For we
5   shall show that it is impossible for the origin of existents to be any
one simple thing, be this unlimited or limited. He has shown in a very
circuitous fashion that the unlimited cannot be one simple thing, if
indeed it is wholly impossible for the element to be one, whether it
be unlimited or limited. For if the element should be some one thing,
then coming to be will be generally eliminated and so will all alteration; and if this is absurd, it is therefore impossible for the element
10   to be one. For if it were some one of the four – fire, for example, as
Heraclitus said, or any other – it will have in itself a portion of
contrariety, such as warmth, and, in this case at any rate, nothing
perhaps will prevent it from altering to the contrary state, since every
alteration is from contrary to contrary. But it will either conserve in
the alteration the contrariety in respect of which it occurs (if, for
example, it should be fire, it will maintain its warmth in the altera-
15   tion to air, which is cool, and thus be at the same time in the contrary
states, which is impossible), or else, abandoning the warmth, it will
admit the coolness, and thus fire would no longer be preserved. But
the first origin must be preserved and be unalterable. And why, pray,
is air not the element rather than fire? For fire no more alters to air
than air to fire. It is therefore impossible that one of the simple
entities should be the element.
20   Therefore it is all the more impossible that the unlimited should
be some one of the simple entities, since the unlimited, if it exists, is
undoubtedly an origin and primary element. That it cannot be one of
the other four elements has been shown; that it can no more be the
intermediary, as Anaximander held, has already been shown, but will
435,1   now be shown also by the same method as the rest. For if that
intermediary has no contrariety to any of the four, neither could it
alter to any of these, and thus neither could anything arise from it.

It will therefore exist pointlessly; but nothing is pointless that is eternal.

Perhaps one might say, then, that we also are falling into the absurdities of Anaximander, by making matter deficient in all contrariety; or is there a great difference between the alteration of a thing itself and its being the medium of alteration? Therefore [we reply that] it is impossible for anything to change if it does not also possess a contrariety; but what argument prevents the alterations of contraries to contraries from occurring in it? Thus for us matter, though being one thing, is present in everything that comes to be, which [claim] is not preserved by those who propose that the element is one. And we do not say that matter subsists in itself in the absence of every quality,[170] but that it is always completely occupied by some form (and on this account, since it possesses a certain quality, it is through the affection of this by its contrary that we say that objects come to be and alter); Anaximander, however, in saying that the body without qualities subsists in actuality, is altogether under the necessity of proposing that it is not affected by anything (for if the affected subject is affected by its contrary, but there is nothing contrary to that [body], since it has been produced entirely without respect to any contrariety, it is presumably necessary that it should not suffer any affection from anything); in consequence, neither will anything come to be from it.

205a6 For everything alters from contrary to contrary.

This is the demonstration that none of the simple entities can be an unlimited element, neither one of the four nor the intermediary. For if there were some one element, how could there be generation or destruction when all alteration is from contrary to contrary? And how this is impossible, we have shown.

205a7 And in every case our inquiry into the possibility or impossibility of there being [an unlimited body] should be based on these facts.

Since he has formulated his argument with regard to fire and the intermediary (for he has mentioned Heraclitus, who posited fire as origin and said on this account that everything would at some time be resolved into it, since the whole will at some time suffer combustion), for this reason he has added that by the same means you will show that it is not possible for any of the others to be the origin either.

205a8 And that it is wholly impossible for there to be any unlimited perceptible body is obvious from these facts.

10   Having shown from the natural powers that it is impossible for there
to be any unlimited body, he now wishes to establish the same point
also from natural places. And he again uses the same division, viz.
that the unlimited is either simple or composite, and first he shows
that it is impossible for it to be simple. And first he takes a certain
pair of axioms: first, that every sensible body, which is the same as
15   to say every natural body, exists in a place (for each of the four
elements occupies a certain definite place); second, that whatever is
the place of the whole, the same is also the place of the portion. For
where all earth is naturally liable to be, there presumably the clod
both is and is naturally liable to be; and likewise, wherever fire is
naturally liable to be in its entirety, there also the spark is naturally
20   liable to be. On these assumptions, then, he shows that it is impossible
for the unlimited to be any natural body; for the subject of the present
inquiry, as I have often said, is whether there is among natural bodies
anything unlimited in extension. For, as for what is outside the
universe, he will show in his work *On the Heavens* that there is nothing
outside it,[171] whether a body or a void or anything else. That it is
25   impossible, then, for a natural simple body to be unlimited in its
extension, he shows in this way. If there were an unlimited body, it is
obvious that it will occupy every place, and if it occupies every place,
every place would seem to be germane to it. For if it were not germane
to it, [the unlimited] will always be in an unnatural place but nothing
437,1   that exists is always in an unnatural place; for it is easier for a thing
not to exist than to be always in an unnatural place. So that the whole
of place would seem to be germane to the unlimited.

But if every place is germane to the unlimited as a whole, then it
is obvious that the same place would be germane to the part too. Now,
5   it is patently obvious that the whole will be immobile (for, being
unlimited and occupying every place, it will have nowhere to move,
since there will be need of another unlimited place if it is to move),
but of the part I shall ask if I take a certain portion of the unlimited,
will it move or not? If, then, it will not move, neither would the
unlimited seem to be a natural body (for none of the natural bodies
10   is immobile both as a whole and in its parts); and if it will move,
whither will it go? Everywhere, perhaps, since every place is germane
to it? In that case, it will no more move downward than upward, at
least if its upward tendency and its downward one are alike –
granting also that we should admit an upward and downward in the
unlimited at all, for this will be the next thing that we examine.

It is necessary, then, that either: (a) the portion will be everywhere
15   simultaneously and will come to be in every place by one and the same
motion (for if it has a tendency in every direction, then just as
heaviness, say, causes it to move downwards, so at the same time
lightness will cause it to move upwards); or (b) the portion will

simultaneously occupy every place, which is impossible; or (c) it will stay, while being drawn to contrary places; or (d) it will be pulled asunder. And the same inquiry will arise again with regard to the sundered portions. For we know from patent fact that the place of the whole and of the portion is the same.

In any case, if it will move, how far will it go? For each of the things that are natural and in the domain of generation moves whenever it departs from its natural place, and carries on moving up to the point when it recovers its natural place, on reaching which it stays. If, now, (a) the portion of the unlimited moves at all, and (b) it moves in its natural place, and (c) every place is germane and natural to it, as it is to the whole, how far will it go? For it will not stay here rather than there, when every one is equally natural to it, so that it will go on for ever. For it will not cease when it has gone to its natural place, since every place alike is natural to it. Yet it must be naturally liable either (a) to abide everywhere, since everything abides when in its own place, and therefore it will not move anywhere but will be immobile; or (b) to go everywhere, and nowhere will it retain its position. But each is impossible; for no motion is eternal, except that in a circle, but every motion is for the sake of something (for a thing moves for the sake of attaining its natural place), and it is not possible for the unlimited to describe a circular motion. For to say 'circle' is at the same time to say 'limited', since everything that has shape is limited, and on this account it is not possible that any unlimited thing should be of the class that go in a circle.[172] It is therefore absurd that the portion should be always moving; for why are not all the portions also always moving? And if all are moving, then so will that which they all comprise. But it is impossible for the unlimited to move (Melissus too was at any rate, quite right to deny the motion of the unlimited).[173] Yet it is impossible for no portion of the unlimited to move (for then it will not be a natural body either), and to deny motion universally (a thing so patent and witnessed by perception) is unreasonable and in need of no refutation. If, then, being a natural body, the unlimited does not move, that is absurd; and if it moves, the aforesaid absurdities will follow.

It is impossible, therefore, for the unlimited to be any simple body. But if the unlimited should be composite, then obviously it is composed from contraries (for every natural body is of this kind), so that the components are also in different and contrary places. Since, then, every natural body that is composite is composed according to mixture, it will follow that the components are in a place unnatural for them, as is also the case with our bodies and with all the rest. For the fire and the air in us abides under constraint and in an unnatural place. It will therefore follow that many of the components of the unlimited are always in an unnatural place, for the unlimited is

20

25

438,1

5

10

15

20

25

eternal. But it is impossible for anything to be always in an unnatural place, for it is easier for something not to exist than for it always to be in an unnatural place. If, now, each is isolated and goes in its natural place, it will follow that the unlimited is made up of things in contact, but no natural body is composed of things in contact. Thus the unlimited will not be some single and continuous body, but every natural body is continuous.

439,1

And alternatively, if the unlimited is composite, it will either be composed of unlimited forms and unlimited individuals,[174] or from limited forms and unlimited indivduals. If, then, it is from limited forms and unlimited atoms, it is necessary that the individuals falling under one form should be unlimited. For otherwise it is impossible that, the forms being limited, the things that come from them should be unlimited. But if the atoms are unlimited, and the power of unlimited things is also unlimited, as has recently been said, it will obviously consume the rest, and thus the whole will again be simple and not composite.

5

Then, since he perceived that he had again undertaken the proof from powers, though his proposed aim was to prove from places that the unlimited cannot exist, on this account [Aristotle], wishing to refute the proposition from the difference in places, summons those very people who propose the existence of the unlimited as witnesses to his own words, speaking virtually as follows. Each of the natural bodies occupies a certain definite place, the heavy occupying the lower place and the light the upper;[175] but, if this is so, it is impossible for any one of the elements composing the unlimited, such as fire or earth, to be itself unlimited in magnitude. For if it should be unlimited, it will not have a certain defined place, but the place of each of the natural bodies is defined. Therefore it is not possible for any one of the components of the unlimited itself to be unlimited in magnitude. For then the unlimited will not have a defined place.

10

15

20

On this account, he says, all the physicists who proposed the existence of an unlimited body, did not propose that the origin which they also held to be unlimited was either fire or earth, but either air or water or the intermediary. For the place of fire and of earth is defined (for one is above, one below), whereas the place of air and water seems to be indefinite. At least, air and water subsist in the hollows of the earth, and also are both alike seen in the places above the earth. Water at least appears to come down from above. Since, then, the place of the unlimited is indefinite, and to them the places of these elements also seemed to be indefinite, they reasonably located the unlimited in these. If, now, the place of the unlimited must be indefinite, but none of the natural bodies has an indefinite place, it is therefore impossible that one of these should be unlimited.

25

30

Neither, then, is it possible that the unlimited should be from limited forms but unlimited atoms.

Perhaps, then, it is from both unlimited forms and unlimited atoms, one atom falling under each form, so that in this way the proposition may become more reasonable. That this also, then, is not   440,1 true, is obvious from the following remarks. First, the unlimited will be doubled, if indeed the forms should be unlimited and the atoms under them are also unlimited – an argument that he himself let pass – then, he says, if the simple forms of which the unlimited consists are unlimited, then, since things that differ in form also have differ-   5 ent places assigned to them, it is necessary that their places will also be unlimited. But this is impossible, for the places are limited. In the primary and most proper sense there are two, 'above' and 'below'; but in all there are six – these two, 'on the right' and 'on the left', and 'before' and 'behind'.[176] If, now, the natural places are limited, it is impossible for the elements to be unlimited, at least if the places of the elements are also distinguished along with the forms. But it is   10 not only by the forms, he says, that the places are distinguished, but also by distance. If, now, the places are limited both in number and in magnitude, the bodies in them will also be limited. For it is no more possible for a body to be larger than its place than for the place to be larger than the body.[177] For if the body should exceed the place, it will follow that not all of the body is in a place. Now it will either be in   15 the void or nowhere: for it to be nowhere is ridiculous, while he will show in the following book that there is no void among the exis- tents.[178] Likewise, if the place is larger than the body, it will again follow that there is a void.

But someone may wonder, how can he say that if the forms are unlimited, the places too must be unlimited? For what prevents it   20 from being the case that, just as now there are two places, above and below, but many bodies are in each (fire and air above and below earth and water) – that, similarly, even if the elements were unlimited, some would be in the lower and some in the upper place? For if the same place is at all naturally liable to receive two heterogeneous bodies, what prevents the same place from receiving even more? But   25 against this I say: How is it possible to distribute the unlimited among the limited? For this is impossible, since either in each of the places the forms will be unlimited, or in each they will be limited, or they will be unlimited in one and limited in the other. If, then, they should   441,1 be limited in each, then what comes from both will be limited as well. And if they should be unlimited in each, the unlimited will be doubled and will be the double of itself. And if they are unlimited in one but limited in the other, the unlimited will be increased by the addition of the limited, and will be larger than itself. And anyway if the   5 unlimited should indeed be in some place and not in another, the

unlimited will not occupy every place. It is therefore not possible for the places of the unlimited forms to be limited. For what we have said regarding two is the same as I shall say with regard to more also. And if it is impossible for the places to be unlimited, then it is presumably also impossible for the forms which are to be in them to be unlimited.
10 So that, if it is impossible for the unlimited to be either simple or composite, it is not possible for it to exist at all. You now have, then, an elimination of the unlimited on the basis of difference in place.

205a10 For every perceptible thing is naturally liable to be somewhere.

The first assumption is that every natural body is in place, a natural
15 body being what is subject to generation and destruction. For now we are inquiring whether there is something unlimited of this kind, which is such as to be an element of things that are generated and destroyed, as we now say that there are four elements of all the other things, and that things are generated from them and resolved into them. The argument now inquires whether perhaps there is some other thing before these, or one of them, or another apart from these,
20 unlimited in magnitude, from which both the elements and the rest come into being. Every body of this kind, then, is in a place, though that is not true of all *simpliciter*. The fixed sphere at least is not in place, since there is neither body nor void surrounding it, but it is in itself, as being itself, so to speak, its own place.[179]

205a11 [And each has some place] and that of the portion and of the whole is the same. {Thus, continues Aristotle, the place of the clod is that of earth, the place of the spark that of fire.}

25 The second axiom is that the place of the whole is the same as that of the portion. The same, obviously, not in quantity, but in form, such
442,1 as the upper or the lower. For just as if you should displace the whole of earth from the centre, it will go on up to the point at which it occupies the centre, in the same way the clod, if it is released from above, will have a tendency toward the same point.

205a12 So that if it is homogeneous, it will either be immobile
5 or will go on for ever. {The following words are quoted below as 205a13. Aristotle continues: 'I mean, for example, if there should be a clod, where will it go? For the place of its own kind of body is unlimited.'}

Here begin the demonstrations that the unlimited does not exist, and first that it is impossible for it to be simple. For this is what he means by 'homogeneous'. Now the words 'either it will be immobile or it will go on for ever' are not said by him of the whole of the unlimited, but of the portion of it. And he has given his proof next by examples, saying 'I mean, for example, if there should be a clod, where will it go? For the place of its own kind of body is unlimited.' That is, if the unlimited should be earth, then will the part of it, such as a clod, move forever or abide forever? For each answer will seem to be necessarily true. For if (a) the part also goes where the whole does, and likewise (b) stays where the whole does; if also (c) the place of its own kind of body (I mean of the entirety of the unlimited) is unlimited, and (d) the place of the part would also necessarily be the same: then – granting that the part of the unlimited is naturally liable to move in its proper place – since its place is unlmited, it will presumably be naturally liable to move everywhere (for why should it move rather in this way than in that, when every place is equally germane to it? But if it moves in the unlimited, it will follow that it goes on forever, and never stays). But if it is not naturally liable to move in its proper place, but to stay (which is what we rather observe in natural entities), then since again the unlimited place is the one germane to the part, it will stay in every place, so that it will be immobile in any direction. It is therefore necessary that the portion should either be always in motion or always in the same position, but each is absurd.

But the argument admits of a certain objection. For we have said that the place of the whole and of the part is not the same in respect of quantity, since the whole place in which the whole of earth is is not also the same place where the clod is (for by this token the part will be equal to the whole), but the same in form, e.g. 'below'. To illustrate: if you conceive the earth being increased so as to reach the lunar sphere,[180] you will say that all the place within the sphere is that of earth, but you will not say *simpliciter* that the whole belongs to it by nature, but that the inclination to the centre is by nature, and that it follows on account of its continuous magnitude that it spreads far out from the centre under its own support (since now too the parts of the earth in the region of its convex surface, which we too inhabit, do not abide where they are as being naturally liable to remain so far from the centre, but because they are supported by the continuity from the centre of the earth. At least, if you dig into the parts in the region of the surface, the parts dug up around the excavation will go downward). Just so, [the clod of earth] is not naturally liable to abide in the place where it is in the absence of any force, but is supported by its own kind of body. So that even should it be increased as far as the heavens, so as to contain the place of the light bodies too, all the place within the sphere would be likewise said to belong to it as a whole; nevertheless, it would not be naturally liable to abide in the whole of the place, even without the fact of its being held in from the middle.

15   The clod, then, is rightly said to move in the whole of this place if the meaning is that it is naturally liable to go from the surface of the heavens as far as the centre; for if you were to say that, because the earth contains the whole of both the place above and the place below, the clod on this account also ought to go in every direction equally,

20   above as well as below, because its entirety is everywhere; this would no longer be reasonable. For it is not even now the case that, since the earth spreads in its entirety as far as the surface of the air that contains it, and the place of the whole is from there as far as the centre, the clod on this account ought presumably to go in every direction within this place. For the clod in the centre, even if it got

25   room, would not be moved from there to the surface of the earth. In the same way, it is not reasonable to say of the unlimited that the part of it goes everywhere because the unlimited occupies every place

444,1 – at least not if the unlimited has any natural tendency at all. But either it has no natural tendency, and thus is immobile in all directions, or if it has a tendency at all, it is not reasonable to say that the part will either keep its position or go in every direction, just as it is unreasonable now to say this of earth, as has been said.

But it is possible to say in answer to this too, that it is possible at

5   present to say what we have said because the earth is limited and so is the place that contains it; if, now, there should be some unlimited place, how is it possible to divide up the unlimited and say that this is its natural place, but this not? For as he himself said in his previous remarks, how is it possible to say of the unlimited that some is above and some below, some before or behind? For the unlimited is on all

10   sides like itself. Therefore it is impossible to determine a portion or point of the unlimited place and say that this is the natural place of the unlimited body, as we presently say that the centre is the natural place of heavy things. The remaining possibility, then, is to say that the whole of place without limit is reasonably the place of the unlimited body; but if the whole should be its natural place, then the

15   things that Aristotle has said will follow.

'So that, if it is homogeneous, it will be immobile.' It is possible to take 'it will be immobile' as a consequence only of being uniform. For if (a) the unlimited is simple and homogeneous, and (b) all place is germane to it and (c) the same place is germane to the part, and if (d)

20   none of the bodies that go straight moves in its own place: then the portion of the unlimited will not move. This, then, follows plausibly from the proposition that the portion of the unlimited is immobile, since it is in its own place and this is the unlimited. But if someone will not grant this, sc. that it is immobile, so as not to deny motion, he will at any rate grant that it will go on forever. For this is what he

means by 'or it will go on forever' – that if we deny that it stays forever, it follows that it will move forever, since the argument that shows it to be immobile, if someone does not accept it, will necessarily show that it is always in motion. For if (a) it is naturally liable to move in its own place, as the proposition states, and (b) its place is that of the whole, and (c) this is unlimited, it will therefore move in the unlimited place. So that it will not stay in one place (for the motion is in an unlimited space), and will not go that way rather than this, but everywhere equally.

25

445,1

205a13 But that is impossible; for why should it be down rather than up or in any other direction?

He says that it is 'impossible' to be in motion forever, and then infers why it is impossible. For why will it move upward rather than downward at the same time and in the same place? For if (a) all place is germane to it and (b) there is in every place the above and the below (for this I apprehend from patent fact), then at the same time and in the same place it will no more move up than down, if it is indeed naturally liable to go everywhere. But it is impossible to move in contrary directions at the same time. For if (a), on account of its having an impulse to move towards every place, it goes where the impulse leads it on being parted from the whole;[181] (b) it goes equally towards everything; but (c) it is impossible for this to happen: therefore it is impossible even to move. For it is necessary, if it moves, that it move thus.

5

10

205a16 Will it then occupy the whole of place? And how?

That is, will it, because it is naturally liable to go toward every place, move everywhere at the same time, both upward and downward? But this is impossible, for it would thus be moving in contrary directions at the same time.

15

205a17 What then, and where, is its permanence and its motion?

That is, either where and toward what place will it move, or in what sort of place will it stay?

'Will it abide everywhere? It will therefore not move. Or will it move everywhere? It will therefore not stay [205a18].' If it is at rest, he says, it will be at rest everywhere (for it will not be at rest when it arrives in its own place, since every place is germane to it and it will therefore be everywhere at rest.) But if this is so, it will not move at all. Again, if it will move, it will move everywhere equally, since

20

once again all place is germane to it. But how, if I am to agree that it
moves in every direction, is it possible to avoid the conclusion that
25   when in motion it never stays?

446,1   **205a19** And if the whole is diverse, then the places too are
diverse.

Having shown that it is not simple, he now shows that it is not
composite either. If, now, it is from non-homogeneous [components],
it is necessary that the places of these also should be many. For when
things are heterogeneous their places are also different. But if this is
so, first it is absurd that the places of the whole should not be
5   continuous, but from things that are in contact. And how this comes
about I have already explained by saying that, if heterogeneous
things should be mixed, they will always be in the unnatural place;
and, if this is impossible and each must occupy its own place, the
unlimited will be from things in contact. But no natural body is of
this kind.

{And so, Aristotle argues, the all will not be one except by
contact.}

10   **205a22** That these [components] should be limited, then, is not
possible; for then some will be unlimited and some not, if the
whole is unlimited.

It is impossible, he says, that the unlimited should be composed of
limited forms. For it is necessary that one of the things that fall under
the form should be unlimited either in amount or in magnitude. For
if the individuals under the forms should be limited, then that which
15   they all constitute will also be limited. If again all or some should be
unlimited, the unlimited will be multiplied two or many times. The
remaining possibility, then, is that the atoms under one form should
be unlimited. But this is also impossible; for, first, here too there
arises an increment in the unlimited, through the addition of the
limited to the unlimited, then (as we have just said) the limited will
20   be consumed by the unlimited. For the power in the unlimited is
unlimited.

205a25 And on this account no one [among the physical theo-
rists] said that the one and unlimited element was fire [or
earth]. {Aristotle adds that they made it water, air or their
intermediary, since each of the former had a determinate place.}

The handling of the argument is rather elliptical (for, as I have said, he added these remarks because he wished to refute the proposition on principles which they accepted). For he should have said that anyway it is not possible for one of the elements in the composition to be unlimited, since the natural place is defined for each of the elements, but the unlimited does not have a defined place. Thus it could not be the case that one of the elements is unlimited. And that the place of the unlimited is indefinite the physicists also prove; at least 'it was on this account that no one said that the one and unlimited element was fire' – and so on.[182]   25

205a28 But these [viz. water and air] occur both above and below.   447,1

However, they ought to be aware that it is not only water and air that are seen in the places foreign to them, but also earth and fire. In many places, at least, there are craters of fire, as in both Etna and Cilicia,[183] and they say that thunderbolts take shape above and go downward.[184]   5 But it is obvious that they cannot go in foreign places according to their actuality, but in so far as they are in process of becoming, since everything undergoes alteration to everything.

205a29 But if they are unlimited and simple, then their places will also be unlimited.

He turns to the other proposition, which is that the forms are unlimited, since it is obvious that the individuals will also be unlim-   10 ited, at least if the smallest single individual falls under one form. If then the components of the unlimited should be unlimited in form, then, since the places of things that differ in form are also different, the places will necessarily also be unlimited. But this, he says, is impossible; for all natural places are limited, and, if the places are limited, then necessarily the bodies in them will also be limited; and,   15 if the bodies are limited, it is necessary that what they constitute should be limited also. But why, if the places are limited in number, is it necessary that the bodies in them should be limited, not only in amount, but also in magnitude? Because every place is limited in magnitude (for it contains the body which is in place), and if the place is limited, it is necessary that the body in it be limited also. For   20 neither, he says, can the place be larger than the body (for then it is void), nor can the body be larger than the place, since then there will be body not in place.

205a30 And the elements will be unlimited. [And if this is impossible and places are limited, so then must the whole be.]

This by itself has the power of a demonstration. For if the unlimited
25　is composed from unlimited forms, it is necessary that the elements
also be unlimited. But this he has also shown to be impossible in his
arguments against Anaxagoras in the first book,[185] and he will show
it also in his work *On the Heavens*, and particularly in that *On
Generation*.[186] For there it is said that, if the elements should be
448,1　unlimited, the unlimited will be doubled with its substrata, and that
will put an end to generation and in general to all alteration (for the
alterations must be unlimited if there is to be generation of anything);
but this is impossible. We must therefore add the phrase 'and if this
is impossible' to the words 'the places also are unlimited'.[187] The
5　phrase 'and if this is impossible' means, if it is impossible that the
places should be unlimited.

{205a32 Body and place must go together, 'for neither can the
whole place be larger than the body can be ... neither yet the
body larger than the place'. After the first impossibility Aristotle
adds the following parenthesis.}

205a34 and at the same time, neither will body be unlimited.

To the words 'for neither is the whole place larger than the body is
able to be', we must annex 'neither yet is the body larger than the
place', and so on; then 'at the same time, neither will the body be
unlimited'.[188] For this is, as it were, the conclusion to which the other
10　remarks converge. For if the place is not larger than the body, nor the
body larger than the place, and every place is limited, then it is
necessary that the body too be limited. No body, therefore, will be
unlimited.

205b1 But what Anaxagoras says about the permanence of the
unlimited is absurd; for he says that the unlimited sustains
itself.

15　Anaxagoras, he says, gives an absurd reason for the abiding and
immobility of the unlimited, this being in his view the composite of
the homoeomeries, which were unlimited; and this [composite] he
said Mind had begun to separate out after a certain time.[189] Saying
then that this whole mixture was immobile, Anaxagoras gave the
following reason for the immobility. It was not by virtue of being
20　always in its natural place that it was immobile (for he even denied
that it was in place at all, in order not to make it also limited as an
immediate consequence), but the cause of its immobility was that it
sustained itself, that is, it offered resistance to itself and rested on

itself; and this property belonged to it because it was neither in nor contained by anything, but was itself in itself and constituted its own place. And [Anaxagoras] maintains this, says [Aristotle], on the ground that everything, wherever it is, is also there by natural liability. For if it stays, not because it is in its natural place, but because it sustains and is in itself, it is presumably possible that it should exist and stay elsewhere, so long as it sustained and was in itself. But this is false; for the reason why earth abides is not that it sustains itself and is attracted to itself. For if this were the reason for its permanence, then if in supposition I raise the earth and take it up as far as the fiery sphere,[190] since there too it is in and sustains itself, it ought presumably also to be immobile. But this is impossible, for it will keep going until it reaches its natural place, and this is the middle. Thus the cause of its present abiding is not that it sustains itself.

And alternatively: to sustain itself and be in itself and contained by nothing will not suffice to make the unlimited naturally immobile. For on the contrary this is the cause of enforced permanence. For it fails to move through lacking a place and having nowhere to move to, not through having no liability to move. For it is not apparent whether it would be at rest if there were a place. Our reason, at any rate, for saying that earth abides by nature is that, even though there is place available everywhere, it nevertheless moves nowhere. Since, then, having somewhere to move, it nevertheless does not move, we say that therefore the cause of its abiding is its natural liability to be in the centre. Just as, then, if we advance the proposition that the earth is unlimited ...[191] as it now is, while it was possible to say that it sustains and is in itself and contained by nothing, yet still this was not the cause of its natural immobility, but rather 'that it was held together by the middle' and inclined toward it: so I say also in the case of the unlimited, that even if it sustains itself and is contained by nothing, this is not the natural cause of its immobility. For, on the contrary, the permanence is enforced. For why is it that if it had a place it would not move? Anaxagoras ought therefore to have given a natural reason for the immobility of the unlimited, since the cause which he gives – that it is a mixture out of all things – does not explain the nature of the unlimited, but its magnitude. For if it were natural for the unlimited to be immobile, then it would presumably also be natural for each of its parts. For what is natural for the whole of earth is also natural for each of its parts, and what is natural for the whole of water, as being such a nature and constitutive of its essence, is also natural for a single measure.

Is it therefore natural for each of the parts to sustain and be in itself, or is it not? For if it is natural, then the portions of it would also be immobile; but neither does he believe this, nor does sense

449,1

5

10

15

20

450,1

5

10

agree. If, on the other hand, the portions are able to move in virtue of being limited, then it is not because of the nature of the body that immobility is a property of the whole, since this would also be a property of the portions, granting that the mixture is homogeneous
15   (for everything is equally in everything);[192] but the reason would be its magnitude. But this is not to give a natural cause. And all in all, if the unlimited were naturally liable to be in itself and be its own place, then also each of its parts ought to be its own place and be in itself. For the places of the whole and the parts are similar, as has already been said. If, now, the place of the unlimited is to be in itself,
20   then the same would also be the place of the part, and the cause of the immobility would be that it is in itself and its own place. And the parts would therefore be immobile along with the wholes; but this is both false and impossible.

And anyway, if the place of the parts is to be in themselves, since it is so for the whole as well, nothing prevents fire from existing below and earth above (for each of these is in itself, wherever it may be);
25   but this is impossible. This, then, is not the natural place of the parts, and neither, therefore, is it that of the whole; for the place of the whole and of the part is formally the same.

451,1   **205b3** And this is because in itself ... [wherever it may be, it is naturally liable to be there].

For this reason, he says, the unlimited sustains itself, that it is not in place and is not contained by another thing, but is in itself. So that 'wherever it may be, it is naturally liable to be there'. He says this in
5   ridicule: since everything, he says, wherever it is, is also naturally liable to be there, so he says it is with this as well. For if being in itself were the cause of permanence, then, even if fire were not above but below, it would abide in the place below through being in itself. But this is false. In the same way, even the suspended clod is not naturally liable to be aloft, but below. If, then, the place of each thing were not
10   defined by nature, earth and fire ought not to abide above any more than below.

{205b5 It is not true that the everything is in its natural place, since it might be somewhere under compulsion. So if the whole is the immobile *par excellence*, we must say why it is naturally so. A parenthesis explains the assumption of immobility.}

205b6 For what is self-sustained and in itself is necessarily immobile.

Even if we grant this, he says, that what is sustained by itself and is in itself through being contained by nothing is necessarily immobile, yet still this is not the cause of its natural immobility. For it is able to be immobile in this way through having nowhere to which it can move, but if it has nowhere to move, there is nothing to prevent its having at least a natural liability to move. He ought, then, to give the cause of its natural immobility, and not of that which is enforced and unnatural.

> **205b8-10** A thing might be in fact immobile yet naturally liable to move, since earth also does not move, [and would not] even if it was unlimited, being held together by the centre.

Just as, he says, if earth were unlimited, its failure to move would not be the result of its being unlimited and having nowhere to move, but of its being held together at the centre (it was possible, now, to say that it is immobile for this reason, that it sustains itself and is contained by nothing; but he proves that this is not the cause of its immobility from the fact that at present it does at least have somewhere to move, but nevertheles does not move) – just so, then, even if the unlimited should not move, a natural cause should be stated for its immobility. For that which he has given lies in its magnitude.

> {205b12 The cause of the earth's immobility is its weight, not its unlimitedness; so too the cause of the immobility of the unlimited might be something else.}

> **205b18** And at the same time, it is obvious that every portion whatever would have to abide.

For if the cause of the immobility of the whole were its being in itself, this ought also to be the cause of the immobility of the part. For the place of the whole and of the part is the same. If, then, it is also natural for the part to sustain itself, all would be immobile; but if it moves because of the limitation of the part, therefore immobility did not belong even to the whole by nature, but because it had nowhere to move.

> **205b24** And in general it is manifestly impossible to say at the same time that the unlimited is a body and that there is a certain place for bodies. {Aristotle goes on to argue that all perceptible bodies have weight or lightness and therefore motion, which implies the distinction of places, which cannot occur 'in an unlimited body' (205b35). He then maintains that absurdities result from the denial of the unlimited, and thus infers the need for an 'arbitrator' (206a12).}

Having shown by consideration of powers and places that it is impossible for there to be an unlimited body, he now demonstrates this same thing also by considering the weights in accordance with which the natural bodies are moved. For there are two forms of motion in the whole, that in a straight line and that in a circle; and of motion in a straight line one sort is upward, that of light things, and the other downward, that of heavy things.[193] If therefore it has been shown that none of the bodies that are moved either in a straight line or in a circle describes a single and unlimited motion, but every motion that is single is limited, it is obvious that there will not be an unlimited place either; and if there is not an unlimited place, then neither will there be a natural body that is unlimited. For every body is in a place. Here, then, he shows that there is no unlimited motion in a straight line and, in his work *On the Heavens*,[194] that no circular motion can be unlimited either. But if every body is moved either in a circle or in a straight line, and both motions are limited, then necessarily the things in motion will also be limited.

He shows here, as I have said, that none of the bodies that move in a straight line can be unlimited, and he shows this first through a hypothetical syllogism.[195] For if, he says, there is any perceptible body that is unlimited, it will have either weight or lightness (for every perceptible body has either weight or lightness), and yet it is impossible for the unlimited body to have either weight or lightness and, therefore, it is not at all possible for an unlimited body to be among the things that move in a straight line. Whence [comes the conclusion] that it is impossible for the unlimited body to have either weight or lightness? Because if it should be heavy, he says, the whole of it will be below, and if is should be light, the whole of it will be above. The absurdity[196] of its being either entirely above or entirely below is so clear that he does not even establish it (the first reason is that bodies are not only heavy, but also light; and the second is that if it occupies only the place above, the place below will be vacant, and if it occupies only the place below, the place above will be vacant: how, then, can that be unlimited which does not occupy all places?). He does, however, consider, or rather he reduces to absurdity, the proposition that part of it is heavy and part light.

For if part of it should be heavy and part light, part of it will be above and part below. How then will you divide the unlimited, he asks, so that you can also give a portion to each place? Will you say that half is heavy and half light, or adopt some other solution? And how is it possible for there to be a half or two-thirds of the unlimited, or any portion at all? Then how in general is it possible for there to be an above and below in the unlimited? Where will you begin and end in marking off the part above, and the same with the part below? For this is impossible with respect to the unlimited. And if in general it has an above and a below, it will also have extremes; for these are extremes. But if it has extremes, it could not be unlimited. And it is possible to say here what was said also with regard to powers, that they will be either mixed together or in contact, and then the previous arguments will follow.

This, then, is the first demonstration. The second is again from places. Every natural body, he says, is in a place, and there are six 25 different kinds of place: the places most properly so are two, the above and the below, and beside these there are four others – before, behind, right and left. I spoke first of the above and the below, because 454,1 together they eliminate all the rest and are not eliminated. For if these do not exist the others cannot exist either; whereas nothing prevents the existence of the above and the below in the absence of the others. For when there is breadth or depth, it is altogether necessary that there should also be length, but if there is length, the others do not follow necessarily. But this he shows more accurately in the treatise *On the Heavens*.[197] There are, then, six different kinds 5 of place, and these, he says, do not exist only in so far as they are posited and with respect to ourselves, but also exist by nature in the whole. And the above and below are manifestly so, while the right and left are obviously so in particulars (for some of the parts are on the right by nature, and some on the left), and in the whole the things on the right are those in the east, as being the originators of motion, 10 and the things on the left are those opposite.[198] So too the poet calls them, for he says:[199]

> Whether they go to the right, towards the dawn and the sunrise,
> Or to the left, and make for the region of mist and darkness.

These, then, are the things on the right and on the left, and by analogy the things in the north are before, and those in the south are 15 behind. It is therefore necessary that, if there is an unlimited body this will be in a place, and being in a place will have one of these dimensions. But it is impossible to grasp these differences 'in an unlimited body'. For which of the parts of the unlimited will you mark off for which of the places? For it necessarily follows at once that it is limited if it is divided into portions along with the differences in place. For either some of the portions will be unlimited and others limited, 20 or all will be unlimited, or all limited. And if all are limited, then the combination of all of them will also be limited; but if one of the other possibilities should be true, the unlimited will be either multiplied or increased.

Third. Every place is limited by nature (for there is a limit of what surrounds); if then every body is in a place and every place is limited, every body is therefore limited. And negatively:[200] if every body is in 25 a place, and an unlimited place does not exist, then no body will be unlimited.

The fourth demonstration that he posits is as follows. It is altogether necessary, he says, that when we predicate the genus of something we also predicate one of the species (for nothing is a genus in itself, but it is observed in its species, nor is there any animal which is not at all events a man or a horse or another of the animals falling under a species).[201] If, therefore, the unlimited is in a place, then at all events it will also be in one of the species of place, either in the place above or that below or in some one of the others (for there is no place apart from the aforesaid ones), and it has been shown repeatedly that it is impossible for the unlimited to be in any of these. Such then are his reasonings here, but in the work *On the Heavens* he establishes by many demonstrations that unlimited circular motion is equally impossible,[202] since the circle itself cannot be unlimited either; of these I shall mention two or three, the ones that are most easy in conception even for those who have not been trained in the study of geometry.[203]

It has been shown at any rate in geometry that if two straight lines from one point are produced without limit, the interval between them will be increased without limit, and if you conceive the straight lines as becoming actually unlimited, then the interval between them will be actually unlimited. This being so, if you conceive of two straight lines produced without limit from the centre of the earth, one to the south and the other to the east, then if the interval between them is unlimited, it follows that, since the sun moves through such an interval in six hours – I mean from the east to the south – it will move through an unlimited interval in a limited time; which is impossible.[204] The interval between the straight lines is therefore not unlimited but limited. The same result will follow also if we produce two straight lines from the centre to the south and to the west. Hence the interval from the south to the west will also be limited. And the same result follows for the other hemisphere. Therefore circular motion cannot be unlimited either.

He shows the same thing also in this way. Just as, he says, a triangle or a square cannot be said to be unlimited, but at the same time as I refer to these I conceive of some particular figures (one limited by three borders, one by four), so it is equally impossible either to speak of a circle as unlimited or of figure *simpliciter*. For the very concept of the shape is significant of a border and a limit. If, then, it is impossible to speak of a circle as unlimited, it will be much more impossible yet that circular motion should be unlimited; for it is necessary that what is true of the path of the motion should also be true of the motion. If then it is not possible either for bodies that move in a straight line or for those that move in a circle that their motion should be unlimited, it is obvious that there cannot be an unlimited place either. No body, therefore, either of those that move in a circle or of those that move in a straight line, can be unlimited.

Having said this, then, and having shown by all these considera- 456,1 tions that it is impossible for any body to be unlimited in actuality, he next proceeds to the proof of the opposite. For if, he says, the unlimited should not exist anywhere in any way, countless impossibilities will follow, just as he also said before. For neither will time be eternal, he says, but there will be some origin and end of it – an impossible state of affairs. For to say that time once began to be is to 5 say nothing else than that there was a time when time was not. For all that comes into being comes to be in time, and the term 'when' is predicated of time. And motion is also shown to be eternal, time being its concomitant.[205]

This then is one absurdity that ensues for those who utterly refuse to allow the unlimited; another is that things which are continuous will not admit division without limit, and a third is that number will 10 come to an end as it is increased. If, then, he says, both the arguments that deny the unlimited and those that maintain it are true, there will be need of 'an arbitrator' who will arbitrate between the contrary arguments, and show in what respect they are true and in what respect untrue. For unless the unlimited subsists in one respect but not in another, it would not be the case that each of the arguments appeared true. Having said this, he next arbitrates, verbally dividing 15 what exists.

But first let us consider the arguments about time. If some absurdity follows on the statement that there was once when there was no time[206] – viz. that there was a time when there was no time – and this negation is false for this reason, that both the terms 'was' and 'once' are temporal appellations, which we declare to have subsisted 20 before time, it is presumably necessary that the corresponding affirmation is true and that no absurdity follows from it, I mean that which states that there was once when there was time. For in every case either the affirmation or the negation is true. But, since the terms 'was' and 'once' indicate time, the affirmation means nothing other than that there was a time when there was time. What there- 25 fore the difference is between these times, the time which was and 457,1 that which existed in it, even one who wished could not imagine. For just as if one were to say 'there was once when Socrates was', he has spoken of one thing that is the time and another that is the Socrates who existed in that time, just so presumably when he says 'There was once when there was time', he says that there was one time in another. One therefore must be the substratum and the other must 5 inhere in that.

But if someone were to say 'I apply to the same thing the terms

"was", "once" and "time" ', he must know that, as well as deserving ridicule, he has destroyed the affirmation by making the same thing the subject and the predicate.[207] For just as if one were to say 'Socrates was when Socrates was', he would be ridiculous, not utter-
10 ing an affirmation, in which the subject term must always be other than the predicate, but one and the same term circling back on itself – just so presumably he who says 'There was once when there was time', if he thinks to express the same time in the subject and in the predicate, will deserve the same ridicule. And another argument is that if the affirmation and the negation employ the same terms in
15 identical senses, and in the negation the terms 'was' and 'once' imply a time subsisting before time, then presumably the same sense must be preserved in the affirmation also. There will therefore be a certain time in which a certain other time subsisted. An 'x' will therefore be in an 'x'; but that is impossible.

As far, then, as concerns these lofty reasonings,[208] the contradic-
20 tion will be false, since an absurdity follows both upon the negation and upon the affirmation. But the reason of your error was not to be aware that it is impossible to predicate anything of anything without a certain temporal connotation, on account of our weakness … .[209] but not even in the case of those very things that are divine. Now how is it not ridiculous to think that the terms 'was' and 'is' are in every case predicated of time, but not also of a subsistent entity,[210] as when I
25 say that 'Socrates was' or 'the Lyceum was',[211] if time is also indicated therewith in a certain way? Presumably we say that there is a God, yet hardly predicate time of Him.[212] For even if they say that the term 'to be' used of God is not in contrast to the other parts of time, it is at any rate true that this word is used in contrast to 'was' and 'will be',
30 yet nevertheless the mind corrects the weakness of the word. So it is,
458,1 then, when I say that 'There was when there was no time' (for I suppress the term 'once' as being more easily turned to bad account), I apply the term 'was' to some subsistent entity, not to time, meaning, say, that there was eternity[213] or certain other divine essences.

And I correct the weakness of the term in the following manner, by saying that 'was' is single as regards being a term, but not so in sense. For it signifies both the subsistence of whatever thing it is
5 predicated of, and also signifies a certain portion of time that is past. The sense, then, in which it shows the thing to subsist I accept, but that in which it means a segment of time I accept no longer. Just as, then, they say with regard to the term 'is' that it signifies both that with parts, which is also predicated of God, and a part of time – since,
10 despite the fact that the word in itself signifies a segment of time, we have nevertheless made a contrast between the senses from that between the subjects of which they are predicated – thus I say it is also with the term 'was', that, since it signifies both time and the

subsistence of a thing, when I say that 'There was when there was not time', I predicate the term 'was' of a certain subsistent entity, not of time. And it is possible to escape those ridiculous mischief-makings by saying that 'There was not always time'. It was, indeed, possible 15
to expose the fatuity of such arguments at greater length, but even these remarks are sufficient for a digression.

Now to say that everything that comes to be does so in time – this too is false. By that which comes to be I mean simply everything that once did not exist, but later existed. And that such things [i.e. which come to be without time] are countless Aristotle himself shows in the last part of this work.[214] Such, for example, are points, contacts, and 20
not these only, but also all the forms. For these come to be in their subjects and depart from them timelessly. And another argument is that even if they deny the coming-to-be of time *simpliciter*, yet they will not therefore deny that a certain time comes to be, such as the current year, since equally they deny that man *simpliciter* comes to be, yet say that a certain man comes to be; and obviously those things 25
all of whose particular instances suffer destruction. Since, then, this day or this year comes to be, they must in every case come to be in time, at least if it is true *simpliciter* that all that comes to be does so in time; there would then have to be another time in which the day will come to be. There will therefore be two times, as for example two days. And what is the difference of one from the other? But even to say these things is worthy of ridicule; and that motion has not been 30
shown to be necessarily eternal I have shown sufficiently in my studies of the eighth book of this work.

But we must return to the point from which we set out. Arbitrating 459,1
between the arguments about the unlimited, Aristotle offers the following division between existents. Of existents, he says, some exist potentially, some actually, and of the potential some exist in such a way that they can pass in their entirety into actuality and utterly lose their potentiality, while others never completely lose their potential- 5
ity, but their essence consists in this – that they always exist potentially. An example of the former case is the potential grammarian who becomes so in actuality; an example of the latter is when we say that matter is potentially all things. For this never comes into actual being in its entirety, so as no longer to possess anything in potential; for even if it should receive one form, all the rest exist potentially. 10
Again, of those things that are actual, some are such as to acquire actuality in their entirety, such as the actual man, while others are such as to acquire actuality part by part, as when we say that the day or the contest are actually present, not by virtue of the whole day being present at once, but by virtue of part of it being so; and so too we say that the contest is present, by virtue of the boxing or the wrestling or some other competition. 15

These things being so, it has already been shown sufficiently that, as regards magnitude, there is no unlimited body that is untraversable in magnitude. There is, now, one that is infinite with regard to division and its converse, addition. For we say that things continuous are potentially divisible without limit,[215] not potentially in the same way as we say that bronze is potentially a statue, because at
20 some time it will be an actual statue; for it could never become unlimited in actuality. For in the case of the bronze and the statue the potentiality ceases when the actuality supervenes, for the statue which has come to be no longer has the potential to become a statue. For in such cases the thing in potential is named with regard to the thing in actuality, so that it is possible for the potential thing to progress to the actuality in regard to which it is also named; but in
25 the case of those things whose existence consists in being potentially existent, it is impossible ever to progress to such an actual state as to be completely rid of the potentiality. Just as it is with matter, which is said indeed to be all things in potential, but will never progress to such an actual state that its potentiality wholly disappears: so it is also in the case of the unlimited, for the magnitude is said to be divisible without limit, but this does not mean that this will ever come
30 to pass, but that it is always observed to be in the process of coming to be.
460,1 The potential and the actual, then, are the same for the unlimited, but the actual in the same way as we say that the contest and the day exist in actuality, not by virtue of the whole having come to pass, but by virtue of its coming to be part by part. It is therefore in this way that the unlimited exists in actuality, that some part of it is always present, and it is always possible to take something else outside what
5 has already been taken. If, then, one wishes the unlimited to exist in *entelechy* in this way – that being a certain form and shape it can also be taken as a whole[216] – this man is seeking nothing other than a limit of the unlimited, or rather its destruction. For if he wishes divisibility without limit to to be present as a whole in magnitude so that there is no remainder with the potential for division, he has destroyed its unlimited potential for division;[217] for it does not remain
10 at all divisible. So that this *entelechy* is the destruction of that of which is *entelechy*; and this is impossible, since every *entelechy* ought to preserve the substratum.
Now just as we show that the *entelechy* of what is changeable, in so far as it is changeable, preserves the potentiality of the cause of change, so the *entelechy* and perfection of the unlimited is the potential to go ever further and not to reach an end. And if its potentiality
15 should ever cease, then its being unlimited will cease forthwith. For just as, if things whose existence consists in the process of coming-to-be stop coming to be, they exist no longer – such things as the contest,

the day, the time and the flame – so those things whose existence consists in being potentially, if they lose their potentiality, *ipso facto* lose their existence along with it. If, then, when we say that magnitude is divisible without limit, someone were to wish that this unlimited process should actually come to pass, he has *ipso facto* destroyed the potentiality for unlimited division. For no limit is ever set to the unlimited, since if you should set a limit to the sections, you have made them limited, not unlimited.

For we do not say that magnitude can be divided into an unlimited number of parts, but rather that it is divisible without limit, and these statements differ immensely. For to divide into an unlimited number of parts is impossible (the process being destructive of itself, because if it is divided it is never into an unlimited number, since the unlimited cannot be traversed and everything traversable is *ipso facto* also limited. And it can also be argued that if it is divided into an unlimited number of parts it is also composed of an unlimited number, and what is composed of an unlimited number of parts is unlimited. Now that this is impossible, we have just ceased saying). On the other hand, nothing prevents unlimited division, since the remainder always has the potential to be divided.

However, the potential and the actual in the case of the unlimited can be considered in the same way as in the case of the potential and the actual statue. For when it has not yet begun to be divided, it is potentially divisble without limit in the same way as the bronze is potentially a statue, but when the division commences, it then comes to be actually divisible to infinity, as the bronze comes to be actually a statue. Except that at the same time the actuality is not as in the case of the bronze, but as in that of the contest, the day and matter – by virtue of being present part by part. Let no one therefore seek the *entelechy* of the unlimited as a thing similar to that of a bed and a house, but, as I have said, to that of the contest and the day. For he must not think that the division occurs all at once or is able to happen simultaneously, but that it takes place part by part, the remainder being always capable of division.

And so it is too with the unlimited increase of number, by virtue of its always being possible to take a number greater than the one that has been taken, and what is taken will always be limited. But if you wish number to be increased without limit, so as to traverse in actuality the unlimitedness in increase, you have *ipso facto* destroyed the unlimitedness. For having halted the increase, you have set a limit to the unlimited. And it is not only in number that there is no limit with respect to increase, but also in magnitudes – not in such a way that the increased magnitude exceeds all the others (for that is impossible, as it is impossible for there to be a body greater than the universe),[218] but if the increase occurs in the opposite manner to the division. For if I take a limited straight line and bisect it, and then proceed with the division of one, adding whatever I cut from one to the other, just as the division of one comes to pass without limit, so too will the increase of the other proceed without limit, but in the opposite manner. For what we take from the former we add to the other. And so the increase does not expire, becoming greater than everything, nor does it even become equal to the whole of the thing itself that is being divided; for a certain magnitude is always left, which was a portion of the whole that is undergoing the division.

205b24[219] And generally it is manifestly impossible at the same time to assume the unlimited body and that there is a certain place for bodies.

It is impossible, he says, for one who proposes that there is an unlimited body at the same time also to propose that there is a natural place for each of the bodies. Now if the place of each of the natural bodies is obvious, it is therefore impossible for there to be an unlimited body. And that it is impossible for there to be an unlimited body, if every natural body has a place, he proceeds to show.

{All perceptible bodies have weight or lightness, and hence move up or down.}

205b28 But it is impossible that the whole should be affected in either way or half in each.

It is impossible, he says, for the whole of the unlimited to be either, whether heavy or light, or for half of it to be affected in each way – that is, for each of its halves to be subject to one of the affects and for one half to be heavy, the other light.

205b29 For how will you divide it? Or how will there be part of the unlimited that is above, and part below, or an extremity and a centre?

For if you allot all the parts of the unlimited to places, you *ipso facto* make it also limited. For how can there be part of the unlimited that is above and part below? From where to where will the part above be, and the same for the part below? And, to argue otherwise, if it has an above, it *ipso facto* also has an extreme and a middle. For the above and the below are extremes, and the middle is what is surrounded by these; but what has centres and extremes is not unlimited.

205b31 Moreover, every perceptible body is in a place. {In every body, Aristotle continues, there is above, below, before, behind, right and left. These are not conventional, but in the things themselves, and even in the whole, but cannot be in the unlimited.}

[This is] another proof. If every body, he says, is in a place, and the differences of place are the aforesaid six, the unlimited also will necessarily be divided according to these places. But this is impossible, as it will necessarily be *ipso facto* limited. Therefore it is impossible for there to be an unlimited body. 25

205b35 And generally, if it is impossible for there to be an unlimited place, and every body is in place, it is impossible for there to be any unlimited body.

463,1

A third proof. It is impossible, he says, for place to be unlimited. For every place limits what is in place and contains it, but what gives limit, or rather is itself a sort of limit of what is within it, is not unlimited. And one can argue otherwise, that if the above and below are differences of place, it is impossible for there to be an unlimited place. For if either should be unlimited, it will not allow the other to exist. But it is impossible for there to be only the above or the below, for how could the unlimited place as a whole be said to be either above or below? If, now, places are limited, and every body is in a place, then every body is limited. 5

10

206a2 But surely what is somewhere is in a place, and what is in a place is somewhere.

This is the fourth proof; but it is continuous with those before it. For since he has shown that it is impossible for the unlimited to be either above or below, or in any of the other places, he will not let anyone say that while it is not in these places it is in place *simpliciter*; for this reason he says in these words that where the genus is predicated,[220] one of the species is necessarily also predicated of the same things, and conversely. Now the genus is being in a place, the species is being somewhere. For when I say 'somewhere', I signify a certain definite place, either the above or the below. 15

206a3 If, then, the unlimited cannot even be a quantity; for it will always be of some quantity, such as two or three cubits {so, Aristotle continues, if it is somewhere, it is limited through being extended in one of the six directions, and this is not

20

possible for the unlimited. Hence there can be no body that is
actually unlimited.}

He has used the example of quantity. The first occurrence of 'quantity'
(*poson*), then, is to be read with the accent on the second syllable
(*posón*), as it indicates the genus of quantity, while the second is to
be read with the accent on the first syllable (*póson*), as in 'bastard'
(*nóthon*).[221] And this indicates the definite quantity, such as two or
three cubits, as he himself has said. What he means is something like
25   this. If each thing which has some genus predicated of it will also have
in every case some one of the species which fall under the predicated
genus (for in no case is there a colour which is not either white or
black or some one of the other forms of colour), the unlimited too, if
464,1   it is to be in place, will in every case also be in one of the species of
place, such as the above or the below. But surely it is impossible for
it to be in one of these, as has been shown. It cannot, therefore, be in
place at all. Yet surely every body is in a place; it is therefore
impossible for any body to be unlimited. For just as there can be no
quantity which is not in every case a certain quantity – I mean two
5   or three cubits [etc.] – so there can be nothing in place which is not
somewhere, and by 'somewhere' I mean, for example, above or below.
That, then, which cannot be somewhere is unable to be in place.

206a9 On the other hand, it is obvious that if there is no
unlimited even in any other sense, many impossibilities follow.

10   It has been shown that the unlimited in respect of magnitude cannot
exist; but if, he says, the unlimited cannot exist in any other way,
many impossibilities will follow.

{206a10 The impossibilities are that there will then be a beginning and end of time and magnitudes will not be divisible into
magnitudes, and number will not be unlimited.}

206a12 But since, when these conclusions have been determined, neither alternative seems possible, there is need of an
arbiter.

15   Since, he says, the non-existence of the unlimited seems plausible,
and so likewise does its existence, there is need of an arbiter for the
arguments to assess the truth in each. 'And it is obvious that in one
sense it exists and in another does not.' For if the unlimited were
non-existent in one respect but not in another, it would not have been
the case that each of the arguments seemed to have plausibility.

{206a13 Clearly the unlimited has being in one sense and not in another.}

206a14 Being is spoken of both as potential and as actual, and 20
the unlimited exists both by addition and by division. {Aristotle
then reminds us of his view that magnitude is not unlimited in
actuality, but (potentially) by division.}

Here he acts as arbiter to the arguments, and his assumptions are
(a) that of things existent some exist in potential and others in
entelechy, as has been shown repeatedly, and (b) that the <unlim-
ited> exists in magnitudes in respect of division and addition; one of
the meanings of 'the unlimited' was that with respect to addition and 25
division. Having made these assumptions, he proceeds to show in
what sense the unlimited exists and in what sense it does not, and
he says: it has been sufficiently shown that the unlimited in magni- 465,1
tude does not exist, but we also say that the unlimited exists in
respect of division, since magnitude is divisible without limit. For
that the line is not composed from indivisible lines (as was proposed
erroneously by those who wished to solve Zeno's difficulty) – this, as
was said in the first book, he declares to be easily shown.[222] For an 5
entire book has been written against Anaxagoras about indivisible
lines,[223] saying that it is impossible for there to be indivisible magnitudes. For if it has been shown by the geometers that a given straight
line can be cut in two, it is presumably impossible for a line to be
indivisible or composed of indivisible ones. For if it should be composed of an odd number of indivisible ones, it will not be cut in two,
and it has been shown that everything composed of indivisibles – 10
which is the same as saying things without parts – will itself be
without parts. We have said in the first book that some conjectured
that Xenocrates introduced indivisible lines and we have shown that
the conjecture is false.

206a18 The remaining possibility is therefore that the unlimited also exists in potentiality. {We should not, says Aristotle,
take potential being to mean that, as in the case of bronze
converted into a statue, 'thus also is that unlimited which will
be in actuality'. Rather, 'since being is in many ways', as in the
case of a day and a contest which are continually coming to be,
so too with the unlimited.}

For if it has been shown to be impossible for it to exist in *entelechy*, 15
and magnitude is also divisible, it is obvious that it will exist in
potentiality and not in actuality. But the potential must not be taken
to mean what will be.[224] One should not think, because I have said

20 that the unlimited exists in respect of division, that the whole of this potentially existent thing will pass into actuality. We say that the bronze is potentially a statue, and that this potentiality passes at some time into actuality; but we do not mean the same in the case of the unlimited also. For it will never be divided into an unlimited number of parts, for this is not even potentially the case with magnitudes.

He says 'but since being is in many ways …'. By this he means that existence in actuality sometimes has the actuality all at once (as with a man, a horse and similar entities), and sometimes has it coming to be part by part and never being present at the same time. (Entities
25 of this kind are those that have their existence in coming-to-be, such as a day, a contest and similar things.) In this way I say that even the unlimited exists in actuality, not by existing in its entirety at one time, but by virtue of some portion of it always being present. 'Thus also is that unlimited which will exist in actuality'. I do not mean, he says, potentially unlimited in the same sense as when I say that the
466,1 bronze is potentially a statue. For I say that the bronze is potentially in the sense that it will also come to be so at some time in actuality; but the unlimited is not likewise potentially what it will be in actuality, but always remains in its potential state.

206a23 For in these cases also [viz. the day and the contest] there is potential and actual existence.

5 That is, obviously, in the case of the contest and the day. For before they come to the full, they exist in potential, but when they begin to come into being, in actuality. But their actuality is that of things subsisting part by part. Now it is possible to grasp the potentially existent even in the very [process of] actuation; for the day exists in actuality in that it is already present, but potentially in that it does not exist at one time, but has its existence always in the process of coming-to-be.

10 **206a25** And the unlimited appears differently in time and in the case of men[225] and in that of the division of magnitudes. [For generally the unlimited exists in this way, that one always takes another part, then another, and the part taken is always limited, yet there is at any rate always a different one and another different one.]

He has stated how the unlimited exists, viz. by virtue of coming to be in parts, which happens both in the division of magnitudes and in the case of time and of number (for time also, and generally number, are
15 increased potentially without limit, but in actuality never, as with

the division of magnitude). But these cases, he says, differ in a certain way with regard to one another. For the unlimited inheres in one way in men and in time, he says, as they are increased without limit, and in another in the division of magnitudes. Then, having undertaken to state the difference between them, he first explains what they have in common, and then their difference.

And he says 'For generally the unlimited exists in this way, that   20
one always takes another part, then another, and the part taken is always limited, yet there is at any rate always a different one and another different one.' This signifies generally, and for all cases, that whatever the unlimited inheres in, whether in numbers or in magnitudes, it inheres not by being present at one time, but by virtue of a different portion and then another always being taken; the portion   25
taken is always limited, yet never the same, but always another and then another. For as number is increased it is always possible to take another and yet another portion, such as 5, 10, 100 and so sequentially, but it is not possible to take (number) at once as a whole, nor to take the same portion twice. Likewise too in the case of bisection, it is impossible to cut the whole at one time, but there is always a different piece being cut and all the pieces created by this process are   30
limited. That then is what the cases have in common.   467,1

But someone might find this difficulty in the argument: what does he mean by saying that the portion of the unlimited that is taken is always limited? For in the case of number and the division of magnitudes, the argument is true if we start from the monad (for the sections of magnitude are always limited, as are the monads of number); but in the case of time and men that is no longer so. For if   5
the universe is eternal, it is not the case that every portion taken either of the unlimitedness of time or of the number of men is limited. At any rate, if I took the whole of time that has passed up to this day, or all the men, the number of these would not be limited, yet they constitute a portion of those things that are unlimited in themselves.

Now then, either (a) the universe is not without a beginning, so   10
that time and the number of men should not be unlimited in both directions and it should be impossible for us to take a portion of the unlimited that is also itself unlimited; or (b) it is unlimited in both directions, even though it is impossible to take an unlimited quantity in both directions, either with respect to number or with respect to the division of magnitudes. For if it were possible to take a number in both directions without limit, the unlimited would be traversable   15
(for all number begins from the monad, and only in one direction is there unlimitedness in number);[226] and Aristotle says otherwise, in keeping with what occurs in the case of numbers, viz. that the part of the unlimited that is taken is always limited. If, then, someone were to say that it is possible to take the unlimited in both directions,

20   he says nothing other than that an unlimited number can come to be
in actuality. For, as one regresses from the present year to the
previous one, I find that an unlimited number of years has come to
pass in actuality.

And yet it is impossible, not only for us, but for nature, to traverse
an unlimited number; for the unlimited is untraversable by its own
nature. And if the unlimited in one direction can come to pass in
25   actuality, why not in the other too? And the result will be that the
unlimited is not only multiplied, but is always being increased, and
that there is an unlimited quantity greater than an unlimited quantity. For, since the number of years is unlimited, the number of
months multiplies the unlimited, since it will possess the unlimited
twelve times over. And indeed much more so [in the case of] the
number of days, and still much more so the number of hours. And yet
it is impossible for the unlimited to be multiplied. And surely it also
follows that in each [of these] the number of the unlimited is increased
468,1   by the coming-to-be of time. If, however, it is impossible for the
unlimited to be either increased or multiplied, or for there to be an
unlimited number in actuality, it is impossible for time to be without
a beginning. This is said in view of Aristotle's statement that the part
5   that we take of the unlimited is always limited – and the statement
indeed is true. For in its own nature the unlimited is untraversable.

> **206a29** Moreover, existence is spoken of in a number of senses
> [so that the unlimited is not to be taken as something in
> particular, like a man or a house, but as the day and the games
> are spoken of, whose existence is not some essence, but always
> in generation and destruction, but always at any rate a different
> [part] and another different one].

The passage from here up to 'but always a different one and then
10   another' is not in the more accurate copies; for they are in all respects
identical in what they say. It must therefore be deleted.[227]

> **206a33** But when this occurs in the case of magnitudes, what
> is taken endures, whereas in the case of time and men it is
> destroyed.

15   Having stated what is common to the unlimited in magnitude and in
number, I mean the unlimited with respect to division and to addition, he now wishes to state the difference between them. And he says
that in the case of time and men what is taken from the unlimited is
destroyed and does not endure (for all past time and all past men have
been destroyed), but in the case of the division of magnitudes the
20   sections taken are not destroyed, but endure, for which reason they

are added, on the opposite principle, to the other portion of that which is being divided.

206b3 But the unlimited with respect to addition is in some sense the same as that with respect to division. {Aristotle explains that division without limit produces unlimited additions to a determinate amount.}

Having stated what is common and what is different in the case of time and men (and when I say men, I mean all individuals *simpliciter*[228] with regard both to ensouled and unsouled beings, comprehending all in the superior class) – having stated, then, what is common and what is different about the unlimited in these things with reference to the unlimited regarding division in magnitudes, since there is also the unlimited in respect of increase, he therefore says that this is almost the same as that in respect of division. For if I take a certain limited magnitude, then divide this in two and proceed with the bisection of the one [half], the extent to which the division of the one occurs is the extent to which the addition of the other occurs. If, then, the division were without limit, so too the addition would be without limit, but on the opposite principle. For what we take from the former we add to the latter. So that the unlimited in respect of division is in a sense the same as that with respect to addition, for both come to be in one and the same act of division.

206b6 In the same proportion we see an addition to the determinate quantity.

'The determinate quantity' is his term for the half of the magnitude that has remained uncut, [so called] either because it remains indivisible or because, even if it receives increments without limit, it is nevertheless impossible for what is being increased to exceed the whole magnitude; on the contrary, there is still a larger magnitude. The smallest quantity can never be taken, but the part that is being diminished goes on diminishing without limit; yet it is not true in the same way that the greater quantity grows without limit, but the greater body, the universe, is determined within the whole. It was for this reason, therefore, that he called what is being increased 'determinate'.

206b7 For if in the limited magnitude one takes a quantity determined by the same ratio and adds it, not taking in the same magnitude by this ratio, he will not traverse the limited quan-

25

469,1

5

10

15

20

tity. {But if, says Aristotle, you take the same magnitude rather than the same ratio, you will traverse the whole quantity.}

Since he has said that the division, as it proceeds without limit, being one and the same [ratio], diminishes one quantity without limit and increases the other without limit, but that this is not the effect with every division, so that one is diminished without limit and one increased without limit: he now says what kind of division proceeds

25 without limit and what kind does not. For if, he says, taking a certain magnitude, say a cubit, you (a) cut off a certain determinate portion

470,1 from it, such as a tenth or a half (and let it be a half), and again (b) cut the remainder (I mean the half-cubit) in the same ratio, i.e. the half, and again (c) bisect the remainder, and (d) do this without limit, the division will never come to an end, but one quantity will be

5 diminished without limit, and one will be increased without limit. But if you do not cut in the same ratio, always (say) taking off the half or indeed the tenth or some other constant ratio, but always cut off some determinate magnitude from the quantity being cut, taking the same magnitude, not magnitudes in the same ratio, you will consume the whole by the process of cutting, and that process will come to an end.[229]

10 If, for example, you take a magnitude of a thousand cubits and constantly subtract from this a certain determinate magnitude, say a finger's breadth, the whole will vanish under the cutting process, and thus neither the division nor the addition will be without limit. Now magnitude and ratio work on converse principles. For if you always subtract the same magnitude, you will not divide according

15 to the same ratio, but an ever greater one; but if you conserve the same ratio, you will not subtract the same magnitude, but an ever smaller one. If, for example, there were a piece of wood ten cubits in length and you cut off from this the tenth part, say one cubit, if you always cut off the same magnitude from the remainder, you will increase the ratio. (For in taking a cubit from the nine-cubit length, you will no longer be subtracting the tenth part, but the ninth, and

20 the ratio of the ninth to the whole is greater than that of the tenth. And likewise, if you subtract a cubit from the remaining eight, you will again increase the ratio. For you have taken off an eighth. And so, if you do this constantly, the division will come to an end.) But if from the ten-cubit length of wood you subtract the cubit, i.e. the tenth part, and wish to subtract the same ratio from the remaining nine

25 cubits, you will not subtract the cubit, but a smaller magnitude. And so, doing this constantly, always conserving the same ratio as you cut, but not subtracting the same magnitude, you will never consume the whole.

206b12 The unlimited does not exist in another way, but in this way, in potential and by reduction. {Its *entelechy*, says Aristotle, is like that of the day and the contest, its potentiality like that of matter.}

For that there is no unlimited body in actuality has been shown, but the unlimited exists, he says, in potential. He has added in what sense it exists potentially, that it is the unlimited in division, which is the same, inversely, as the unlimited in addition, as he has already said. But, he says, the unlimited has not only potential but actual being.[230] Just as we say that the day is present in actuality – not because the whole exists at one time, but because some portion of it does, and likewise the Olympic games are present in actuality by virtue of a part of them existing in actuality, either the boxing or the wrestling or some other event – so also the unlimited division is actually present, not by occurring all at once, but by virtue of a certain portion being divided. Then, since he has said that it is the same in potential and in actuality, and has confirmed the manner of its actual existence by the example of the day and of the contest, but has not yet established how it is that this same thing exists potentially – for this reason, he resumes the account of that which exists potentially, and says 'by the potentially existent I mean what is divisible without limit', just as we also say that matter is potentially all things. With matter, then, when we say that it is potentially all things, we do not mean either that it will ever become all things together in actuality, or that it has no form in actuality, but that, while it has some form in actuality, it is naturally liable to receive all things in part but not all together; so it is with what is potentially divisible without limit, that it is capable of unlimited division, but the divisions always exist in part and never all together.

206b15 [and it exists potentially,] not in itself [like the limited].

For just as, even if matter receives the form, the form nevertheless does not inhere in it through its own nature and by the essential principle of matter, but rather supervenes on its essence, so too the limited inheres in the unlimited, but not through its own nature. For if it were a property of what is divisible without limit to be limited as well, it is not limited in as much as it possesses unlimitedness, but in as much as the limited supervenes upon the unlimited. For as he will say shortly, matter is the unlimitedness of magnitude, and so we shall see in that discussion.

30
471,1

5

10

15

20

25

206b16 And indeed the unlimited by addition in this way
potentially is. {Aristotle adds that in a some sense it is the same
as the unlimited by division.}

472,1   Since he has given his account for the case of the unlimited with
respect to division, he has therefore added that we shall speak
similarly also in the case of the unlimited with respect to addition.
For it will likewise exist both in potential and in actuality, just as the
former does. And the reason why the same arguments apply to this
case he has also explained: it is the one that he gave in the foregoing
words, which is that 'it is the same in a certain way as that with
5   respect to division'. And in what sense it is the same, we have said,
namely that in one and the same division there is addition to one
quantity and subtraction from the other. If, however, it is the same,
then it would be fitting to say the same things in this case too, but
not the same without qualification. For this reason he added the
words 'in some sense'. What, then, the difference is, he goes on to say.

10   **206b17** For while it is always possible to take something beyond, this does not, for all that, exceed the whole magnitude [of
the universe],[231] as it does exceed the whole determinate quantity in respect of division. {But, says Aristotle, by addition it
cannot even potentially be such as to exceed the whole, unless
its unlimitedness is merely that which the physical theorists
predicated as an accident of some element outside the universe.
There cannot be in actuality such a perceptible body, and the
unlimited by addition can exist only as the inverse of that by
division, as just explained.}

Even if it is common, he says, to the thing undergoing division and
the thing to which the divided portion is added, that it is always
possible to take some different quantity beyond that which has come
15   into being (for it is always possible to make another division beyond
the division, and likewise it is always possible to make another
addition beyond the addition, when the division occurs according to
the same ratio, as we have already said) – even so, there is a certain
difference between what is being increased and what is being diminished, in that it is possible for what is being diminished to be
diminished without limit (for there is no smallest magnitude, in that
every magnitude is divisible, and for this reason it is possible to take
20   a quantity smaller than any determinate magnitude, and the dimi-
nution never comes to an end). In the case of what is being increased,
however, it is not possible for what is being increased to exceed the
whole determined magnitude [of the universe]; for the universe is the

largest body within the whole, and it is impossible for there to be a
greater magnitude.

So it is possible to take a quantity smaller than any determinate
magnitude, if not in actuality, then in potential, but it is not possible   25
even potentially to take a greater magnitude than the determined
whole, since no body can be even potentially greater than the heavens.
For it has been shown that it is impossible for there to be any
unlimited body outside the heavens, such as the physicists declared
to exist[232] and which they stated to be either air or water or another
[element]. Now if it has been shown that what is unlimited in this
way cannot exist, it is obviously not possible, even potentially, to take   30
a greater magnitude than the determined whole. For this was the
consequence if it was possible for there to be an unlimited body in
actuality. For even if it is not actually possible to take a smaller
quantity than any determinate one, then at least it is not impossible   473,1
as regards the nature of magnitudes – at any rate, not if every
magnitude is *ipso facto* divisible; to take a greater quantity than the
determined whole is, however, not even potentially possible, because
there cannot be an unlimited body.

> **206b27** {There cannot be unlimitedness by increase inde-   5
> pendently of division} seeing that, Plato also posited two kinds
> of the unlimited for this reason, that it also seems [possible] to
> exceed through increase right up to an unlimited degree.

For this reason, he says, namely that the unlimited pertains both to
increase and to division, Plato also used to posit two kinds of the
unlimited, the great and the small, of which he used to say that the
great is that which pertains to increase, while the small was that
which pertains to the division which is the converse of this.[233]   10

> **206b30** yet, having posited two, he does not use them. {For in
> numbers, says Aristotle, Plato allows neither unlimited subtrac-
> tion nor unlimited increase, his termini being the monad and
> ten.}

He reproaches Plato for saying that there were two kinds of the
unlimited, the great and the small, but using neither among his
principles. Now according to him [Plato], the principles are numbers,[234] but in these numbers there is neither the unlimited through
division nor that through addition. For numbers do not possess the   15
unlimited through division (as the division stops at the monad), and
he himself does not allow the increase through addition to reach the
unlimited. For he says that number is increased as far as the decad,
but the decad itself circles back upon itself. It should be noted that

20 he himself [i.e. Aristotle] stated in the earlier discussion that the great and the small meant to Plato the indefinite and matter,[235] but now, as he himself is speaking with regard to numbers, he attacks the account on the principle that he clearly follows everywhere, of refuting the apparent [meaning], not the intention of the ancients.[236]

> **206b33** And the unlimited proves to be the contrary of what they say. {It is not that, Aristotle explains, beyond which there is nothing, but that beyond which there is always something. After various examples, taken up in this long comment by Philoponus, Aristotle makes incompleteness the criterion of the unlimited, so that 'Parmenides must be thought to speak better than Melissus' when he says that the whole is limited, 'evenly balanced from the midpoint' (207a15-16). The unlimited does not contain, 'but is contained' (207a25), and it is manifest 'that the unlimited falls under the account of the portion rather than of the whole' (207a26-7).}

Having shown in what sense the unlimited exists and in what sense it does not, namely that there is not, as the physicists said, a body
25 unlimited in extension, but there is unlimitedness with respect to division and its converse, addition, he now wishes also to refute the definition of the unlimited which the physicists gave. For when they
474,1 defined the unlimited they said that that is unlimited beyond which nothing can be taken; but I, says he, affirm on the contrary that that is unlimited of which some quantity can always be taken beyond what has been taken. And as a token of this he advances also common usage – a token, I mean, that the unlimited is that beyond which another
5 quantity can always be taken. For rings which have no seal, he says, are called unlimited, on the grounds that they have no determined limit. For the seal (which is unlike the whole in form) is a sort of limit or origin, but those which have no seal (which are called hoop-rings), being uniform with themselves, do not have any determined limit, but when a portion is taken it is always possible to take a homogene-
10 ous one beyond it. And for this reason, since they have a certain similarity to the unlimited, such rings are called unlimited.

Though indeed they do not resemble the unlimited in all respects; for this is not, in fact, the only property that must inhere in the unlimited, that there is something of it beyond what has been taken, but it must also be impossible to take the same portion twice. And this is not a property inherent in the ring, since we repeatedly take the same portion, as often as we twist it round. Moreover, he says,
15 people call the unlimited 'complete' and 'whole' and 'all-containing', speaking in this lofty manner,[237] whereas I say on the contrary that if it is both whole and complete, it is not unlimited. For that is whole

of which there is nothing beyond the ingredients that comprise it, just as we say that a man is whole when no portion of him is missing; but we have declared the unlimited to be that beyond which there is always something. But the complete also, he says, is either the same as the whole or close. For we say that a contest is complete when it 20 has reached its completion, and when none of its ingredients is missing; and we say that a man is complete when he has achieved the completion of his nature, and I say indeed the complete and ultimate actualisations of his nature which it is the function of his nature to effect.

But with the unlimited the contrary obtains. For that is unlimited which has no limit, but there is always something left beyond. From 25 these remarks he therefore weaves together the following syllogism;[238] what is whole is complete, what possesses completion possesses limit, what possesses limit is not unlimited, therefore the whole is not unlimited. So that their argument has again come round to the contrary position; for they said that the unlimited is complete and whole, but he has shown, on the contrary, that if it is complete and whole, it is not unlimited. And next he will show also that it does not contain everything, as they asserted, 'but' on the contrary 'is 30 contained', and that 'the unlimited falls under the account of the portion rather than of the whole'. For this reason, he says, 'Parmenides must be thought to speak better than Melissus.' For Melis- 475,1 sus, he says, blending the unblendable,[239] stated that the whole is unlimited, while Parmenides says that the whole is limited. For he says that it is 'equally balanced from the midpoint',[240] that is it is equally distant from the middle in all directions, so that he can show it to be spherical; but the spherical, and everything *simpliciter* that 5 has been given a shape, is limited.

Having said this, he proceeds to explain the reason for their error in making the unlimited identical with the complete and the whole. For he says that matter, being indefinite in itself, is also unlimited, and I mean unlimited in as much as it has no definition or form of its own, but on the contrary is the cause of dispersion, indeterminacy 10 and unlimited division even for the forms.[241] For when it receives the principles of the forms, which are partless in themselves, it pulls them apart. For receiving in itself the principle of magnitude, which is properly indivisible, and pulling it apart, it leads it on to indefiniteness, and becomes the cause of its unlimited division. And likewise in the other forms it is, to a greater or lesser degree, the cause of 15 dispersion. Such, then, is matter, but the form is a sort of limit and a whole. For it limits and circumscribes matter, and makes whole and complete that in which it comes to be. For bronze, as being the matter of bronze artefacts, is in this respect something indefinite and not such as to be called whole and complete; when, however, the form of

20 the tripod or the statue arrives, it determines it to a greater or lesser degree and makes it a particular thing that is complete and whole – a whole statue or a whole cauldron. Thus [the unlimited] can be spoken of more properly in relation to matter than to the forms.

Since, then, (a) the form is a certain whole and complete thing, (b) the matter is indefinite and in that sense unlimited, (c) the matter is the form in potential, and (d) we often call potential things by the

25 names of those that exist in actuality (we say at any rate that the bronze is a statue, often when it has not yet acquired the form, and the wood a bed, wheat bread and the sperm a man): for this reason, they predicated of matter what pertains to the form, because it is all things in potential. And that the unlimited is in matter is obvious from the division of magnitudes; for the division does not occur with

30 regard to the form (at any rate, even after the division, the form of bronze or wood or flesh is preserved), but with regard to the substratum, in which the form too was in its discrete state. Being, therefore,

476,1 unlimited in itself, matter is limited and receives definition when it is circumscribed by the form. If, now, the form limits and matter is limited, and what limits contains, while what is limited is contained, again the very contrary of their position follows – I mean that the unlimited is contained and does not, as they believed, contain.

5 And if matter, which is the unlimited, is a certain portion of the composite, it could not be a whole, as the portion is not a whole. And it can be plausibly said that matter is unknowable by virtue of being unlimited, for the unlimited is unknowable in its own nature. And having shown from the facts themselves that the opposite of what they said is the case – I mean that the unlimited does not contain but is contained, and is rather a portion and not a whole – he shows the

10 same thing also by the *reductio ad absurdum*.[242] For if, he says, the unlimited contains and is not only among the perceptible phenomena but also among the intelligibles (for Plato posited it also among the Ideas)[243] it is plausible that, just as it contains in perceptibles, so it will also contain in intelligibles.[244] But he says that it is 'absurd'[245] and 'impossible' for things that are the cause of knowledge and

15 constitute proper knowledge[246] and are the cause of definition in all things to be contained by what is unknowable in its nature, I mean by the unlimited. Or it can also be argued thus: if they say that the unlimited contains all things, and the intelligibles are in the class of all things (not only those intelligibles which are in the universe, but those above it), it is obvious that the unlimited would also contain the intelligibles, either all of them *simpliciter* or at least those in the universe.[247]

207a4 [Rings without a seal are called unlimited] ... speaking   20
in respect of a certain similarity, but not properly.

'Speaking': obviously, the majority in their usage. And in what sense
they make them unlimited 'in respect of similarity', but 'not properly',
he has inferred. It is, he says, because the unlimited must not only
have this property, that something can be taken beyond what has
been taken, but also that the same cannot be taken twice; this second
property does not belong to the ring.

207a7 That, then is unlimited of which, when we take from it   25
in respect of quantity, it is always possible to take something
beyond.

With the words 'when we take from it with regard to quantity' we
should also understand 'some part', so that it will be 'That then is   477,1
unlimited of which, when we take some part from it with regard to
quantity, it is always possible to take something beyond.' And this is
a definition of the unlimited. So that if this is the unlimited, whereas
to be whole and all there and complete is to have nothing beyond,
then the unlimited is not whole and complete. For it is both true in
the case of numbers that, as they are increased without limit, it is   5
always possible to take a different number beyond what has been
taken, and true in the case of the cutting of magnitudes that it is
always possible to take a different section beyond the section that has
been taken. And he rightly said 'in respect of quantity', for the division
does not take place in respect of the form. At any rate, the same form
is seen in everything produced by the division. For all the segments
are either lines or surfaces or bodies.

And alternatively [we can show that] the form is not preserved in   10
every instance of division. For he himself has shown in the earlier
discussion that it is not just any form that can exist in just any
magnitude,[248] since the form is not preserved in division up to every
point, but as it proceeds the division destroys it. At least, flesh can
be divided without limit as a magnitude, yet not any longer as flesh.
And one might have a difficulty about whether the definition of the
unlimited would not also fit the whole and the complete and generally   15
everything that is limited. For in the case of the complete as well, it
is possible to say that it is that of which, when we take some part
from it in respect of quantity, it is always possible to take something
beyond. For if I take the portions by way of bisection, it will be possible
to go on without limit taking quantities beyond what has been taken.
But this is not true in the case of things that are limited. For in the
case of the unlimited it is not simply if I take this or that portion that   20
I do not traverse it, but whatever portion I take; but it is not so with

the limited. For if I always take some determinate portion, I annihilate the whole.

And in another way it is not true that it is always possible to take some portion beyond what has been taken. For if I take the portions next to the limits, it is no longer possible to take something different
25   beyond these, but in the case of the unlimited it is not possible to take the extremity. So that, even if it is true in taking some portion that the same result follows also in the case of the limited, the same thing is not true of the whole process that is true of the unlimited. And generally, this occurs in some degree even in things that are limited, because they partake of the unlimited. So that, even if, according to some way of taking, it should be possible in the case of the complete
30   to go on forever taking something beyond what has been taken, this result does not follow for it in so far as it is complete, but in so far as it partakes of the unlimited.

478,1   **207a10** For just as it is with each, so it is with what properly is: that is whole in the proper sense of which there is nothing beyond. {Aristotle uses the examples of a man and ship. The proper usage is of particulars: they are whole when there is nothing outside them.}

5   Just as, he says, in the case of whole particulars, such as a man or a ship, we say that they are whole when none of the ingredients that compose the subject is absent, so also in the case of what is whole in the proper sense, I mean the all, we say that it is whole and all there when there is nothing beyond, e.g. a whole universe, where none of the things that conduce to the composition of a universe lies beyond. For this is the whole and the all in the proper sense, since if some part of it should be absent, even if it be just any one, it is not whole, nor even all there.

10   **207a13** 'Whole' and 'complete' are either the same as 'all' or close [in meaning].

For the term 'whole' is used of what is continuous, as we say the whole wood or the whole bread, while the term 'all' is predicated of what is discrete, as we say 'all men'. But the term 'complete' is common to either kind, when none of its parts is missing. Now if the terms 'whole' and 'all' are not identical, but 'complete' is identical with both, then
15   'whole' is not in every respect identical with 'complete', and this is because 'whole' is used to denote the concourse of all the parts, while 'complete' is used to denote the attainment of completion. Both, however, are predicated of the same subject, and in this way both might appear to be one and the same universally.

207a17 [Parmenides speaks better than Melissus] for one can- 20
not combine the unlimited with the all and the whole as one
combines flax with flax.[249]

Melissus, he says, blends the unblendable, and not, as the proverb
has it, 'flax with flax', which have a natural propensity to combine.
For it is not possible for the whole and the all to be at the same time
unlimited, as he has shown.

207a18 Since they adopt their lofty diction about the unlimited 479,1
from this [saying that it 'contains all' and 'has all in it' because
of having some similarity to the whole]. {But the unlimited, says
Aristotle, is so in potential only, as the matter of magnitudes,
divisible by subtraction, inversely increasing by addition, never
whole and limited in itself.}

This he said, was the reason why they called the unlimited whole and
complete, that they might assign to it the lofty property of being
complete and containing everything. Then he proceeds to show the
cause of their aberration, what it was that deceived them into saying 5
that the unlimited is whole and complete. For the unlimited, he says,
seems to have some similarity to the complete and the whole. And
what the similarity is he goes on to explain: 'For the unlimited is the
matter for the completion of the magnitude and is whole in potential,
but not in *entelechy*.' By magnitude he means the composite. Of 'the
completion of the magnitude', he says – that is, of the form, according
to which everything has its being and its own completion – the 10
unlimited is the matter, and the matter is potentially whole and
complete, that is form, but not in *entelechy*. For in itself it is unlimited
and indefinite. Yet it is potentially whole and complete, for it can
receive the form, and from these arises the composite. That, then,
which belongs to it potentially, he says, they predicate of it as if it
belonged in actuality. And that the unlimited is in matter, he shows 15
in the words that follow. For, he says, division without limit, and its
converse, addition, belong to magnitude by virtue of the matter. For
in themselves forms are indivisible. This [divisibility], then, belongs
in itself to matter, but to be whole and complete, when it meets a
definition, belongs to matter not in itself but by virtue of something
else, namely the form. 20

207a24 And it does not contain, but is contained, in so far as it
is unlimited.

For in so far as it is matter, the unlimited is defined and limited by
the form; but what is defined and limited does not contain but is

contained. And if it is contained, it is manifest that the unlimited is
25   not some whole, as they said, but on the contrary a portion of the
whole, which is composed from the containing and the contained.

> **207a25** Thus it is also unknowable, in so far as it is unlimited;
> for matter does not have a form.

For if the knowledge of each thing is according to the form, and matter
480,1 is formless, it is quite clear that it is also unknowable. Hence Plato
too said that it was apprehensible by a 'bastard reasoning'.[250] For this
reason it is impossible to know matter by direct apprehension, but by
abstraction from the forms we come to a conception of it. So that the
enlightened way of knowing it derives from the forms.

5   > **207a29** [The unlimited is a portion rather than a whole, as
> matter is a portion of the whole and bronze of the statue,] since,
> if it were to contain in the world of perceptibles, it ought also to
> contain the great and small in the world of intelligibles.

By these remarks he confirms that he was right to say that matter is
contained and does not contain. For if the unlimited is found among
the intelligibles in the same way as it is among the perceptibles, it is
plausible that, just as it contains among the perceptibles, so too it
10   will contain among the intelligibles. But this is impossible, viz. that
the causes of definition and knowledge should be contained by the
unknowable and indefinite. Thus the unlimited does not, as they
asserted, contain. Now the great and small are in matter, to which
they assigned the unlimited; and Plato called matter great and small.

15   > **207a33** It accords with reason that the unlimited by addition
> should seem not to exist in such a way as to exceed every
> magnitude, but that by division [should seem to] exist. {Aristotle
> goes on to say that number has a lower limit, but no upper one,
> while the case with magnitudes is the reverse. Magnitude is
> thus potentially unlimited, but not actually so, while the un-
> limitedness of number is continually coming to be, never present
> at once. This unlimitedness is not the same thing in number,
> time and magnitude. This reasoning does not negate the study
> of mathematics, since they do not need to take an unlimited line,
> but only 'as much as they wish that is limited' (207b30).}

From this point he wishes to advance more theorems which concur
with the arguments already given about the unlimited, and first that
the result in the case of division and addition is in keeping with the
20   arguments that we have given about the unlimited – I mean that in

division it is not possible to take the smallest part, but it is possible to take a quantity smaller than any determinate one, whereas in addition it does not carry on being possible to take a larger quantity than the whole, because in the whole the largest magnitude is determined, and this is the body of the universe. For it has been shown that there exists no magnitude unlimited in extension. And the reason for this is that the unlimited does not contain, but is contained, and it is the whole and complete that contains, and this is the form. For since addition takes place outside and division within the limits, quite reasonably, on the one hand, it is impossible to add from outside without limit, since the form is a definition and a limit (increase must therefore stop when the form is arrived at, nor, if it occurs, does it occur outside the form, which contains it), and, on the other hand, matter, being contained within what is being cut, lends itself to being cut without limit.

Hence in division the form often comes to an end because it has a certain limit, with regard to the smaller as to the greater (for it has been said that forms are not naturally able to remain in every magnitude), but because of matter the cutting does not come to an end. And, he says, it is reasonable that number also should be determined at the minimum (for it encounters the extreme of small-ness at the monad, which is indivisible), but has no limit as to greatness; for it is possible to increase number without limit. But in the case of magnitudes the contrary has occurred, that there is a limit to being greater, but none to being smaller. And the reason is that number is composed of units,[251] and whatever elements something is composed of, it is also resolved into them; number is divided into the monads, and these, in as much as they are monads, are indivisible, for everything that is one is indivisible in so far as it is one. For a man in so far as he is one man is indivisible, since even if he is divided as a magnitude, it is nevertheless not as a man that he is being divided, for he is not being divided into men but into portions. But he is not one in respect of this, but in so far as one particular form has been composed from all [the constituents], which cannot further be divided into homogeneous fractions. If, now, the monad is indivisible, but number is divided into monads, it is obvious that the division will stop, and the extreme and limit of it is the monad. For this reason the division of number does not go on without limit, but, quite reasonably, the addition goes on without limit, because this is the combination of monads. Since therefore unlimited combinations of the monad with itself are possible, the unlimited increase of number is a reasonable result.

But magnitude is not also composed of henads, but of magnitudes. And the division of them therefore never encounters indivisibles, but always magnitudes naturally admitting of division, and thus the

25

481,1

5

10

15

20

25

cutting goes on without limit. But the increase is not without limit, for it encounters the whole and complete. For nothing can be greater than the universe, which is that which is properly whole and all there. For this reason, then, the case with number is the contrary to that with magnitudes. And this follows also from what has previously been shown concerning the unlimited. For number possesses the unlimited
30   not in itself, but on account of matter. For the unlimited division of magnitudes, taking place in the matter, is the cause of the unlimited increase of number, and for this reason it also encounters the monad
482,1 at the limit, because the continuous before division was one thing, which was potentially unlimited, and became the cause of the unlimited increase of number through its unlimited division. The unlimited is thus in all things on account of matter.

Next he inquires, since the unlimited occurs in a number of things
5   (for we say that a magnitude is unlimited through its being divided without limit, and that change is unlimited and that time is unlimited), how does the unlimited inhere in these things? Is it or is it not as a genus and a single nature predicated commonly of them all? And he says that the unlimited is not predicated of them as a genus, but that the meanings stem from one case and tend to one point. For
10   howsoever the subjects are ordered, I mean magnitude or change or time, thus it is with the unlimited in them. It is primarily magnitude, then, that is continuous, and because of this the change that befalls it is continuous, whether this be locomotion, mutation or increase, and on account of the change the time also is continuous. The unlimited is thus primarily in magnitude; and because of the magnitude, in change; and because of the change, in time. And at this point
15   he takes these things as agreed – that magnitude is continuous and undergoes partition not into indivisibles but into magnitude, and that change is continuous on account of magnitude and time on account of this – but subsequently he will also prove these positions in the sixth book of this work.[252]

After this he says that we do not negate the bases and proofs of
20   geometry when we eliminate the actual unlimited from existent things. For someone might have raised the difficulty that mathematics arises by abstraction from things in nature, and with geometers it is a sort of basis to take an unlimited straight line (for they are continually saying 'let this be produced without limit',[253] and when this is given the geometrical proofs proceed), yet since there is no natural magnitude which is actually unlimited, it is not even possible
25   to abstract an unlimited straight line from things in nature; and, if this is so, then, with the elimination of the unlimited straight line which the geometers used as a basis in their proofs, the geometric proofs will be eliminated also. Yet it is absurd to eliminate the most beautiful and accurate of the sciences.

This difficulty, then, Aristotle resolves with the greatest subtlety, saying that we do not negate the proofs themselves when we have shown that there is no unlimited magnitude in actuality. For neither do the geometers use the unlimited in their proofs, but they take the unlimited for this reason, that they may be able to abstract 'as much as they wish' from 'that which is limited'. So that if at any rate it were permissible for them to take as much as they wish, they would not need even the unlimited. And the strongest token that the unlimited straight line does not contribute even to geometrical proofs is that, having taken from it whatever limited quantity they wished, they have used this in the proof of the present theorem, but not the unlimited. If, then, the greatest straight line should be given to them, such as the diameter of the whole, they will no longer have need of the unlimited. For from this it will be possible to abstract 'as much as they wish'. So that if they have been using the unlimited in their proofs, the argument which eliminates the unlimited has really been negating their science; but if they have not used it, this is not true any more.

Next he inquires under what class of causes the unlimited should be brought. For, since (1) he has shown that if the unlimited exists it is wholly necessary for it to be an origin, not from an origin, and (2) it has been shown that if there is no unlimited in extension there is still that in respect of division and its converse, addition: he reasonably inquires into what class of origins the unlimited should be brought. Now the origins are four – matter, form, the maker and the final.[254] He says, then, that it is as matter that the unlimited is an origin and he shows this both from the argument and from the witness of the ancients. For that it cannot be a principle as a form is patently obvious, since the form is a definition and a limit, while the unlimited is indefinite and untraversable. Nor could it be an origin even as a making cause, for the making cause must exist in actuality, but the unlimited exists in potentiality. And it is clear that it could not be an origin as a final cause, first because the form often comes to be the same as the end, secondly because the final cause is an end and limit of that whose final cause it is, while the unlimited has no end. It thus remains for the unlimited to be a material cause; and reasonably so. For matter is in privation and the unlimited too is in privation[255] (for the unlimited does not even have a form, as the form is both a definition and a limit), so that if the unlimited is in privation by its own nature, and matter is in privation, then the unlimited is matter. And all those, he says, who proposed the existence of the unlimited, proposed it as matter. For they said that the unlimited is air or water or the intermediary or whatever else [they called it], from which as from matter the things that come into being were thought to arise.

483,1

5

10

15

20

25

30

484,1

5   Having said this, as he approaches the limit of the book, he uses
the remainder to solve the difficulties which made it seem necessary
that the unlimited should be one of the things that exist, so that the
difficulties may not remain to cloud popular understanding.[256] And
they were five in number: first, that raised by the unlimitedness of
time; second, that raised by the unlimited division of magnitudes;
third, that raised by perpetual generation; fourth, that raised by the
10   claim that every limited thing terminates in relation to something;[257]
fifth, (and this he called the most important cause of the popular
belief in the existence of the unlimited), that raised by conceptualisation through the fact that conceptualisation never has a limit, but
it is always possible to conceive of something further beyond what
has been conceived. Of these difficulties, then, he says that some
contain no necessary proof of the existence of the unlimited, either in
15   actuality or in part or in potential.

And the first [that is true] at any rate is the difficulty arising from
perpetual generation. For it does not even follow, just because generation is perpetual, that there is some unlimited body from which
come the things that come to be. For if the generation of one should
be the destruction of the other, and the destruction of one the
generation of the other, it is possible that they all be limited, but that
generation and destruction never come to an end for this reason.[258]
20   So that this kind of difficulty contains no necessary proof. For it is
not necessary on account of this that the unlimited should exist
actually or potentially or in part.

But there is not even any necessary [force] in the objection that
every limited thing terminates in relation to something; for this is
false. For if to be limited were the same as to be in contact, it would
really be necessary that everything limited was *ipso facto* in contact
with something beyond it and was circumscribed by this, but as it is,
25   to be limited is not the same as to be in contact. For to be in contact
is one of the relations (for what is in contact is in contact with
something, since it is in contact with the contiguous), so that what is
in contact is and is said to be in relation to something beyond it; the
limited, on the other hand, is spoken of not with respect to something
else, but to itself. Just as, then, not even the unlimited is spoken of
30   with respect to something else, but to itself, so neither is the limited
referred or related to something else. For contact means that some
particular thing is touching another, but limit consists in the fact that
485,1 the thing itself has some extreme. So that if to be in contact and to
be limited are not the same, it is not necessary that the limited
terminate in relation to something; rather some of the things that are
limited can terminate in relation to something and be in contact with
something beyond them, yet even for these to be in contact and to be
limited are not the same, but only for those limited things to which

contact is incidental because there is no void.[259] Those things, then, 5
that are limited internally are also always in contact with something,
because, as I have said, there is no void; but those things that are
limited externally (and all existent things are of this description) are
not necessarily also in contact with something. For those things that
are limited externally and in contact with something are not wholes
but parts of the all. These things, then, are in contact, not in that they 10
have a limit, but in so far as they are parts of the whole, and there is
no void in the universe. But if anything is properly whole and all
there, it is not necessary for it to terminate in relation to something
else, but rather this is impossible, as it would not be properly whole.
Of such a kind is the fixed sphere, being limited, since it is also a
sphere (and every figure is obviously limited), but it is in contact with
nothing beyond it, since there is nothing beyond it. So this argument 15
also does not necessarily entail the existence of the unlimited.

But neither does that from conceptualisation. For it is true that
conceptualisation can always add something from without to the
magnitude that has been taken, and can always go on doing this. Yet
it is not necessary that the nature of things should follow our conception, but, on the contrary, it is necessary rather that true knowledge 20
should follow the nature of things. For it is not even necessary, just
because it is possible to conceive of Socrates as outside Athens,[260] that
he should be outside Athens, nor even, because I can imagine him a
hundred cubits high, does that make it necessary for him to be so. For
not everything that we may wish to conceive *ipso facto* exists, seeing
that some imagine themselves to be kings and lords of all the earth, 25
but it is not necessary that things should conform to their conception.
And so indeed even if I can conceive of some body being increased
without limit, it is not necessary that there be such a body.

These arguments then do not contain any necessary proof that the
unlimited must exist; but the other two, that from the unlimitedness
of time and that from the unlimited division of magnitudes, do
possess some plausibility. And yet it is not necessary, if there should 30
be no actually unlimited body, to eliminate either the increase of time
without limit or the unlimited division of magnitudes. For it is not in 486,1
such a way that time or the division of magnitudes is unlimited, that
either time or the divisions of the continuous should be entirely
present all at once, but in being taken part by part and never coming
to an end, and through the potential, not the actual, existence in them
of the unlimited. Thus we have affirmed, and the aforesaid arguments necessarily entail, the partial subsistence of the unlimited, and 5
its existence in potentiality, not in actuality; but the existence of the
unlimited that the physicists spoke of – that which subsists as a whole
at once, and in actuality, not potential – is not shown to be necessary
by these arguments. So that, since the unlimited exists in this way,

10 I mean potentially not actually, and partially not altogether, there is therefore no absurdity in the fact that conception also should come to an end. For this too cannot conceive it all at once, since it conceives it as limited, but always makes a limited addition to what is taken, which is limited, until it stops through fatigue. So we shall concede that it increases potentially without limit, but not in actuality, and 15 shall allow what is taken always to be limited, but never unlimited.

207a33 It accords with reason that the unlimited should not seem to exist by addition.[261]

That is, it appears so plausibly and following on what we have said about the unlimited, viz. that the unlimited is contained but what contains it is the whole and the all. Thus it is reasonable that there should never be an end to the cutting of a magnitude, since every cut 20 takes place within the limits; for the unlimited, being contained within the limits, gives to the process of cutting an unlimited continuation. But it is not possible to add without limit, for the addition comes from outside, and it is impossible to add to the whole and the all. So that, when the addition arrives at this, it quite reasonably stops.

25 **207b1** And it is plausible also that there should be a minimum limit in the case of number, [while in the direction of increase it exceeds every multiplicity; in the case of magnitudes, however, every magnitude can be exceeded in respect of division but not in increase of size].

There is another theorem that follows concerning the unlimited, viz. that number is limited as to the minimum (For the minimum limit 487,1 of number is the monad), but has no limit to being greater (for it is possible to take a number greater than any that has been taken), but the contrary obtains in the case of magnitudes. For magnitudes have a limit to being greater, but as to the minimum it is not possible to take an extreme. And he goes on to explain the reasons.

5 **207b5** And the reason is that the unit[262] is indivisible, whatever the unit may be, [for example, a man is one man and not many].

The cause of there being a minimum limit to number is that number is nothing other than an aggregate of monads. Since, therefore, (a) number when divided arrives at some extreme, the monad (for whatever a thing is composed of, it is resolved into that), and (b) the monad in so far as it is a monad, is indivisible, quite reasonably it 10 will not go on without limit to the minimum. For the division ceases when it arrives at the monad. For the same reason it also has no limit to being greater, since if it is a composition of monads, and nothing prevents our adding the monads to one another without limit, and always doubling the ones that have been taken, quite reasonably it has no limit in respect of increase. And this is true of it because of the nature of the unlimited, which was found to consist in the unlimited cutting of magnitudes. For it is on account of the unlimited cutting of magnitudes that number increases without limit, and it is because the cutting of the continuous begins from the monad that the numerical minimum also is a monad. For it is as a unit that the continuous is thus divided.

But what does he mean by saying that the unit is indivisible 'whatever the unit may be'? Do we not, then, say that animal, being one genus, is divisible into many species? For if it is one in so far as it is a genus, yet in virtue of being a genus is divided into species, therefore it is divided in virtue of being one. And the same argument applies to the continuous; for the continuous is one thing in so far as it is continuous (for we speak of one wood and one stone), and again the continuous in so far as it is continuous is divisible without limit, and therefore the unit in so far as it is a unit is divisible. For what in general is divided but the unit? For the many have been divided already, and are not being divided. I say, then, that both the genus and the continuous are not only one, but also potentially many. As being one, each of these is indivisible (for if it were divided under the description that makes it one, it would be divided into many similar things, the genus, for example, into genera, and the cubit length into many cubit lengths); but as being potentially many (for the genus embraces within itself many species, and the continuum many continua), in this respect it is divided. But in numbers the monad alone is one and in no sense many; so that it is indivisible in every way. But it is perhaps safer to inquire yet again, if every unit really is indivisible in so far as it is a unit.

207b7 But number is a plurality and certain quantities of one; so that it must necessarily stop at the indivisible.

That is, number is nothing other than a monad taken many times over. The phrase 'and certain quantities' is a parallel expression of the same thing, that is certain monads in certain quantities. If, however, number is nothing other than a plurality of monads, it is necessary that the division of it should arrive at the monad. For whatever ingredients a thing is composed of, it is resolved into them. For if it is also divided into portions, yet it is not in respect of these that it is one. But if the cutting of number stops at the indivisible, there is therefore some limit of it at the minimum.

207b8 For three and two are derivative terms[263] [and so too is each of the other numbers].

That number is nothing other than a composition of monads he establishes from the names of numbers. For from the three monads, 20 he says, the number three is derivatively named, and from the two the number two, and likewise in the case of the others. So that it is nothing other than the monads.[264]

207b10 And it is always possible to conceive of more; for the bisections of magnitude are unlimited.

Having shown that there is some limit to being smaller in the case of 25 number, he now shows that there is none to being greater. For it is always possible to conceive of a number greater than the one that has 489,1 been taken. Then he has also concisely given the reason why this property belongs to number, which is that one can cut magnitudes without limit.

207b11 So that [the unlimited] has potential but not actual being.

For if number never has a limit to being greater, but it is possible to 5 take one greater than that which has been taken, it was rightly said on our part that the unlimited does not actually exist, but does potentially. For the number that is actually taken is always limited, but the increase has no limit.

207b12 But what has been taken always exceeds every determinate amount.

10 The term 'determinate' stands for 'taken'. Thus he says that every one that is taken is exceeded by the one about to be taken, and the process of taking does not come to an end.

207b13 But this number is not separable, nor does the unlimitedness remain, but it is always coming into being, as also are time and the number of time.

15 Since he has contrasted what happens in the case of magnitudes with what happens in that of number, he therefore says that these facts do not imply that number can be separated, nor that it is something other than the things that are numerable, but it is in thought that we separate those things that are by nature inseparable. And it is not the case that, as the segments of the continuous remain, so, as

number is increased, do the previous numbers remain, but just as   20
time has its existence in the process of coming to be, so too does the
number of time. For the portion that is taken exists when the previous
one no longer endures. Thus indeed, in the case of number also, its
increase has its existence in coming to be, for when twenty is the
number taken, the number ten does not remain. So that the unlimitedness of number does not have an existence that consists in its
remaining, but in its coming to be.   25

207b15 But in the case of magnitudes the contrary is [true].   490,1
{Aristotle explains that the continuous is divided without limit,
but cannot increase without limit in size.}

Having said that the contrary holds for number as against magnitudes, and having shown how it is with number, and having added
the reasons, he proceeds to show also what holds of magnitude, and
why it has no limit to being smaller but has one to being greater.   5

207b17 For to whatever extent it can be potentially, it can also
be actually to the same extent. {A perceptible body that was
unlimited in magnitude, says Aristotle, would exceed the whole
heaven.}

He shows why it is impossible to increase magnitudes without limit.
For had it been possible for it to be increased without limit, he says,
it would also have been increased without limit in actuality. And yet
there is nothing that has either been increased or is increasing   10
without limit (for nothing is greater than the heavens), nor therefore
is it possible for anything to be increased without limit. For as has
been said in the foregoing remarks, in the case of things that come to
be and are destroyed, there is nothing surprising in the failure of the
potential to pass into the actual, but in the case of the whole of nature,
which is eternal, if what is potential were without limit, it is altogether necessary that the actual would be also. But the consequent   15
is not true; therefore neither is the antecedent.

But someone might raise a difficulty: is there then in the whole of
nature no potentiality for unlimited division? How, therefore, is
nothing divisible without limit in actuality? For if nature has created
such a potentiality, why has she not also created the actuality? I say,   20
then, that we do not say that a thing is potentially divisible into
unlimited parts (for this does not hold even potentially with magnitudes), but without limit. This, then, is its actuality, not to cease being
cut at any time. Nor, therefore, does it cease. It [the divided thing]
exists therefore in potential before it begins to be cut, but in actuality
when it has already been cut. And if you should say that none of those

things [which are being divided without limit][265] has unlimited
25   division in actuality (for we are not able to divide without limit, but
we stop at some time), yet this is the result of our weakness, not of
the nature of the thing. For nature has presented us with magnitudes
of such a kind that the cutting of them never stops according to their
own definition, and nature herself divides to the extent that is
491,1   necessary for her workmanship.[266] And in another way, nature has
made magnitudes divisible even without limit, so that it is possible
to make a division at any point whatsoever, and this is possible in
actuality. For the straight line can be divided at any point whatsoever. What, therefore, magnitude has potentially, it can also have in
5   actuality. And this is true not only of increase, but also of division.

> **207b21** But the unlimited is not the same thing in magnitude
> and change and time [... it is predicated in change on account
> of magnitude, in time on account of change].

Another theorem: whereas the unlimited exists in the case of magni-
10   tude, change and time, the unlimited is not predicable of all these as
a single genus (for it is not equally ranked in all of them), but
howsoever each of these is in respect of its nature, so will the
unlimited be in each of them. In time, then, the unlimited is present
because of change, since its existence also derives from this, and in
change it is present because of magnitude. Primarily then, the
15   unlimited is in magnitude, since it is magnitude too that is primarily
and in itself continuous. It is in change secondarily, since change also
possesses continuity on account of magnitude. It is in tertiary place
in time, since on account of motion time too is continuous. And let it
now, he says, be taken as agreed that these things are so, but a little
later we shall prove these also. And he will prove these things in the
20   eighth book of this work.[267]

> **207b27** But the argument does not negate the studies of mathe-
> maticians, when in this way it eliminates the existence of
> anything unlimited in such as way as to be actually untrav-
> ersable with respect to increase. {We need only grant them, says
> Aristotle, 'as much as they wish' of a line 'that is limited'.}

[He means] that we do not in fact eliminate the principles of geometry
25   by saying that there is nothing unlimited in actuality. For neither is
it the unlimited that they use in their proofs, but the limited. But
they propose the unlimited [line], so that they can take 'as much as
they wish that is limited'. If, then, what they are seeking is granted
to them, they will not need the unlimited.

207b31 For it is possible to cut a different magnitude of any size   492,1
in the same ratio as the greatest magnitude.

Alexander is right to say here that Aristotle, having shown what sort
of unlimited the geometers do not need for their proofs, viz. that they
do not need the unlimited in respect of extension, now states what   5
sort they use, viz. that in respect of division.[268] For it is possible, he
says, to cut another magnitude of any size in the same ratio as the
greatest magnitude. For example, just as it is possible to bisect the
greatest magnitude, so too another magnitude of any size can be
bisected. For what is being shown is that it is also possible to divide
a portion of any size in the same ratio as the whole. And if it is possible   10
to bisect every magnitude, then magnitudes are divisible without
limit; for otherwise it would not be possible to bisect every magnitude.

207b33 So that taking it thus will make no difference to their
proofs, but it is in existing magnitudes that it exists.

It is obvious, he says, from what has been stated that as regards their   15
proofs 'it will make no difference' to the geometers, whether the
unlimited is 'thus' or not, I mean that it is that with respect to
extension, but the unlimited cannot be at all in anything other than
actually subsisting magnitudes, and these are the limited ones. And
obviously it is in these with respect to division.

207b34 Now since the causes are divided fourfold.   20

He is inquiring in this passage to what kind of cause the unlimited
belongs, and he says it is to material causes. For even originally[269] it
was said that if the unlimited exists it is an origin and not from an
origin.

207b35 [it is clear that the unlimited is the cause as matter]
because its existence is a privation, but the substratum in itself   25
is the continuous and perceptible. [All the others appear to have
used the unlimited as their matter, so it is absurd to make it the
container and not the contained.]

From this point he shows that the unlimited is matter, but he shows
this in two ways, from the very nature of the unlimited and from the   493,1
witness of the ancients. For matter, he says, is privation by its own
definition (for it has no form of its own), and the unlimited is in
privation (for the form is the cause of definition and limit), so that
the unlimited would seem to be matter. Yet even if the unlimited is
in privation and has to do with matter, matter none the less neither   5

subsists in itself nor acts as substratum for unlimited division, but it is the perceptible body which subsists in itself and acts as substratum for unlimited division. For the thing to be divided must exist in actuality. What, then, do we mean by saying that the unlimited division of magnitudes takes place with respect to matter? That, when the composite body is divided without limit, since the cutting

10 does not take place with respect to the form (for that remains the same), it is necessary that the division should take place with respect to matter, but with respect to matter which has undergone formation and is something in actuality. And all the ancients, he says, who proposed the existence of the unlimited proposed it as matter. For they said that everything came to be from it and was resolved into it.

15 And this some said to be air, some water, some another thing.

> **208a5** The remaining task is to address those arguments which make the unlimited exist not only in potential but as a determinate thing.

The remaining task, he says, is to consider from this point the difficulties which made it appear that the unlimited exists, not merely in potential nor as something which has its existence in

20 limited things, but also exists in actuality and marked off in itself.

> **208a6** For some of them [have] no necessary [force] and some admit of other true responses. {'Neither,' says Aristotle, need we postulate an unlimited perceptible body 'in order that generation may not come to an end', as there may be exchange by generation and corruption between the elements, while the whole remains determinate.}

Of the difficulties, he says, which made it appear that the unlimited exists,[270] some have no necessary force in proving the existence of the unlimited, while others do possess a certain truth, and do not contra-

25 dict our discussions about the unlimited. 'For neither in order that generation should not come to an end ...'. This means that it is not necessary to introduce the unlimited on the grounds that generation is perpetual. For it is possible, even if the whole is limited, for generation to be perpetual, if the coming-to-be of one thing is the destruction of another.

494,1 **208a11** Moreover, to be in contact and to be limited are different. {Aristotle explains that contact is 'in relation to' and 'of something', while limitedness is not.}

[He means] that the argument stating that the limited is a limit with respect to something, being false, is another that has no necessary force. For if the limited were a limit with respect to something, to be in contact and to be limited would be the same thing; but, as it is, there is some thing which is limited but in contact with nothing (for 5 such is the fixed sphere[271]), and therefore to be limited is not the same as to be in contact. Nor therefore does the limited terminate in relation to something. 'The former is in relation to and [a touching] of something.' To be in contact, he says, is one of the relations (for what is in contact is in contact with something), but the limited is not in a relation, but even if it should happen that one of the limited things is in contact because there is no void, yet it is not the same 10 thing for it to be in contact and to be limited, since everything limited would then be *ipso facto* also in contact; but as it is, that is not so, as has been said.

208a14 Nor can anything be in contact with just anything.

That being in contact is one of the relations he shows from the fact that nothing can be in contact with just anything. For it is not the 15 case that anything is in contact with just anything. For a line is not in contact with a surface, nor a surface with a body, nor is a line in contact with a sound, but line is in contact with line and surface with surface. For even if a line is in contact with a surface, it is with respect to a line, not a surface. And it is not only our opinion that to be limited is not the same as to be in contact, but this follows also on the 20 propositions of Democritus;[272] for the atoms that move in the void are limited, but in contact with nothing. And those who propose a void outside the heavens make the heavens limited, but in contact with nothing. Thus to be limited and to be in contact are not the same; and so neither is it true that the limited is a limit with respect to something.

208a14 And it is absurd to rely on conceptualisation. {For then, 25 says Aristotle, 'the excess and defect are not with regard to the thing, but to the conception'. The longer text adds that it is not by being thought to be 'outside the city' or 'of a certain magnitude' that one becomes such, but by being so; the shorter says simply 'beyond a certain magnitude'.}

Neither does the difficulty raised by conceptualisation have necessary force. 'For the excess and defect are not with regard to the thing, but to the conception.' From the fact that conception can conceive an unlimited magnitude, it is not, he says, immediately necessary that such a magnitude should exist. For neither, he says, if you were to 495,1 conceive Socrates increased without limit would it be immediately

necessary that Socrates is this size and exceeds the three-cubit magnitude that he possesses[273] because of the conception; nor if we were to imagine him 'outside the city', would it be immediately necessary that he is outside. For neither is true that objects follow on
5   conceptualisation, but conception (at least it is when correct) supervenes on the objects. And the most accurate copies do not read 'outside the city', but only 'beyond the magnitude', that is, the magnitude that we men possess.[274]

> **208a20** But time and change are unlimited, and conception, when it does not imply the permanence of what is taken.

10   [He means] that the difficulty raised by time and change introduces the unlimited, but not the sort that we have demonstrated to be non-existent, the unlimited which subsists in actuality and all together. For time is not unlimited all at once, nor does what is taken from it remain, but its unlimitedness subsists part by part in the process of coming to be. But even if you wish to increase time
15   conceptually, you will not in this way take its nature all together, but part by part.

> **208a21** And magnitude is not unlimited either by reduction or by conceptual increase.

For magnitude is divisible without limit, but it is impossible for the division to result in unlimited parts. But neither can it be increased
20   without limit, as has been shown. So here too the unlimited is in the process of coming to be and part by part; but not as a whole at once.
    [Philoponus finds it superfluous to comment on the final sentence: 'But about the unlimited, in what way it exists, and in what way it does not, and what it is, I have finished speaking.']

Notes

Abbreviations

DK   H. Diels, rev. W. Kranz, *Die Fragmente der Vorsokratiker*, vols
I-III, Berlin 1952 (Zurich 1966).

Aristotle (English names supplied where used in text)

An. Pr.	*Analytica Priora*
Cael.	*De Caelo* (*On the Heavens*)
Cat.	*Categoriae* (*Categories*)
DA	*De Anima* (*On the Soul*)
EN	*Ethica Nicomachea*
GC	*De Generatione et Corruptione* (*On Generation*)
Int.	*De Interpretatione* (*On Interpretation*)
Metaph.	*Metaphysica*
Meteor.	*Meteorologica*
Phys.	*Physica* (*Physics*)
Sens.	*De Sensu et Sensibilia*
Top.	*Topica*

Plato

Euthyd.	*Euthydemus*
Phil.	*Philebus*
Rep.	*Republic*
Symp.	*Symposium*
Tim.	*Timaeus*

Plotinus

Enn.	*Enneads*

Porphyry

De Antro	*De Antro Nympharum*

Proclus

Elementa	*Elementa Theologiae*
in Alc.	*In Platonis Alcibiadem*
in Eucl.	*In Euclidis Elementa*
in Parm.	*In Platonis Parmenidem*

Simplicius, Themistius

in Phys.	*In Aristotelis Physica*
SVF	Von Arnim (ed.) *Stoicorum Veterum Fragmenta*

1. *arkhê* is sometimes rendered 'principle', but for this part of the *Physics* I have found 'origin' the more intelligible word in most contexts. Aristotle's opening sentence takes up the conclusions of *Physics* 2, 192b22ff. The words *kinêsis* and *metabolê* are, according to E. Hussey, *Aristotle's Physics* (1983), 55, largely interchangeable in *Physics* 3; I have used 'alteration' for *metabolê*, rather than for *alloiôsis*, because it seemed best to render the commoner Greek by the commoner English term.

2. *ta phusika* are the subjects of the verb *phuein*, which means literally 'to grow'. In this translation, *phusis* is rendered as 'nature', but the term 'natural science' or 'natural philosophy' is now too archaic to be used as an equivalent for *ta phusika*, and I have therefore followed convention in using 'physics'.

3. *hulê* is defined at *Phys.* 2, 192a31: 'the first substratum of each thing, from which it comes, and which does not inhere in it as an accident.' Cf. *GC* 320a2-9.

4. In Aristotle's tutor, Plato (428-348 BC), the *eidos* or *idea* is the universal form of any particular, sometimes conceived as a separable paradigm. In Aristotle the *eidos* is a form that does not exist apart from matter, except in the case of God.

5. The word *kinêsis* stands for all forms of change, including change of place. I have used the term 'change' throughout, except where it is clear that only motion is in question. Note that *kineô* in Greek is transitive, *kinoumai* being the intransitive form; because the verb 'change' is ambiguous in English, I have used 'cause change' for the former and 'be changed', 'suffer change', 'undergo change' for the latter. English lacks words for the agent and subject of change, though it can speak of the cause of motion as a 'mover'; my renderings of *kinoun* ('cause of change') and *kinoumenos* ('subject of change') are therefore necessarily cumbersome.

6. Place (*topos*) is discussed at *Phys.* 208a27-213a11, and is defined at 212a2-14 as the limit of the containing body. This solution, which does not allow for empty space or void (213a12-217b28), was rejected by Philoponus and even by more faithful Aristotelians: see Sorabji, *Philoponus* (1987), 15.

7. Time (*khronos*) is discussed at *Phys.* 4, 217b29-224a17, and is held to depend on motion. This principle is invoked in the latter parts of Philoponus' commentary on *Physics* 3.

8. Book 1 has considered the substratum of natural process, Book 2 its causes and ends, both of which involve the notion of form.

9. *allôs* ('otherwise').

10. See *Phys.* 227a10-15 for a definition of *sunekhês*; 228a20 for the axiom that motion is continuous; 239b5-240b7 on Zeno's denial of motion; 250b10 for prolonged discussion.

11. *apeiron* means 'having no limit (*peras*)', and is contrasted with '*peperasmenon* (limited)'. The alternative English renderings, 'infinite' and 'finite', do not admit of a corresponding verb. The meanings of *apeiron* are to be expounded shortly in this work. The statement that the unlimited is contained in the account of the continuous may be a pun, since later we shall hear that the unlimited is contained and not containing.

12. *Phys.* 222b30-223a15.

13. Or 'natural philosophers', those who make no use of the concepts aired in the *Metaphysics* of Aristotle, and explain the world by material and efficient, rather than formal and final, causes. Sometimes used to distinguish certain Presocratics from Plato, the Eleatics and the Pythagoreans.

14. 'Motion' = *kinêsis* (see n. 5). For arguments against motion in the void see *Phys.* 213a11-217b27. Philoponus disagreed with Aristotle on this question: see his *Corollaries on Place and Void* (tr. 1991) and the summaries by David Furley and David Sedley in R. Sorabji (ed.) *Philoponus* (1987), 130-53.

15. Because matter has no properties and hence 'is not'. See n. 21, and, on ancient anticipation of Berkeley's objections to the concept of matter, R. Sorabji, *Time, Creation and the Continuum* (1983), 287-96.

16. For Platonists this would include at least the Forms and the rational soul. For Aristotle, the only subsistent incorporeal being is the Prime Mover, i.e. the ultimate final cause who is called God: see *Metaph.* 1074b34, where this being is called the 'thought of thought' (*noêsis noêseôs*).

17. *Int.* 23a23.

18. The word is Aristotle's invention. W.D. Ross, commenting on *De Anima* 402a26, writes: 'It appears that strictly speaking *energeia* means activity or actualisation, while *entelecheia* means the resulting actuality or perfection. For the most part Aristotle treats the two words as synonyms.' Quoted in J. Urmson, *The Greek Philosophical Vocabulary* (1990).

19. See *Cael.* 270a13-270b25 on the aethereal body of the heavens, a fifth element believed to be the outer limit of the universe, and to be incorruptible and in constant rotatory motion. Philoponus does not question the need for a fifth element here, although that will be a central thesis of his later *contra Aristotelem*. Aristotle's universe is geocentric, the earth being surrounded first by water, then by air, then by a transparent belt of fire, and then by the transparent aethereal spheres which carry round moon, sun, planets and finally the fixed stars.

20. See e.g. Plato, *Rep.* 476E-478E on the difference between the objects of knowledge and opinion; *Tim.* 27D on being and becoming. Plato contrasts a realm of things that are necessarily and eternally what they are with the world of material phenomena, in which every object is what it is contingently and is subject to continual transformation.

21. The verb *esti* stands for both the copulative and the existential uses of the verb to be, i.e. to say 'F is not' may mean either 'F does not exist' or 'F is not x, y, z etc.' Often no clear distinction is made, and so I have usually avoided the term 'exist'. On the exploration of the concept of not-being in Plato's *Sophist* see G.E.L. Owen, 'Plato on Not-Being' (1970).

22. A category is a predicate: according to Aristotle's *Categories* 1b25f, there are ten such, namely substance, quantity, quality, relation, place, time, position, state, action and affection.

23. The term *ousia*, in the sense of substance, covers both individual beings (primary *ousia*: *Cat.* 2a11ff.) and their species (secondary *ousia*: *Cat.* 2b7ff.). *Metaphysics* 1017b24-5 points out that the noun may refer both to the substratum and the form of an existent thing. Sometimes it means the substance *of* something, in other words, its essence.

24. i.e. the state of being perfect or complete in its own kind, the attainment of the form. On ancient and modern etymologies of *entelekheia* (which can hardly in fact contain the word *hen*) see D.W. Graham, *AJP* 110 (1989).

25. i.e. what can be used for building, materials such as wood, stone, etc.

26. Perhaps a reference to Plato, *Timaeus* 57E, where motion is said to arise from inequality.

27. At *Cat.* 2a16 the *genos* is the class that subsumes the individual species (*eidê*). *Top.* 102a31: 'predicated of many things differing in species in the category of substance.' Philoponus' discussion presupposes the notion of 'focal meaning' (*Metaph.* 1003a33ff.), which explains how the many senses of terms like 'being' are neither synonymous nor merely homonymous, but as it were related to one centre.

28. See *Phys.* 8, 260a23ff.

29. A *hupographê* is a general illustration used in place of a definition: Von Arnim, *SVF* p. 75ff.

30. See *DA* 412b4-5 and 414b20ff., where Aristotle argues that the definition of soul, like that of figure, cannot be given for the general case, but only for each order of soul.

31. Philoponus often repeats lemmata because his discussion is broken into two parts, first a *protheôria* (424,4-13) which discusses the *doctrine* of an Aristotelian passage, and then a discussion of the text itself, broken into portions by lemmata which partly repeat the original lemma. Vitelli sometimes fails, as here, to print the textual lemmata as separate headings. See n. 219 below. The situation is explained by É. Évrard in *L'école d'Olympiodore et le composition du 'Commentaire à la Physique' de Jean Philopon*, dissertation, Liège 1957.

32. No doubt is implied by this use of the verb *dokein* such as 'seems' would imply in English.

33. By Philoponus in his commentary on *Categories* 48,7ff. and 199,14ff.

34. At *An. Post.* 84a12, Aristotle distinguishes two senses of *kath' hauto* for attributes: (a) they are included in the account of the *hupokeimenon*; (b) the *hupokeimenon* is included in the account of them. Cf. 34,22 of Philoponus *in Phys.* (book 1).

35. *hupokeimenon* is said to have two usages at *Metaph.* 1038b5: either as an animal underlies its passions, or as matter underlies form. For the former case the rendering 'subject' is preferable; otherwise 'substratum' is preferred in this translation.

36. See *Cat.* 4b20-5a15 for frequent recurrence of this criterion.

37. This passage refers primarily to motion. On the motion of atoms in the void see Leucippus (5th cent. BC) Fr. A6 DK (Aristotle, *Metaph.* 985b).

38. The syllogism is defined at *An. Pr.* 24b18-19 as a discourse in which a conclusion follows from stated premisses. Syllogisms in the species 'demonstrative' are differentiated from their non-demonstrative congeners, not by any difference of form, but by material features of their premises (e.g. truth – see *An. Post.* 71b20). However, the usual form of the demonstrative or apodeictic syllogism (*An. Post.* 74b11) expressed in English idiom is: all A's are B, all B's are C, all A's are C, where B is the explanatory term, and the necessity of the premises shows the necessity of the conclusion. The example has no special relevance; any pair of genus and species would have sufficed.

39. On *Phys.* 189b30 (pp. 151-2 Vitelli) Philoponus explains that one cannot give a generic account of 'coming-to-be' (*genesis*), and that the 'general (*katholou*)' treatment of it will deal in fact with what is 'specific but applicable to many things (*pleiosi epharmattonta*)'. He also states that by an overall definition of genesis, Aristotle includes its incidental presence in other things. Here he seems to exclude the first kind of generality, leaving only the incidental predications.

40. On the incorruptibility of the heavenly bodies see *Cael.* 279b5-283b22. Aristotle held that these bodies were of aether; cf. n. 19 above.

41. See n. 27 on *Metaph.* 1003a33ff. and esp. n. 30 on *DA* 414b20ff.

42. Alexander of Aphrodisias (fl. AD 200), one of the earliest extant commentators on Aristotle. For this reference cf. Simplicius, *in Phys.* 403,13f.

43. cf. *Cat.* 1a16-18, 2a6 and *Phys.* 185a30-4, where it is asserted that the categories, other than substance, cannot exist independently.

44. Themistius (AD ?317-88), one of the later commentators on Aristotle, frequently used or quoted by Philoponus: *in Phys.* 206,22f.

45. These words of Aristotle's are more accurately quoted when Philoponus resumes his piecemeal commentary at 354,23.

46. The Greek reads to *kinoun phusikôs kinêton* ('the causing-change naturally changeable'); ambiguity arises because the verb 'to be' is left, as often in Greek, to be inserted by the reader. Philoponus does not make it any more lucid by substituting *kinoumenon* ('subject of change') for *kinêton* ('changeable').

47. See *Phys.* 198a35-6. Aristotle adds that the non-natural one is that which has no principle of motion in itself (e.g. the Prime Mover, who acts as final, not efficient cause).

48. See especially *Phys.* 257a31-260a19 on the Unmoved Mover. The bread as given as an example below is desired, not eaten.

49. See n. 42. For this reading cf. Simplicius, *in Phys.* 422,23. Ross's edition follows the text of Aspasius, which yields a different rendering from either: 'It is the fulfilment of the potential when it is already fully real and operates not as itself but as movable' (Hardie and Gaye).

50. Hyperbaton is the transposition of words and clauses within a sentence, more common in an inflected language like Greek than it can be English.

51. See Aristotle, *DA* 418b-419a on light as the actuality of the transparent, in other words as the state of the medium in which one can actually, not merely potentially, see through it.

52. On Aristotle and the Pythagoreans see H. Cherniss, *Aristotle's Criticism of Presocratic Philosophy* (1935). His testimony will be considered in detail below.

53. Socrates (469-399 BC), the tutor of Plato, was frequently cited in examples by Aristotle (*Int.* 20a25 etc.), perhaps in imitation of his own practice, in Plato's dialogues, of using the names of himself and his companions (*Phaedo* 102B7ff. etc.)

54. See *Metaph.* 986a20ff., where a table of ten opposed contraries is given, the positive term being always in the left-hand column, the negative in the right.

55. See on Aristotle and the Pythagoreans in general, W. Burkert, *Lore and Science* (1972), 28-53. It is unlikely that Pythagoras (fl. ? 500 BC) is responsible for the theories expounded by Aristotle; but, as Burkert shows, they have at least not yet been fully assimilated to Plato's 'unwritten doctrines'. For a collection of Aristotelian testimonia see 58 B5-B13 in Diels-Kranz.

56. On the syllogism see n. 38 above. In this instance, the major premiss follows the minor premiss, but the logical form still holds.

57. Usually called *modus tollens*: if p, then q; but not-q, therefore not-p. If form, definition; but no definition, hence no form (privation).

58. See *GC* 319a4-5, 323b1-324b3, 326b29-327a29, 331a6-331b10.

59. See *DA* 417b2-16, 421a2-26, 429a13-430a26.

60. See *GC* 317a32-320a10 on the unity of matter.

61. cf. *Phys.* 255a31 for the two senses of *dunamis*. Nature is said to be the source of all *taxis* (the arrangement or scheme of things) at *Phys.* 252a12.

62. Substituting *anisotês* ('inequality') for *tautotês* ('sameness'), to yield both good sense here and consistency with the rest of the discussion.

63. *kinoumenoi*, a play on words. The word translated 'consideration' here is *enoias* in the MS: some would correct to *aitias* ('cause'), but the correction to *ennoias* is supported by 366,8.

64. See *Cat.* 12a1-14a25 on the logical rules that govern contraries.

65. See *Cat.* 12a26-12b16. Blindness would be a privation of sight, not-seeing its negation. Privation always implies that the possession of the absent quality would be proper to the subject (e.g. a man can be blind, but a stone cannot, because stones can never see).

66. Themistius, *in Phys.* 214,11ff.

67. Vitelli supplies: 'and he says that it is in the subject of change.'

68. Philoponus was a vigorous polemicist against the Arian heresy, which maintained that the Second Person of the Trinity (the Son of God) was a creature. He may here have in mind the contention of the anti-Arian writer of the fourth century, Marius Victorinus, that the Son is the actuality of which the Father is the potential.

69. See *An. Pr.* 25b31-2ff. The first type (or figure: *skhêma*) is one in which the predicate term of one premise is the subject-term of the other premise. 'All B is A; all C is B; therefore all C is A', OR 'No B is A; all C is B; therefore no C is A'. Aristotle also includes: 'All B is A; some C is B; therefore some C is A' and 'No B is A; some C is B; therefore some C is not A'.

70. A well-known road between two major cities of the Greek mainland; but the phrase is perhaps suggested by the remark of Heraclitus (6th cent. BC) that 'the road up is the road down' (Fr. 60 DK; see especially the interpretation by the Peripatetic Theophrastus).

71. *lôpion* and *himation* in the Greek. The distinction is roughly that between identity of extension and identity of intension in modern philosophy. W.V. Quine and others throw doubt on the viability of such a distinction.

72. I have attempted to retain the correspondence of *logikê* and *logos*, though the latter term here means merely 'argument'.

73. See *Cat.* 1a1-12. When two things have only a name in common, they are homonymous; when the same definition (*logos tês ousias*) can be applied to both, they are synonymous. (Note that in Aristotle's terminology 'man' and 'horse' can be synonyms because both belong to the genus 'animal'.)

74. Philoponus is able to refer here without demur to Aristotle's divine prime mover, because Ammonius, the teacher of Philoponus, had argued that Aristotle viewed his God as a Creator. That is, Aristotle's God did not just inspire celestial motion by being an object of love, or final cause, but was in addition an efficient cause or maker (*poiêtikon*) who maintained the universe in beginningless and endless existence. (See Richard Sorabji, *Matter, Space and Motion*, ch. 15.) There was only one thing with which Philoponus, as a Christian, need disagree. Ammonius took Aristotle's God to be a Creator in the sense which the Neoplatonists believed they found in Plato, that is, a God beginninglessly responsible for the existence of a beginningless orderly cosmos. Philoponus himself believed that God was a Creator in the Christian sense of one who gives the universe a beginning. He insists on this beginning below at 428,16-430,10 and 467,15-468,4. It has been suggested by Verrycken that even this disagreement would not have been included in the AD 517 edition of the *Physics* commentary, but would have been added in a revision after 529 (see Konraad Verrycken, 'The Development of Philoponus' Thought and its Chronology' in Richard Sorabji, ed., *Aristotle Transformed*, pp. 233-74).

75. *DA* 405b33-407b26 denies all motion to soul, and especially natural motion (406a21-7); but the power to cause motion is the characteristic of soul in Platonism, e.g. *Phaedrus* 245C.

76. The preternatural alternative is canvassed here and in the *contra Proclum*. But the rotation of the fiery belt is considered *natural* earlier in the *de Anima* and later in the commentary on the *Meteorologica* and in the *contra Aristotelem*. In fact, the latter allows for fire to have two natural motions after all, upward and circular (Simplicius *in Cael.* 35,14-16).

77. The expression *ta analutika* seems to stand for logical method in Aristotle: on the value of this see *An. Pr.* 48a1ff., *Metaph.* 1005b4.

78. On the motion of the fiery sphere see 384,29ff. below and nn. 76, 79.

79. Here Philoponus extends the idea of an impetus, i.e. an internal force impressed from without, which Thomas Kuhn has treated as a scientific revolution in its medieval context, from the case of projectiles (*in Phys.* 641,13) to the case of the firebelt. The rotating heavens impress a force into the firebelt below. The

Neoplatonist language is well explained by Michael Wolff in 'Philoponus and the Rise of Preclassical Dynamics', 1987, at 110, and *Fallgesetz und Massbegriff* (Berlin 1971) 88-9.

80. On this question see H.F. Cherniss, *Aristotle's Criticism of the Presocratics* (1935) p. 17 n. 68.

81. i.e. the 'triangle' 1+2+3+4, often arranged in rows of concrete units, with the 4 at the base and the 1 at the apex. See W. Burkert, *Lore and Science* (1972), 72.

82. See *Philebus* 16C and 23C-26D on the role of the *apeiron* in producing entities. On the theory of the *apeiron* in Plato see C. de Vogel, *Philosophia* (1970), 378-95. The second half of this summary is curious, since *Phaedrus* 247C2 speaks expressly of 'the things outside the heavens'; but this refers to the incorporeal forms, and the existence of anything corporeal outside our universe is no doubt precluded by *Timaeus* 31A, which argues that there can be only one world.

83. *Phil.* 16C and 64A imply that the Platonic form or idea is discerned in the mixture of limit with limitlessness.

84. See *Metaph.* 986a18 for the unlimited, 987b25 for the Dyad. For the great and small see *Metaph.* 998a8. Aristotle and his commentators are our chief source for these 'unwritten doctrines' of Plato, the existence of which is denied, e.g., by H.F. Cherniss, *Aristotle's Criticism of Plato and the Academy* (1944), but maintained, e.g., by H.J. Kramer, *Plato and the Foundations of Metaphysics* (1990). See further W.D. Ross, *Plato's Theory of Ideas* (1951), 142-63 and J.N. Findlay, *Plato: The Written and the Unwritten Doctrines* (1974).

85. It was a major objection of Aristotle's to infinity existing in the sense of more than finite quantity that then a mere part of this quantity would be equally infinite (*Phys.* 3.5, 204a20-6). We ourselves accept that the odd numbers form a more than finite series just as much as the series of all whole numbers. But Aristotle's rejection of such a possibility is exploited by Philoponus too.

86. Or 'a perfect essence' (*autoousia*). Cf. Plotinus, *Enn.* VI.8.12, where the first extant use of this term occurs.

87. Wholes are by definition finite for Aristotle, because they have nothing left over outside them, whereas there is always something more to take in an infinity, *Phys.* 3.6, 206b33-207a10, with Philoponus comments below 440,6; 473,23-477,31.

88. W. Burkert, *Lore and Science* (1972), 466-8 collects the relevant testimonia: *Cael.* 268a11, *Metaph.* 985b29-30, 986a8, 990a23, 1078b22-3.

89. Though *Metaph.* 986b6 finds difficulty in the application of the concept. W. Burkert, *Lore and Science* (1972), 57-8 collects post-Aristotelian testimonia which show a greater degree of assimilation to the 'Platonic' position.

90. The view that Plato was a Pythagorean is represented e.g. by Hippolytus, *Refutatio* VI.21 and Numenius Fr. 1 (Des Places). Timaeus, in Plato's dialogue of that name, was generally held to be a Pythagorean, as are Simmias and Cebes in the *Phaedo*. See e.g. J. N. Findlay, *Plato* (1974), 57ff.

91. See *Phys.* 187a17.

92. *Cat.* 5b 1-2.

93. Euripides, *Orestes* 25. As the most sententious of the great tragedians, Euripides (480-405 BC) is the favourite of philosophers.

94. See further *Phys.* 213b22, Simplicius *in Phys.* 651,26 and Stobaeus, *Ecl.* I.18.1c, quoting a lost work of Aristotle.

95. The demiurge or divine artificer of the world enters philosophy with the *Timaeus* of Plato; in later Platonism he was often identified with a primordial, creative intellect. See J.M. Dillon, *The Middle Platonists* (1977), 366-76 on Numenius of Apamea; A.-J. Festugière, *Hermès Trismégiste* IV (1954), 275-92 on the Neoplatonist interpretations of *Timaeus* 39E.

96. Paraphrasing *proaktikê*, Vitelli's substitution for the *praktikê* of the MS. But this is a rare word, and an equally simple correction would yield *paraktikê*, much the same in meaning, but an established technical term of the later Neoplatonists. Cf. Proclus, *Elementa* 7, E.R. Dodds, *The Elements of Theology* (1963), 194 and *paragein* at 402,24 etc. On the generation of phenomena from the forms see Plato, *Rep.* 509; Plotinus, *Enn.* V.1.6; Proclus, *Elementa* 25.

97. A common similitude: cf. Plotinus (AD 204/5-270), *Enn.* IV.9.4.

98. See *Cat.* 11a5-14, and for the classic exposition of the *gnômon*, Iamblichus, *in Nicomachum* 58,19f. (Pistelli). This may be illustrated by the following diagram:

```
x   x   x   x   x   x

x   x   x   x   x   x

x   x   x   x   x   x

x   x   x   x   x   x

x   x   x   x   x   x

x   x   x   x   x   x
```

Diogenes Laertius, *Vitae Philosophorum* II.2 perhaps means to credit Anaximander (see n. 160) with the invention of this mathematical instrument; he can hardly have been thinking of the material tool.

99. *daktylikoi*, i.e. counted on the fingers; cf. 428,14.

100. On the representation of numbers as magnitudes see *Metaph.* 1080b16-21, 1083b8-18. Aëtius, I.3.19 attributes the beginnings of this doctrine to Ecphantus; for a digest of Pythagorean theories see [Iamblichus], *Theology of Arithmetic* (tr. Waterfield, 1988).

101. Aristotle would think of Anaximenes (late 6th cent. BC) as the proponent of the view that air is the primordial element (*Metaph.* 984a5), and of Thales (fl. 585 BC) as the proponent of the view that it is water (*Metaph.* 983b10-21). His testimony concerning Thales is particularly dubious: see G.S. Kirk et al., *The Presocratic Philosophers* (1983), 76-99. Aristotle ascribes to Anaximander (6th cent. BC) the view that the unlimited itself is the primordial substrate, i.e. is rather a substance than an accident: see Aristotle, *Phys.* 203b7, Simplicius, *in Phys.* 24,13. According to the latter, the properties of warmth, coolness, dryness and wetness emerge from and return to this substrate, paying their debts to one another at the bar of time. On the meagre evidence concerning this early figure see G.S. Kirk, 'Some Problems in Anaximander' (1955).

102. See Empedocles (fl. ? 470 BC), Fr. B6 DK etc. This mystical philosopher and poet was perhaps the first to name four elements.

103. The term homoeomery was probably coined by Aristotle, not by Anaxagoras (fl. 450 BC): *Phys.* 187a25, *Cael.* 302b1. A homoeomery is a whole whose parts are of like substance. M. Schofield, *An Essay on Anaxagoras* (1980), 43-67 argues that Anaxagoras, employing the Parmenidean principle of sufficient reason, deduced that it was impossible for matter to possess one quality rather than another, and then inferred that all things were 'originally' what matter is 'in itself'.

104. For Aristotle's account of the theory of Democritus (fl. 440 BC), see *Metaph.* 985b4ff. The term *atomoi* is the origin of our word 'atoms'.

105. For the term *panspermia* ('seminal mixture of all things') see also *Cael.* 303a16 (and see Simplicius *in Cael.* 242,18ff. on Democritus), *GC* 314a29.

106. See *Phys.* 187a23 and cf. Anaxagoras, Frs B4, B5, B10 DK with n. 98 above.

107. Simplicius, *in Cael.* 295,1 quotes Aristotle as saying that Democritus made substances originate by aggregation of atoms.

108. See *Phys.* 188a10 for this punning criticism.

109. On Mind in Anaxagoras see Frs B1, B9, B13, B14 DK, all from Simplicius, who gives a full account at *in Phys.* 164,24 and 156,13. Both Plato (*Phaedo* 97B) and Aristotle (*Metaph.* 985a18-20) complain that the action of Mind is not sufficiently explained.

110. Reading *mikras* after Vitelli; but perhaps this should be corrected to *merikas* in conformity with 397,21.

111. At *Timaeus* 55E-56C the elements have each a shape assigned to them, and that of fire is *puramoeidês*. The spherical form is reserved for the universe itself.

112. See *Metaph.* 985b15-19.

113. *arkhê* is a term of wide application. For consistency I have generally employed 'origin' as the equivalent, but sometimes 'principle', 'basis', 'beginning' or 'cause'.

114. See *Metaph.* 983a24-b7, and the subsequent presentation of the history of philosophy as the discovery of these four causes which are really four types of explanatory factor. The material cause is the stuff from which a thing is formed; the formal cause is the ground of its identity (roughly speaking, its defining characteristics); the final cause is its goal; the efficient cause is close to its cause in the modern sense.

115. For the dispersion of the form in matter cf. Plotinus, *Enn.* IV.3.19, etc.

116. White differs from black in dividing the sight.

117. For *sumplokê* cf. 398,29, where the Pythagoreans derive all entities from the *sumplokê* of odd and even. This usage in Philoponus may rest either on the Stoic notion of fate as a *sumplokê* of all things (cf. Plotinus, *Enn.* III.1.4), or on the Aristotelian definition of predication as the *sumplokê* of the subject and the predicate (*Cat.* 1a16, *DA* 432a11; cf. 474,25 below).

118. Philoponus here distinguishes the form in matter from that in the mind of the Demiurge, for which Platonists often reserved the name Idea. The question whether the forms can be predicated of themselves is at least implied in Plato: see G. Vlastos, *Platonic Studies* (1981), 335-41. For admonitions similar to those of Philoponus cf. Proclus, *in Eucl.* 54,8, *in Parm.* 890,2ff.

119. 'Formulae' renders *logoi*. For the Platonic Ideas as thoughts in the mind of the Demiurge (the discursive intellect) see A.M. Rich, *Mnemosyne* (1954); on the use of the word *logos* in Platonism to mean a formative and generative principle, see J.M. Rist, *Plotinus* (1967), 84-102, and, e.g., Plotinus, *Enn.* IV.8.8.

120. According to Plato, the artist produces merely copies of copies (*Rep.* 597D), but the Demiurge looks directly at the eternal paradigm (*Tim.* 28B). The image of the painter is used by the Stoic Seneca in his exposition of the Platonic forms at *Letter* 65.7.

121. cf. n. 95 and Apuleius, *De Platone* 6.192-3. At *Theaet.* 194A-195A the percipient soul is compared to wax receiving an impression.

122. On Neoplatonic attempts to synthesise and improve both the Platonic and the Aristotelian theories of predication see A.C. Lloyd, *The Anatomy of Neoplatonism* (1990), 76-122; P. Hadot, in R. Sorabji, ed., *Aristotle Transformed* (1990), 125-40. The simile in the following paragraph may be inspired by Aristotle's comparison (*DA* 430a16-17) of the sun with the 'active intellect' which illuminates the 'potential intellect', and thus makes possible discursive thought; for the commentaries of Themistius and Pseudo-Alexander on this passage see now the annotated translation by F.M. Schroeder and R.B. Todd (1990).

123. Presumably referring to the repulsion between like poles of magnetised units. Plutarch, *De Iside* 376b remarks upon this property of repulsion. Since it is the influence of one object on another that is in question, I have rendered *dunamis*, not by 'potentiality', but by 'power'.

124. Perhaps Philoponus has in mind Alcmaeon (?early 5th century BC), who maintained that the universe was an *isonomia* ('equal polity') of simple properties (Aëtius V.30.1 etc.); cf. the speech of Eryximachus in Plato, *Symposium* 185E6ff.

125. This passage may be illustrated by the following diagram (cf. p. 408,1ff.):

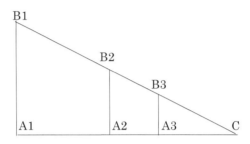

CB2 = B1A1; CB3 = B2A2 etc.

126. See Hippolytus, *Refutatio* I.13.2. Despite Plato (*Tim.* 31A and 92) the plurality of worlds remained a point of debate in Platonism: see e.g. Plutarch, *De Def. Orac.* 422A-427A.

127. See e.g. Empedocles Fr. B17.19-20 DK. Aristotle, *Metaph.* 985a21ff. suggests that love and strife are efficient causes, the universe suffering the alternate dominance of each. For modern doubts as to whether Empedocles posited a cyclical alternation, rather than concurrent activity, of love and strife, see A.A. Long, 'Empedocles in the Sixties' (1974).

128. To the references above (nn. 101-6) may be added Heraclitus (Fr. B90 DK etc.), who opined that all things were transformations of fire. See further n. 149 below.

129. Meaning the Presocratics of the sixth century BC. In reckoning men a thousand years before him as inhabitants of the same period, Philoponus may have in mind the theory of *Timaeus* 22Bff., where Solon is told that civilisation has arisen and been destroyed many times in Greece, the previous cataclysms having effaced the Greeks' recollection of their own longevity.

130. See *Cael.* 278b10-279b2.

131. *Phys.* 187a13-188a4.

132. *GC* 315b25-317a17 denies both the possibility of actual division *ad infinitum* and the existence of indivisible magnitudes.

133. The labyrinth was the maze built in Crete by Daedalus as a house for the Minotaur. This creature was killed by Theseus, who found his way back by following a thread which he had unravelled on the inward journey. The contrast between the 'pathless' (*aporeuton*) and the unlimited in this passage may involve an etymology, or at least a play on words; cf. n. 136.

134. The river Ocean was supposed by many geographers to encircle the whole land mass: see Strabo I.1.3-9. Ptolemy (*Geographia* VII.5.2) affirms that a combination of land and ocean girdles the known world. The only authority known to me for complete encirclement of the Ocean by land is Philoponus' contemporary Cosmas Indicopleustes, *Topographia* 84c. On Philoponus' relation to this cosmology in his *De Opificio Mundi*, see H. Chadwick, 'Philoponus, the Christian Theologian' (1987), 51, and W. Wolda, *La Topographie chrétienne de Cosmas Indicopleustes* (1962), 147-92. Cosmas, a notoriously unreliable author, is interested in the location of paradise and may be influenced by Plato, *Phaedo* 109A-115A, where the visible world is said to lie in a hollow of a greater one.

135. cf. *De Opificio Mundi* 168,25-169,19. The Periplus Maris Erythraei (2nd cent. AD) reveals the interest which these waters held for the ancients. The views of Cosmas were not identical on this point, since he had sailed to India: see Wolda (op. cit.), 264-5.

136. *apeirêkotes*: not so much a pun as an adventure in etymology. It is not certain that there is any etymological relation between *peira* ('trial') and *peras* ('limit'). Cf. n. 133.

137. This may be illustrated by the following diagram:

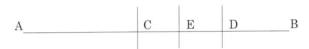

AB = 2CB. CB = 2CD. CD = 2CE etc.

138. On *ousia* see n. 23 above.

139. Vitelli marks a lacuna with a reference to p. 414,7f.

140. That is, it employs a complex premise, in this case a conditonal. Formally, it is an instance of modus tollens (if p then q, but not-q; therefore, not-p), which Philoponus elsewhere calls 'the second hypothetical' (102,17; 505,16; 782,20 – see also 'the first' at 608,19). The ordering is derived from the Stoic list of indemonstrable arguments, but the labels had become customary for Peripatetics as well. But because of the content of the propositions, the standard Peripatetic classification (which Philoponus seems to follow elsewhere – see *'diaretikos'* at 308,1) would make this syllogism an argument 'from the more and less' (*apo tou mallon kai hêtton*). On the Peripatetic classification of hypothetical syllogisms, see Alexander Aphrodisias *in An. Pr.* 265 and 389.

For another example, see n. 195 below.

141. See n. 85.

142. Other MSS supply 'but if it should not be divisible'; Vitelli adds: '[the unlimited] will then be simple; and if simple it will be completely divisible into an unlimited number of parts. But if they state that it is indivisible' etc.

143. See references in nn. 81-4, 88-9 above.

144. Vitelli's text of Philoponus has *molis*; Ross's text of Aristotle has *mogis*. There is no difference in meaning.

145. The Greek dative is used in this passage to indicate attributive predication as opposed to predication of identity.

146. See *Cat.* 2a19-34.

147. See n. 85.

148. *An. Pr.* 26b34-27a1. The second type or figure is that in which some thing belongs to all of one and none of another, or all of both, or none of either. Thus: 'All

B is A; no C is A; therefore no C is B', OR 'All B is A; all C is A', OR 'No B is A; no C is A'. It is obvious that only the first case yields a correct deduction. On the first type see n. 69.

149. The notion of an unlimited (infinite) number perhaps appears first in Plato, *Parm.* 144A.

150. *Cael.* 302b10-303b8.

151. *GC* 329a5-331a5.

152. This generalises the difficulty, referred to in nn. 85, 141 and 147, that a more than finite quantity could be divided into parts that were more than finite. The objection here is to the multiplication of a more than finite quantity. This will be repeatedly exploited below, 428,14-430,10; 446,15; 467,5-468,4.

153. This absurd remark might rest on a single, botched experiment, but is more likely to rest on none. It is probably related to Philoponus' view that if you double the weight, a falling body falls slightly faster, though to his credit, he claims that observation will show it does not fall twice as fast, *in Phys.* 683,1-25. C. Wildberg, *John Philoponus' Criticism of Aristotle's Theory of Aether* (1988), 185 observes that, while Philoponus is apt to answer mathematical arguments with appeals to the phenomena of nature, most of his experiments are 'carried out in thought rather than practice'. (In Wildberg's view the experimental observations at *in Phys.* 683,16ff. are unique.)

154. The word *homoeidês* applies both to homogeneous wholes and to their similar parts. Where the meaning is clear, I have always preferred 'homogeneous'.

155. For *hê arkhaia phusis* cf. Plato, *Symp.* 192A and Plotinus, *Enn.* VI.5.1.16.

156. Meaning presumably Alexandria, where Philoponus was writing, though the logic of the argument is, of course, independent of any locality. On the invariance of intensity with quantity, perhaps an important feature in the case for the fiery nature of the heavens, see *contra Aristotelem* Fr. III/53 and Wildberg (op. cit. n. 153), 168.

157. Since the influence of one body on another is the subject of this passage, I have rendered *energein* by 'be active' and *dunamis* by 'power'. For another case where *energeia* means 'activity' rather than 'actuality' in Philoponus, see *in DA* 332,7-22.

158. Scythia is the land to the north of the Caucasus and the Caspian Sea; Ethiopia is the southernmost extent of Africa as known to the Romans. On the effects of climate in the determination of national characteristics see the Hippocratic treatise *Airs, Waters and Places*.

159. For this use of *khôrein* cf. Proclus, *Elements* 152.

160. Anaximander, Fr. B1 DK, from Simplicius, *in Phys.* 24,13ff. As is clear from the following discussion, the intermediary (*metaxu*) is a stuff partaking of more than one element, not a fifth element.

161. Vitelli marks a lacuna here, since the subject of this paragraph does not follow immediately from the last.

162. *ho arithmôn* – a participle, unless we are to read it instead as the genitive, 'of numbers'.

163. Philoponus was the first Christian to undertake a scholarly polemic against the philosophers who maintained the eternity of the world. See especially his *De Aeternitate Mundi contra Proclum* (ed. Rabe, Leipzig 1899) and R. Sorabji, *Time, Creation and the Continuum* (1983), 210-31.

164. These arguments are paraphrased by Simplicius (*in Phys.* 1178-9) from a lost work of Philoponus against Aristotle. See the fragments of his work *Against Aristotle On the Eternity of the World*, trans. C. Wildberg (London 1987) esp. Fr. 132, as well as his *John Philoponus' Criticism of Aristotle's Theory of Aether*.

165. cf. Aristotle, *Cael.* 283a4-10 on the suggestion that the world might have a beginning but no end. Aristotle claims (though he does not repeat this in later works) that a unidirectional infinity is neither infinite nor finite. This is the theory suggested by a literal reading of Plato's *Timaeus* (esp. 29C-D). With regard to Philoponus' remarks on number, it should be remembered that the Greeks had no sign for zero and no conception of negative numbers.

166. The interpretation of the 'contraries' in Anaximander (if he spoke of them at all) remains uncertain. Aristotle, *GC* 329b25-331a6 maintains that the important contrarieties are warm-cool, wet-dry. Earth is dry and cool, water cool and wet, air wet and warm, fire warm and dry. Hence water is most contrary to fire and earth to air. See on these contrarieties G.E.R. Lloyd, 'Hot and Cold' (1964), and, for the role of polar opposites in early Greek philosophy, his *Polarity and Analogy* (1966).

167. Closely resembling the citation of Anaximander at Simplicius, *in Phys.* 24,17ff., this passage may strengthen the view that we have at least one direct quotation from this Presocratic thinker.

168. See Frs B30, 31, 90 and possibly 67 DK; Fr. 76 speaks of a reciprocal conversion of air and fire. On the *ekpurôsis* or conflagration see Fr. B31 and A1 (Diogenes Laertius 9.8). On this group of fragments see G.S. Kirk, *Heraclitus* (1954), 306-65.

169. *GC* 330b5 etc.

170. Candidates might be *heterotês* ('otherness'), *ametria* ('indetermination'), *aoristia* ('indefiniteness'), *sterêsis* ('privation'), *amorphia* ('shapelessness'). See e.g. Plotinus' treatises on the nature of matter, *Enn.* I.8 and II.4.

171. *Cael.* 278b23-279a11.

172. Here the word *eidos* must be translated 'class'. On the impossibility of rotation for an unlimited body see further *Cael.* 271b26-273a6.

173. Melissus (fl. 440 BC) was a philosopher of the Eleatic school of Parmenides and Zeno. His Fr. B7 DK, taken from Simplicius *in Phys.* 111,18, denies all forms of change to 'that which is', which he believes to be eternal and unlimited.

174. *atoma* here is neuter; when the noun means atoms in the Democritean sense, it is usually feminine, *atomoi*.

175. On the natural places of fire and earth see especially *Cael.* 308a34-310a13. For Philoponus' denial of natural places and of the consequences drawn by Aristotle from his theory, see *in Phys.* 581,14-31 and C. Wildberg, *John Philoponus' Criticism of Aristotle's Theory of Aether* (1988), 106-20. In his works against Aristotle, Philoponus endorsed the Platonic view that there is matter of all kinds in the heavens (*Timaeus* 31B4-33B1), though fire predominates.

176. The motion of the elements is considered at length in the *De Caelo*: 268b27-268b18, 300a20-302a9, 310a14-311a14.

177. This is a corollary of Aristotle's arguments against the existence of void (see n. 178 below). The weakness of these arguments was exposed by Philoponus himself in his *Corollaries on Place and Void*: see D. Furley, in R. Sorabji, ed., *Philoponus* (1987), 130-9. The *Corollaries* have now been translated, with Simplicius' reply, by D. Furley and C. Wildberg (1991).

178. *Phys.* 213b32-216b21.

179. See *Metaph.* 1073b18-1074a32 for theories on the motion of the 'fixed stars' and the planets. Though here and elsewhere in the Classical period (Plato, *Tim.* 40B etc.), the sphere of the fixed stars is spoken of, the expression 'fixed sphere' (*hê aplanes sphaira*) is rare: see *Corpus Hermeticum* II.6 (date uncertain).

180. The moon is taken to be the first planet from the earth, and nothing above it is perishable: *Cael.* 279b5ff. etc.

181. The word *hormê* is found here only in the commentary on *Physics* 3. On the contribution made to science by his notion of impulse see M. Wolff, 'Philoponus and the Rise of Preclassical Dynamics' (1987); ibid., *Geschichte der Impetus Theorie* (Frankfurt 1978); Richard Sorabji, ch. 1 in *Philoponus and the Rejection of Aristotelian Science* (1987), 7-13.

182. Contrast n. 128 on Heraclitus; but maybe Heraclitus did not say that fire was unlimited.

183. Etna in Sicily was the most famous volcano in antiquity: see Pindar, *Pythian* I.20ff.; Lucretius, *De Rerum Natura* I.722-5; Virgil, *Aeneid* III.570-87. The monster Typhon, said to lie under Etna, came from Cilicia in southern Turkey: Aeschylus, *Prometheus* 351-74 etc.

184. On thunderbolts see Aristotle, *Meteor.* 369a13-22.

185. *Phys.* 189a12-17.

186. *Cael.* 302b10-303a3; *GC* 332b31-333a13.

187. It could refer as well to the unlimitedness of the elements or the parts, but, as Aristotle qualifies the statement 'this is impossible' by the assumption that the places are limited, Philoponus would seem to be correct.

188. The syntax might suggest that the third clause followed only from the first (as indeed it logically may).

189. On Anaxagoras see above, nn. 103, 106.

190. See Aristotle, *Meteorologica* 341b10 for this sphere of fire which marks the upper limit of the mutable and sublunary world. See C. Wildberg, in R. Sorabji, ed., *Philoponus* (1987), 202-9, and ibid., *John Philoponus' Criticism of Aristotle's Theory of Aether* (1988) on the evolution of Philoponus' views about the motion of this sphere.

191. Vitelli marks a lacuna since there seems to be no connected argument.

192. Assuming the famous Anaxagorean maxim: see Frs B4, B5, B10 DK and n. 101 above.

193. *Cael.* 271b26-272a8.

194. See *Cael.* 285b1-3.

195. See n. 140 above.

196. Philoponus plays on the literal meaning of *atopon*, 'in no place'.

197. See *Cael.* 284b6-286a2, and for commentary T.L. Heath, *Aristarchus of Samos* (1913), 231-4.

198. The words used denote positions of the sun in its daily motion: *anatolê* ('orient', i.e. rising), *mesemêrinon* (i.e. mid-heaven), *dusis* ('occident', i.e. setting). To be valid the argument requires that the sun's orbit be at the end of the produced lines, i.e. at infinity.

199. Homer, *Iliad* 12.239-40. Homer is the Greek author who is most often called simply 'the poet': e.g. Plato, *Gorgias* 485D, Aristotle, *Rhetoric* 1365a11.

200. That is, substituting a negative premiss for a positive one. Cf. Aristotle, *An. Pr.* 64a14.

201. See n. 27 on species and genus.

202. *Cael.* 271b28ff.

203. Philoponus seems to have known of the inscription reputed to stand over the door of Plato's Academy, 'Let no one enter here unschooled in geometry' (*in DA* 117,29). Nevertheless his own title was *grammatikos*, and his accomplishments in geometry do not justify the prolixity with which he demonstrates them. See n. 153 above on his preference for empirical to mathematical argument.

204. cf. *Cael.* 271b28ff. on the necessary limitedness of a rotating heaven.

205. See *Phys.* 218b21ff. for the arguments that time does not exist without *kinêsis*. Plotinus, *Enn.* III.7.9 and 12, rejects the view that 'time is a measure of motion (change)' in favour of Plato's definition of it as 'the moving image of eternity' (*Tim.* 37B-39B). The questionings of Augustine, *Confessiones* XI, are famous.

206. I have given the literal rendering of a formula which deliberately avoids the duplication of the word *khronos*. Philoponus would be aware that such a formulation had been attempted by the heretic Arius (condemned at the Council of Nicaea in AD 325), who held that Christ was created by the Father, that therefore 'there was when he was not', but did not wish to assert that there was time before the creation of the world, which occurred through Christ. See Athanasius, *contra Arianos* I.11 etc. and the anathemas of the original Nicene creed. On the religion of Philoponus see H. Chadwick, 'Philoponus, the Christian Theologian' (1987).

207. *hupokeimenon*, elsewhere translated 'substratum'; but where employed as a term in logic it is better translated 'subject'. For the same reason *horos* is here translated 'term', though elsewhere 'definition'.

208. The word *semnotês* is often used in philosophical controversy to indicate that the language of an opponent is more impressive than his reasonings: cf. e.g. Plotinus, *Enn.* II.9.14.11 and 16.

209. A typically Christian notion, as expounded at length by Philoponus' contemporary Pseudo-Dionysius in his treatise *De Divinis Nominibus*. It is obviously Philoponus' concern for theological propriety that gives this passage its unusual tone. Part of his indignation has been swallowed by a lacuna which is noted in the translation.

210. *huparxis*: concrete being, as opposed to abstract or notional being. The word may denote either the subsistence or the subsistent entity.

211. The Lyceum, his own school, is used by Aristotle as the subject of illustrative sentences: *Cat.* 2a1 etc.

212. On God's timelessness in both pagan and Christian theology see R. Sorabji, *Time, Creation and the Continuum* (1983), 253-67. Ps-Dionysius (see n. 157) would have agreed with Philoponus: see *De Div. Nom.* V.3.4 etc. For a celebrated attempt to relate the timeless eternity of God to his providence see Boethius (5th cent. AD), *De Consolatione Philosophiae* V.6.

213. On the fortunes of the word *aiôn*, which may denote a long age, everlastingness, eternity or the personified ruler of time, see A.-J. Festugière, *Hermès Trismégiste*, vol. 4 (1954), 152-99.

214. Examples in *Phys.* 225b11ff.; 246b11-12; 247b4; b13; *Metaph.* 1002a28-b11; 1026b22-4; 1027a29; 1039b26; 1043b14; 1044b21; 1060b18; *EN* 1174b10-13; *Cael.* 280b26; *Sens.* 446b4.

215. cf. *GC* 316a15-317a13.

216. With a whole it is not 'always possible to take something else outside what has already been taken'. See below Philoponus on 206b33-207a10 and above n. 87.

217. The received text says 'you have destroyed', which I have corrected in accordance with Vitelli's emendation and the tenor of the whole sentence.

218. See *Cael.* 276a18-277b25.

219. Here, as above (see n. 31) Vitelli had not recognised that a lemma is repeated, as the *protheôria* ends and the commentary on the text begins.

220. On genus see n. 27 above.

221. *pósos*: lit. 'of what quantity?'; *posós*: lit. 'of a certain quantity'. The Greek accent denotes the pitch of the voice, and in certain pronouns and adverbs the position of the accent may determine whether the word is interrogative or indicative, of definite or indefinite extension.

222. Zeno of Elea (b. ?490 BC), a friend of Parmenides, propounded the celebrated paradoxes, sometimes thought to deny the possibility of motion, which are discussed by Aristotle at *Phys.* 233b9-240a18. On the validity of his arguments see G.E.L. Owen, 'Zeno and the Mathematicians' (1957-8).

223. Reference to pp. 83,20 and 84,20 on *Phys.* 187a1 make it clear that the person intended is Xenocrates (396-314), Plato's second successor at the Academy, and perhaps therefore a personal rival of Aristotle. On his contribution to the development of Platonism see J.M. Dillon, *The Middle Platonists* (1977), 22-39. Xenocrates is named below in the text, but, as Vitelli observes, we do not find here any attempt at refutation. See further D. Harlfinger, *Die Textegeschichte der Ps.-Aristotelischer Schrift Peri Atomôn Grammôn* (1971), esp. pp. 97-9 on the significance of this passage in Philoponus. Cf. the pseudo-Aristotelian *On Indivisible Lines*, which starts by summarising five arguments for indivisible lines which it attacks.

224. Probably a loose reminiscence (rather than a quotation, as Vitelli indicates) of *Phys.* 206a19.

225. Some MSS have 'numbers'; the text that follows might support either, but Ross prints *anthrôpôn* (men) in his text of Aristotle. The translation by E. Hussey, *Aristotle's Physics* (1983), suggests that there are two categories, (a) time and men, (b) magnitudes (p. 14). In his commentary, however (pp. 83-4), Hussey seems to treat all three on the same footing. *Phys.* 206b2 supports Hussey's translation, as Philoponus also does (see 468,24 on *Phys.* 206b3).

226. The Greeks did not recognise negative numbers, but this passage envisages, only to dismiss as impossible, something analogous. Aristotle's claim that you cannot traverse, i.e. finish going right through, an infinite quantity would be violated for number, if this were infinite in both directions, because one of the infinities would be traversed by the time it finished at the monadic *one* (corresponding to our minus-one). Equally with infinite division, you cannot take an infinity in both directions. 'And Aristotle says otherwise' 467b16-17 gives the reason (nb. 'for', 467,14) for bi-directional infinity not being possible 'even with respect to the division of magnitudes' (467,13-14). The reason is that Aristotle treats infinite division like infinite number, when he says that infinite quantities are ones of which you can always take a further *finite* quantity. Bi-directional infinities would also violate Aristotle's claim that no infinity is actual, i.e. complete. Infinity is merely a finite quantity to which there can always be added further finite quantities.

227. Ross's text of the *Physics* follows suit. Simplicius *in Phys.* 495,8 notes that the passage is ommitted in some MSS, and claims that this was observed by Alexander of Aphrodisias.

228. That is, men are taken (most recently at *Phys.* 206b2) as a paradigmatic example. The word *atoma* (literally indivisible, individual) is Democritus' word for the elementary particles, but in Philoponus *atomoi* is the usual word for 'atoms'. At 465,24 (on *Phys.* 206a18f.) Philoponus speaks of a man, a horse and similar entities. (Because he varies between the singular and the plural, I have used a plural noun in English rather than 'humanity' or 'the human race'. The conventional translation of *anthrôpos* is 'man', although the word in Greek is supposed to cover both sexes; as is clear from their occasional use of proper names in illustrative sentences, the philosophers had no vivid sense that it also included women.)

229. After a time, of course, the divisions are only potential, and not actual, i.e. not marked out. A numerical series in which each term was half the last could never be written down. (Actual divisions are marked out ones; actual infinities would be complete ones.)

230. 'Actual' here has yet a third sense: presently occurring.

231. Since this appears to be Aristotle's meaning I have made Philoponus refer to 'the whole determined magnitude', rather than 'every determined magnitude' when he uses the expression *pantos megethous*.

232. See nn. 13, 101-4 above.

233. See nn. 82-4 above.

234. See *Metaph*. 987b14-988a15; Ross, *Plato's Theory of Ideas* (1951), 176-205. On the importance of number in the metaphysics of later Platonists see P. Merlan, *From Platonism to Neoplatonism* (1960), *passim*.

235. See *Metaph*. 988a8-15.

236. A remarkable observation, which may be intended to denigrate Aristotle, or simply to facilitate a reconciliation of his views with those of Plato. In the original version of the *Physics* commentary, dated to AD 517, Philoponus may have still been following Ammonius' policy of harmonising Aristotle with Plato as far as possible. After AD 529, Philoponus openly attacks Aristotle, and Verrycken conjectures that the disagreements were added to the *Physics* commentary then. ('The Development of Philoponus' Thought and its Chronology' in Richard Sorabji, ed., *Aristotle Transformed* (London and Ithaca NY 1990), 233-74.)

237. See n. 208 above.

238. In fact, two consecutive syllogisms (cf. *An. Pr.* 42b1-26). First: (a) what is whole is perfect, (b) what is perfect possesses limit, therefore (c) the whole possesses limit. Second: (a) the whole possesses limit, (b) what possesses limit is not unlimited, therefore (c) the whole is not unlimited. Both are syllogisms of the first type (all B is A, all C is B, therefore all C is A), but with the minor premiss preceding the major one. See further n. 48 above. The term 'weaves together' (*sumplekei*) is an anticipatory pun; cf. n. 44 above.

239. Literally 'spinning together the unspinnable'. See Melissus (fl. 440 BC) Fr. A11 DK for supporting references; this passage appears under Parmenides as Fr. A27.

240. See preceding note and Parmenides (fl. 490 BC) Fr. B8.44 DK, cited in whole or part by a number of witnesses. The subject of this fragment has been variously identified as 'being', 'that which is', 'the One', 'the All', 'whatever is a subject of inquiry'. For a review of positions see G.E.L. Owen, 'Eleatic Questions' (1960), J. Barnes, *The Presocratic Philosophers*, vol. 1 (1979), 155-75, A. Finkelberg, 'Parmenides' Foundation' (1988). J.E. Raven, *Pythagoreans and Eleatics* (1948), 21-42 and 112-25, upholds the view that the subject is the One.

241. The colour of the language is rather Neoplatonic than Aristotelian: cf. Plotinus, *Enn*. IV.3.12 and III.6.16-18 for the notion of magnitude as supervenient on matter, and VI.8.18.35 for *skedasmos*.

242. On this method of refutation see *An. Pr.* 45a23-b10.

243. See Plato, *Philebus* 16C.

244. Though *noêta* and *aisthêta* are contrasted at *EN* 1174b34, it was the Platonists who made most of the word *noêton*, which covers the highest objects of intellection, i.e. the Forms.

245. A reference to *Phys*. 207a30, where Aristotle puns on the word *atopon* (literally 'out of place'.)

246. *autognôsis* was a Platonic neologism; cf. Proclus, *in Alc.* 88c and Damascius [Olympiodorus], *in Phaed*. 100,22 (Norvin), where *nous* itself is said to be *autognôsis*.

247. This distinction between *enkosmia* and *huperkosmia* (respectively things within and without the universe) is a Neoplatonic one: see Proclus, *Elementa* 166 and cf. Porphyry, *De Antro* p. 62,10ff. (Nauck). E.R. Dodds, *Proclus* (1963), 284-5 remarks 'there are three grades of divine intelligence: (a) the "unparticipated" Intelligence; (b) the supra-mundane intelligences, which serve as a mean term between (a) and (c); (c) the intra-mundane (planetary) intelligences.' Cf. perhaps the Three Minds (resting, demiurgic, intramundane) of Numenius of Apamea (fl. AD ?150), Frs 11, 16, 21-22 (Des Places).

248. *Phys.* 187b19-22.

249. See Plato, *Euthydemus* 298C for an early citation of this proverb, which continues the spinning metaphor noticed in n. 239.

250. *Tim.* 52B, frequently cited by Neoplatonists: see e.g. Plotinus, *Enn.* II.4.10.11.

251. *henas* is a term for a unified being at Plato, *Phil.* 15A. At Proclus, *Elementa* 6, it denotes (according to Dodds) an indivisible unity; but for the history of the term in Neoplatonic metaphysics see E.R. Dodds, *Proclus* (1963), 257-60.

252. *Phys.* 234b10-235b6.

253. For criticism of the faith which mathematicians place in their hypotheses see Plato, *Rep.* 533B-C.

254. See n. 114 above.

255. In fact, matter and privation are distinguished at *Phys.* 192a3-5. Matter is not-being in virtue of some particular attribute (i.e through being the persistent substrate of all attributes, potentially having all but at any one time actually having certain attributes but not others); privation is simply the non-existence of something, which implies no persistent substrate.

256. For the difficulties see commentary above on *Phys.* 205b15-24. There may be a play here on the word *peras*.

257. i.e. it is limited by something further out, so that it is not, and there is not, an ultimate limit.

258. The principal thesis of *GC* 1, as also of Heraclitus and Empedocles, who are not said to have spoken of the *apeiron*.

259. See nn. 177-8 above.

260. Philoponus perhaps detects a reference to *Phaedrus* 230C-D, in which it is said that Socrates is notoriously reluctant to leave Athens. In the following sentence *phantazesthai* denotes the deceptive power of imagination: for Neoplatonic disparagement of this faculty see Plotinus, *Enn.* I.8.15 and G. Watson, *Phantasia in Classical Thought* (1988), 96-133.

261. Again, Vitelli overlooks the fact that this is the first lemma of the discussion of text and that is why it repeats the lemma of the *pretheôria*.

262. Literally 'the one' (neuter: *to hen*). In translating Aristotle himself I have wished to avoid a term too redolent of Neoplatonism.

263. *Cat.* 1a12 explains that a paronymous term is one that derives from another but differs in termination. See further *Top.* 109b.

264. The terms *duo, tria, tessares* are originally plural adjectives (or rather a dual in the first case), implying that there is some noun to be qualified.

265. The words in square brackets may have fallen out, as Vitelli's apparatus suggests, through haplography, i.e. conflation of two adjacent clauses ending with the same words.

266. For such a personification of nature as demiurge cf. Plotinus, *Enn.* III.8.4.

267. Or better, 'sixth' (Vitelli): *Phys.* 234b10-235b6.

268. Alexander of Aphrodisias: see n. 42 above. Alexander's commentary on the *Physics* is not available for comparison.

269. That is, at the outset of the argument. Yet another uninteresting pun, this time on *arkhê*.

270. Playing on *aporon* and *apeiron*. As at n. 136 the pun may be significant: *apeiria* is the ignorance which leads to the difficulties that seem to necessitate the hypothesis of the *apeiron*. Cf. nn. 133 and 136.

271. i.e. the outermost of the transparent rotating spheres which carries the stars that we called 'fixed' in contrast to the wandering planets.

272. Democritus, Fr. B125 DK etc., requires a void for the motion of his indivisble particles (*atomoi*). On Democritus see nn. 104-7 above.

273. Three cubits appears to have been a normal height for a man (used of soldiers at *Inscriptiones Graeci* II (2nd ed.) 1467.53), so the cubit (the length from elbow to finger-tip) will have been a little less than two feet. Philoponus ignores the smallness of Socrates, to which the latter himself refers at *Phaedo* 102B-E.

274. Ross's commentary (1936), p. 562 agrees, citing this passage.

Select Bibliography

Ackrill, J. 'Aristotle on "Good" and the Categories', in J. Barnes, M. Schofield and
    R. Sorabji, eds, *Articles on Aristotle 2: Ethics and Politics*, London 1977, 17-24.
Barnes, J. *The Presocratic Philosophers*, vols 1-2, London 1979.
Burkert, W. *Lore and Science in Ancient Pythagoreanism*, Cambridge, Mass. 1972.
Chadwick, H. 'Philoponus, the Christian Theologian', in R. Sorabji, ed., *Philoponus
    and the Rejection of Aristotelian Science*, London 1987, 41-56.
Cherniss, H.F. *Aristotle's Criticism of Presocratic Philosophy*, Baltimore 1935.
—— *Aristotle's Criticism of Plato and the Academy*, vol. 1 (sole volume), Baltimore
    1944.
De Vogel, C. 'La Théorie de l'Apeiron chez Platon', in her *Philosophia*, part 1 (Assen
    1970), 378-95.
Dillon, J. *The Middle Platonists*, London 1977.
—— 'Iamblichus and the Origin of the Doctrine of Henads', *Phronesis* 17, 1972,
    102-6.
—— 'Iamblichus and Henads Again', in H. Blumenthal and E.G. Clark, eds, *The
    Divine Iamblichus*, London 1993, 48-54.
——, trans. with comm., Alcinous, *The Handbook of Platonism*, Oxford 1993.
Dodds, E.R., ed. and comm., *Proclus: The Elements of Theology*, Oxford 1963.
Festugière, A.-J. *La Révelation d'Hermès Trismégiste*, vol. 4, Paris 1954.
Findlay, J.N. *Plato: the Written and Unwritten Doctrines*, London 1974.
Finkelberg, A. 'Parmenides' Foundation of the Way of Truth', *Oxford Studies in
    Ancient Philosophy* 6, 1988, 39-67.
Furley, D. 'Summary of Philoponus' Corollaries on Place and Void', in Sorabji, ed.,
    Philoponus, 130-9.
Furley, D. and Wildberg, C., trans. with notes, *Philoponus: Corollaries on Place
    and Void, with Simplicius: Answer to Philoponus*, London 1991.
Graham, D.W. 'The Etymology of Entelecheia', *American Journal of Philology* 110,
    1989, 73-80.
Hadot, P. 'The Harmony of Plotinus and Aristotle according to Porphyry', in R.
    Sorabji, ed., *Aristotle Transformed*, London 1990, 125-40.
Harlfinger, D. *Die Textegeschichte der Ps.-Aristotelischer Schrift Peri Atomôn
    Grammôn*, Amsterdam 1971.
Heath, T.L. *Aristarchus of Samos, The Ancient Copernicus*, Oxford 1913.
Hussey, E., trans. with notes, *Aristotle's Physics, Books III and IV*, Oxford 1983.
Kirk, G.S., ed. with comm., *Heraclitus: The Cosmic Fragments*, Cambridge 1954.
—— 'Some Problems in Anaximander', *Classical Quarterly* 5, 1955, 21-38.
Kirk, G.S., Raven, J.E. and Schofield, M. *The Presocratic Philosophers*, Cambridge
    1983.
Kramer, H.J. *Plato and the Foundations of Metaphysics*, Albany NY 1990.
Lacey, A.R., trans. with notes, *Philoponus: On Aristotle Physics 2*, London 1992.
Lloyd, A.C. *The Anatomy of Neoplatonism*, Oxford 1990.

Lloyd, G.E.R. 'Hot and Cold, Dry and Wet in Early Greek Thought', *Journal of Hellenic Studies* 84, 1964, 92-106.

—— *Polarity and Analogy: Two Types of Argumentation in Early Greek Thought*, Cambridge 1966.

Long, A.A. 'Empedocles' Cosmic Cycle in the Sixties', in A. Mourelatos, ed., *The Presocratics*, New York 1974, 397-425.

Merlan, P. *From Platonism to Neoplatonism*, The Hague 1960.

Owen, G.E.L. 'Zeno and the Mathematicians', *Proc. of the Aristotelian Society* 1957-8, 199-222.

—— 'Eleatic Questions', *Classical Quarterly* 10, 1960, 43-67.

—— 'Plato on Not-Being', in G. Vlastos, ed., *Plato I: Metaphysics and Epistemology*, New York 1970, 223-67.

Raven, J.E. *Pythagoreans and Eleatics*, Cambridge 1948.

Rich, A.M. 'The Platonic Ideas as Thoughts of God', *Mnemosyne* 7, 1954, 123-33.

Rist, J.M. *Plotinus: the Road to Reality*, Cambridge 1967.

Ross, W.D. *Commentary on Aristotle's Physics*, Oxford 1936.

—— *Plato's Theory of Ideas*, Oxford 1951.

—— *Commentary on Aristotle's De Anima*, Oxford 1961.

Schofield, M. *An Essay on Anaxagoras*, Cambridge 1980.

Schroeder, F.M. and Todd, R.B., ed. and trans., *Two Greek Aristotelian Commentators on the Intellect*, Toronto 1990.

Sedley, D. 'Philoponus' Conception of Space', in R. Sorabji, ed., *Philoponus*, 140-53.

Sorabji, R. *Time, Creation and the Continuum*, London 1983.

——, ed., *Philoponus and the Rejection of Aristotelian Science*, London 1987 (introduction pp. 1-40).

——, ed., *Aristotle Transformed*, London 1990.

Urmson, J. *The Greek Philosophical Vocabulary*, London 1990.

Vlastos, G. *Platonic Studies*, 2nd ed., Princeton 1981.

Waterfield, R., trans., *The Theology of Arithmetic*, Grand Rapids 1988.

Watson, G. *Phantasia in Classical Thought*, Galway 1988.

Wildberg, C., trans. with notes, *Philoponus: Against Aristotle On the Eternity of the World*, London 1987.

—— 'Prolegomena to the Study of Philoponus' Contra Aristotelem', in R. Sorabji, ed., *Philoponus*, 196-209.

—— *John Philoponus' Criticism of Aristotle's Theory of Aether*, Berlin 1988.

Wolda, W. *La Topographie Chrétienne de Cosmas Indicopleustes*, Paris 1962.

Wolff, M. 'Philoponus and the Rise of Preclassical Dynamics', in R. Sorabji, ed., *Philoponus*, 84-120.

Appendix
The Commentators*

The 15,000 pages of the Ancient Greek Commentaries on Aristotle are the largest corpus of Ancient Greek philosophy that has not been translated into English or other European languages. The standard edition (*Commentaria in Aristotelem Graeca*, or *CAG*) was produced by Hermann Diels as general editor under the auspices of the Prussian Academy in Berlin. Arrangements have now been made to translate at least a large proportion of this corpus, along with some other Greek and Latin commentaries not included in the Berlin edition, and some closely related non-commentary works by the commentators.

The works are not just commentaries on Aristotle, although they are invaluable in that capacity too. One of the ways of doing philosophy between A.D. 200 and 600, when the most important items were produced, was by writing commentaries. The works therefore represent the thought of the Peripatetic and Neoplatonist schools, as well as expounding Aristotle. Furthermore, they embed fragments from all periods of Ancient Greek philosophical thought: this is how many of the Presocratic fragments were assembled, for example. Thus they provide a panorama of every period of Ancient Greek philosophy.

The philosophy of the period from A.D.200 to 600 has not yet been intensively explored by philosophers in English-speaking countries, yet it is full of interest for physics, metaphysics, logic, psychology, ethics and religion. The contrast with the study of the Presocratics is striking. Initially the incomplete Presocratic fragments might well have seemed less promising, but their interest is now widely known, thanks to the philological and philosophical effort that has been concentrated upon them. The incomparably vaster corpus which preserved so many of those fragments offers at least as much interest, but is still relatively little known.

The commentaries represent a missing link in the history of philosophy: the Latin-speaking Middle Ages obtained their knowledge of Aristotle at least partly through the medium of the commentaries. Without an appreciation of this, mediaeval interpretations of Aristotle will not be understood. Again, the ancient commentaries are the unsuspected source of ideas which have been thought, wrongly, to originate in the later mediaeval period. It has been supposed, for example, that Bonaventure in the thirteenth century invented the ingenious arguments based on the concept of infinity which attempt to prove the Christian view that the universe had a beginning. In fact, Bonaventure is merely repeating arguments devised

* Reprinted from the Editor's General Introduction to the series in Christian Wildberg, *Philoponus Against Aristotle on the Eternity of the World*, London and Ithaca, N.Y., 1987.

by the commentator Philoponus 700 years earlier and preserved in the meantime by the Arabs. Bonaventure even uses Philoponus' original examples. Again, the introduction of impetus theory into dynamics, which has been called a scientific revolution, has been held to be an independent invention of the Latin West, even if it was earlier discovered by the Arabs or their predecessors. But recent work has traced a plausible route by which it could have passed from Philoponus, via the Arabs, to the West.

The new availability of the commentaries in the sixteenth century, thanks to printing and to fresh Latin translations, helped to fuel the Renaissance break from Aristotelian science. For the commentators record not only Aristotle's theories, but also rival ones, while Philoponus as a Christian devises rival theories of his own and accordingly is mentioned in Galileo's early works more frequently than Plato.[1]

It is not only for their philosophy that the works are of interest. Historians will find information about the history of schools, their methods of teaching and writing and the practices of an oral tradition.[2] Linguists will find the indexes and translations an aid for studying the development of word meanings, almost wholly uncharted in Liddell and Scott's *Lexicon*, and for checking shifts in grammatical usage.

Given the wide range of interests to which the volumes will appeal, the aim is to produce readable translations, and to avoid so far as possible presupposing any knowledge of Greek. Notes will explain points of meaning, give cross-references to other works, and suggest alternative interpretations of the text where the translator does not have a clear preference. The introduction to each volume will include an explanation why the work was chosen for translation: none will be chosen simply because it is there. Two of the Greek texts are currently being re-edited – those of Simplicius *in Physica* and *in de Caelo* – and new readings will be exploited by

---

1. See Fritz Zimmermann, 'Philoponus' impetus theory in the Arabic tradition'; Charles Schmitt, 'Philoponus' commentary on Aristotle's *Physics* in the sixteenth century', and Richard Sorabji, 'John Philoponus', in Richard Sorabji (ed.), *Philoponus and the Rejection of Aristotelian Science* (London and Ithaca, N.Y. 1987).

2. See e.g. Karl Praechter, 'Die griechischen Aristoteleskommentare', *Byzantinische Zeitschrift* 18 (1909), 516-38 (translated into English in R. Sorabji (ed.), *Aristotle Transformed: the ancient commentators and their influence* (London and Ithaca, N.Y. 1990); M. Plezia, *de Commentariis Isagogicis* (Cracow 1947); M. Richard, *'Apo Phônês', Byzantion* 20 (1950), 191-222; É. Evrard, *L'Ecole d'Olympiodore et la composition du commentaire à la physique de Jean Philopon*, Diss. (Liège 1957); L.G. Westerink, *Anonymous Prolegomena to Platonic Philosophy* (Amsterdam 1962) (new revised edition, translated into French, Collection Budé; part of the revised introduction, in English, is included in *Aristotle Transformed*); A.-J. Festugière, 'Modes de composition des commentaires de Proclus', *Museum Helveticum* 20 (1963), 77-100, repr. in his *Études* (1971), 551-74; P. Hadot, 'Les divisions des parties de la philosophie dans l'antiquité', *Museum Helveticum* 36 (1979), 201-23; I. Hadot, 'La division néoplatonicienne des écrits d'Aristote', in J. Wiesner (ed.), *Aristoteles Werk und Wirkung* (Paul Moraux gewidmet), vol. 2 (Berlin 1986); I. Hadot, 'Les introductions aux commentaires exégétiques chez les auteurs néoplatoniciens et les auteurs chrétiens', in M. Tardieu (ed.), *Les règles de l'interprétation* (Paris 1987), 99-119. These topics are treated, and a bibliography supplied, in *Aristotle Transformed*.

translators as they become available. Each volume will also contain a list of proposed emendations to the standard text. Indexes will be of more uniform extent as between volumes than is the case with the Berlin edition, and there will be three of them: an English-Greek glossary, a Greek-English index, and a subject index.

The commentaries fall into three main groups. The first group is by authors in the Aristotelian tradition up to the fourth century A.D. This includes the earliest extant commentary, that by Aspasius in the first half of the second century A.D. on the *Nicomachean Ethics*. The anonymous commentary on Books 2, 3, 4 and 5 of the *Nicomachean Ethics*, in *CAG* vol. 20, is derived from Adrastus, a generation later.[3] The commentaries by Alexander of Aphrodisias (appointed to his chair between A.D. 198 and 209) represent the fullest flowering of the Aristotelian tradition. To his successors Alexander was The Commentator *par excellence*. To give but one example (not from a commentary) of his skill at defending and elaborating Aristotle's views, one might refer to his defence of Aristotle's claim that space is finite against the objection that an edge of space is conceptually problematic.[4] Themistius (*fl.* late 340s to 384 or 385) saw himself as the inventor of paraphrase, wrongly thinking that the job of commentary was completed.[5] In fact, the Neoplatonists were to introduce new dimensions into commentary. Themistius' own relation to the Neoplatonist as opposed to the Aristotelian tradition is a matter of controversy,[6] but it would be agreed that his commentaries show far less bias than the full-blown Neoplatonist ones. They are also far more informative than the designation 'paraphrase' might suggest, and it has been estimated that Philoponus' *Physics* commentary draws silently on Themistius six hundred times.[7] The pseudo-Alexandrian commentary on *Metaphysics* 6-14, of unknown

3. Anthony Kenny, *The Aristotelian Ethics* (Oxford 1978), 37, n.3: Paul Moraux, *Der Aristotelismus bei den Griechen*, vol. 2 (Berlin 1984), 323-30.

4. Alexander, *Quaestiones* 3.12, discussed in my *Matter, Space and Motion* (London and Ithaca, N.Y. 1988). For Alexander see R.W. Sharples, 'Alexander of Aphrodisias: scholasticism and innovation', in W. Haase (ed.), *Aufstieg und Niedergang der römischen Welt*, part 2 *Principat*, vol. 36.2, *Philosophie und Wissenschaften* (1987).

5. Themistius *in An. Post.* 1,2-12. See H.J. Blumenthal, 'Photius on Themistius (Cod. 74): did Themistius write commentaries on Aristotle?', *Hermes* 107 (1979), 168-82.

6. For different views, see H.J. Blumenthal, 'Themistius, the last Peripatetic commentator on Aristotle?', in Glen W. Bowersock, Walter Burkert, Michael C.J. Putnam, *Arktouros*, *Hellenic Studies Presented to Bernard M.W. Knox* (Berlin and N.Y., 1979), 391-400; E.P. Mahoney, 'Themistius and the agent intellect in James of Viterbo and other thirteenth-century philosophers: (Saint Thomas Aquinas, Siger of Brabant and Henry Bate)', *Augustiniana* 23 (1973), 422-67, at 428-31; id., 'Neoplatonism, the Greek commentators and Renaissance Aristotelianism', in D.J. O'Meara (ed.), *Neoplatonism and Christian Thought* (Albany N.Y. 1982), 169-77 and 264-82, esp. n. 1, 264-6; Robert Todd, introduction to translation of Themistius *in DA* 3.4-8, in *Two Greek Aristotelian Commentators on the Intellect*, trans. Frederick M. Schroeder and Robert B. Todd (Toronto 1990).

7. H. Vitelli, *CAG* 17, p. 992, s.v. Themistius.

authorship, has been placed by some in the same group of commentaries as being earlier than the fifth century.[8]

By far the largest group of extant commentaries is that of the Neoplatonists up to the sixth century A.D. Nearly all the major Neoplatonists, apart from Plotinus (the founder of Neoplatonism), wrote commentaries on Aristotle, although those of Iamblichus (*c.* 250–*c.* 325) survive only in fragments, and those of three Athenians, Plutarchus (died 432), his pupil Proclus (410–485) and the Athenian Damascius (*c.* 462–after 538), are lost.[9] As a result of these losses, most of the extant Neoplatonist commentaries come from the late fifth and the sixth centuries and a good proportion from Alexandria. There are commentaries by Plotinus' disciple and editor Porphyry (232–309), by Iamblichus' pupil Dexippus (*c.* 330), by Proclus' teacher Syrianus (died *c.* 437), by Proclus' pupil Ammonius (435/445–517/526), by Ammonius' three pupils Philoponus (*c.* 490 to 570s), Simplicius (wrote after 532, probably after 538) and Asclepius (sixth century), by Ammonius' next but one successor Olympiodorus (495/505–after 565), by Elias (*fl.* 541?), by David (second half of the sixth century, or beginning of the seventh) and by Stephanus (took the chair in Constantinople *c.* 610). Further, a commentary on the *Nicomachean Ethics* has been ascribed to Heliodorus of Prusa, an unknown pre-fourteenth-century figure, and there is a commentary by Simplicius' colleague Priscian of Lydia on Aristotle's successor Theophrastus. Of these commentators some of the last were Christians (Philoponus, Elias, David and Stephanus), but they were Christians writing in the Neoplatonist tradition, as was also Boethius who produced a number of commentaries in Latin before his death in 525 or 526.

The third group comes from a much later period in Byzantium. The Berlin edition includes only three out of more than a dozen commentators described in Hunger's *Byzantinisches Handbuch*.[10] The two most important are Eustratius (1050/1060–*c.*1120), and Michael of Ephesus. It has been suggested that these two belong to a circle organised by the princess

---

8. The similarities to Syrianus (died *c.* 437) have suggested to some that it predates Syrianus (most recently Leonardo Tarán, review of Paul Moraux, *Der Aristotelismus*, vol.1 in *Gnomon* 46 (1981), 721-50 at 750), to others that it draws on him (most recently P. Thillet, in the Budé edition of Alexander *de Fato*, p. lvii). Praechter ascribed it to Michael of Ephesus (eleventh or twelfth century), in his review of *CAG* 22.2, in *Göttingische Gelehrte Anzeiger* 168 (1906), 861-907.

9. The Iamblichus fragments are collected in Greek by Bent Dalsgaard Larsen, *Jamblique de Chalcis, Exégète et Philosophe* (Aarhus 1972), vol. 2. Most are taken from Simplicius, and will accordingly be translated in due course. The evidence on Damascius' commentaries is given in L.G. Westerink, *The Greek Commentaries on Plato's Phaedo*, vol. 2, Damascius (Amsterdam 1977), 11-12; on Proclus' in L.G. Westerink, *Anonymous Prolegomena to Platonic Philosophy* (Amsterdam 1962), xii, n. 22; on Plutarchus' in H.M. Blumenthal, 'Neoplatonic elements in the de Anima commentaries', *Phronesis* 21 (1976), 75.

10. Herbert Hunger, *Die hochsprachliche profane Literatur der Byzantiner*, vol. 1 (= *Byzantinisches Handbuch*, part 5, vol. 1) (Munich 1978), 25-41. See also B.N. Tatakis, *La Philosophie Byzantine* (Paris 1949).

Anna Comnena in the twelfth century, and accordingly the completion of Michael's commentaries has been redated from 1040 to 1138.[11] His commentaries include areas where gaps had been left. Not all of these gap-fillers are extant, but we have commentaries on the neglected biological works, on the *Sophistici Elenchi*, and a small fragment of one on the *Politics*. The lost *Rhetoric* commentary had a few antecedents, but the *Rhetoric* too had been comparatively neglected. Another product of this period may have been the composite commentary on the *Nicomachean Ethics* (*CAG* 20) by various hands, including Eustratius and Michael, along with some earlier commentators, and an improvisation for Book 7. Whereas Michael follows Alexander and the conventional Aristotelian tradition, Eustratius' commentary introduces Platonist, Christian and anti-Islamic elements.[12]

The composite commentary was to be translated into Latin in the next century by Robert Grosseteste in England. But Latin translations of various logical commentaries were made from the Greek still earlier by James of Venice (*fl. c.* 1130), a contemporary of Michael of Ephesus, who may have known him in Constantinople. And later in that century other commentaries and works by commentators were being translated from Arabic versions by Gerard of Cremona (died 1187).[13] So the twelfth century resumed the transmission which had been interrupted at Boethius' death in the sixth century.

The Neoplatonist commentaries of the main group were initiated by Porphyry. His master Plotinus had discussed Aristotle, but in a very independent way, devoting three whole treatises (*Enneads* 6.1-3) to attacking Aristotle's classification of the things in the universe into categories. These categories took no account of Plato's world of Ideas, were inferior to Plato's classifications in the *Sophist* and could anyhow be collapsed, some

11. R. Browning, 'An unpublished funeral oration on Anna Comnena', *Proceedings of the Cambridge Philological Society* n.s. 8 (1962), 1-12, esp. 6-7.

12. R. Browning, op. cit. H.D.P. Mercken, *The Greek Commentaries of the Nicomachean Ethics of Aristotle in the Latin Translation of Grosseteste, Corpus Latinum Commentariorum in Aristotelem Graecorum* VI 1 (Leiden 1973), ch. 1, 'The compilation of Greek commentaries on Aristotle's Nicomachean Ethics'. Sten Ebbesen, 'Anonymi Aurelianensis I Commentarium in *Sophisticos Elenchos*', *Cahiers de l'Institut Moyen Age Grecque et Latin* 34 (1979), 'Boethius, Jacobus Veneticus, Michael Ephesius and "Alexander" ', pp. v-xiii; id., *Commentators and Commentaries on Aristotle's Sophistici Elenchi*, 3 parts, *Corpus Latinum Commentariorum in Aristotelem Graecorum*, vol. 7 (Leiden 1981); A. Preus, *Aristotle and Michael of Ephesus on the Movement and Progression of Animals* (Hildesheim 1981), introduction.

13. For Grosseteste, see Mercken as in n. 12. For James of Venice, see Ebbesen as in n. 12, and L. Minio-Paluello, 'Jacobus Veneticus Grecus', *Traditio* 8 (1952), 265-304; id., 'Giacomo Veneto e l'Aristotelismo Latino', in Pertusi (ed.), *Venezia e l'Oriente fra tardo Medioevo e Rinascimento* (Florence 1966), 53-74, both reprinted in his *Opuscula* (1972). For Gerard of Cremona, see M. Steinschneider, *Die europäischen Übersetzungen aus dem arabischen bis Mitte des 17. Jahrhunderts* (repr. Graz 1956); E. Gilson, *History of Christian Philosophy in the Middle Ages* (London 1955), 235-6 and more generally 181-246. For the translators in general, see Bernard G. Dod, 'Aristoteles Latinus', in N. Kretzmann, A. Kenny, J. Pinborg (eds), *The Cambridge History of Latin Medieval Philosophy* (Cambridge 1982).

of them into others. Porphyry replied that Aristotle's categories could apply perfectly well to the world of intelligibles and he took them as in general defensible.[14] He wrote two commentaries on the *Categories*, one lost, and an introduction to it, the *Isagôgê*, as well as commentaries, now lost, on a number of other Aristotelian works. This proved decisive in making Aristotle a necessary subject for Neoplatonist lectures and commentary. Proclus, who was an exceptionally quick student, is said to have taken two years over his Aristotle studies, which were called the Lesser Mysteries, and which preceded the Greater Mysteries of Plato.[15] By the time of Ammonius, the commentaries reflect a teaching curriculum which begins with Porphyry's *Isagôgê* and Aristotle's *Categories*, and is explicitly said to have as its final goal a (mystical) ascent to the supreme Neoplatonist deity, the One.[16] The curriculum would have progressed from Aristotle to Plato, and would have culminated in Plato's *Timaeus* and *Parmenides*. The latter was read as being about the One, and both works were established in this place in the curriculum at least by the time of Iamblichus, if not earlier.[17]

Before Porphyry, it had been undecided how far a Platonist should accept Aristotle's scheme of categories. But now the proposition began to gain force that there was a harmony between Plato and Aristotle on most things.[18] Not for the only time in the history of philosophy, a perfectly crazy proposition proved philosophically fruitful. The views of Plato and of Aristotle had both to be transmuted into a new Neoplatonist philosophy in order to exhibit the supposed harmony. Iamblichus denied that Aristotle contradicted Plato on the theory of Ideas.[19] This was too much for Syrianus and his pupil Proclus. While accepting harmony in many areas,[20] they could see that there was disagreement on this issue and also on the issue of whether God was causally responsible for the existence of the ordered

14. See P. Hadot, 'L'harmonie des philosophies de Plotin et d'Aristote selon Porphyre dans le commentaire de Dexippe sur les Catégories', in *Plotino e il neoplatonismo in Oriente e in Occidente* (Rome 1974), 31-47; A.C. Lloyd, 'Neoplatonic logic and Aristotelian logic', *Phronesis* 1 (1955-6), 58-79 and 146-60.

15. Marinus, *Life of Proclus* ch. 13, 157,41 (Boissonade).

16. The introductions to the *Isagôgê* by Ammonius, Elias and David, and to the *Categories* by Ammonius, Simplicius, Philoponus, Olympiodorus and Elias are discussed by L.G. Westerink, *Anonymous Prolegomena* and I. Hadot, 'Les Introductions', see n. 2 above.

17. Proclus in *Alcibiadem 1* p. 11 (Creuzer); Westerink, *Anonymous Prolegomena*, ch. 26, 12f. For the Neoplatonist curriculum see Westerink, Festugière, P. Hadot and I. Hadot in n. 2.

18. See e.g. P. Hadot (1974), as in n. 14 above; H.J. Blumenthal, 'Neoplatonic elements in the de Anima commentaries', *Phronesis* 21 (1976), 64-87; H.A. Davidson, 'The principle that a finite body can contain only finite power', in S. Stein and R. Loewe (eds), *Studies in Jewish Religious and Intellectual History presented to A. Altmann* (Alabama 1979), 75-92; Carlos Steel, 'Proclus et Aristotle', Proceedings of the Congrès Proclus held in Paris 1985, J. Pépin and H.D. Saffrey (eds), *Proclus, lecteur et interprète des anciens* (Paris 1987), 213-25; Koenraad Verrycken, *God en Wereld in de Wijsbegeerte van Ioannes Philoponus*, Ph.D. Diss. (Louvain 1985).

19. Iamblichus ap. Elian *in Cat.* 123,1-3.

20. Syrianus *in Metaph.* 80,4-7; Proclus *in Tim.* 1.6,21-7,16.

physical cosmos, which Aristotle denied. But even on these issues, Proclus' pupil Ammonius was to claim harmony, and, though the debate was not clear cut,[21] his claim was on the whole to prevail. Aristotle, he maintained, accepted Plato's Ideas,[22] at least in the form of principles (*logoi*) in the divine intellect, and these principles were in turn causally responsible for the beginningless existence of the physical universe. Ammonius wrote a whole book to show that Aristotle's God was thus an efficent cause, and though the book is lost, some of its principal arguments are preserved by Simplicius.[23] This tradition helped to make it possible for Aquinas to claim Aristotle's God as a Creator, albeit not in the sense of giving the universe a beginning, but in the sense of being causally responsible for its beginningless existence.[24] Thus what started as a desire to harmonise Aristotle with Plato finished by making Aristotle safe for Christianity. In Simplicius, who goes further than anyone,[25] it is a formally stated duty of the commentator to display the harmony of Plato and Aristotle in most things.[26] Philoponus, who with his independent mind had thought better of his earlier belief in harmony, is castigated by Simplicius for neglecting this duty.[27]

The idea of harmony was extended beyond Plato and Aristotle to Plato and the Presocratics. Plato's pupils Speusippus and Xenocrates saw Plato as being in the Pythagorean tradition.[28] From the third to first centuries B.C., pseudo-Pythagorean writings present Platonic and Aristotelian doctrines as if they were the ideas of Pythagoras and his pupils,[29] and these forgeries were later taken by the Neoplatonists as genuine. Plotinus saw the Presocratics as precursors of his own views,[30] but Iamblichus went far beyond him by writing ten volumes on Pythagorean philosophy.[31] Thereafter Proclus sought to unify the whole of

21. Asclepius sometimes accepts Syranius' interpretation (*in Metaph.* 433,9-436,6); which is, however, qualified, since Syrianus thinks Aristotle is realy committed willy-nilly to much of Plato's view (*in Metaph.* 117,25-118,11; ap. Asclepium *in Metaph.* 433,16; 450,22); Philoponus repents of his early claim that Plato is not the target of Aristotle's attack, and accepts that Plato is rightly attacked for treating ideas as independent entities outside the divine Intellect (*in DA* 37,18-31; *in Phys.* 225,4-226,11; *contra Procl.* 26,24-32,13; *in An. Post.* 242,14-243,25).

22. Asclepius *in Metaph.* from the voice of (i.e. from the lectures of) Ammonius 69,17-21; 71,28; cf. Zacharias *Ammonius, Patrologia Graeca* vol. 85 col. 952 (Colonna).

23. Simplicius *in Phys.* 1361,11-1363,12. See H.A. Davidson; Carlos Steel; Koenraad Verrycken in n. 18 above.

24. See Richard Sorabji, *Matter, Space and Motion* (London and Ithaca, N.Y. 1988), ch. 15.

25. See e.g. H.J. Blumenthal in n. 18 above.

26. Simplicius *in Cat.* 7,23-32.

27. Simplicius *in Cael.* 84,11-14; 159,2-9. On Philoponus' *volte face* see n. 21 above.

28. See e.g. Walter Burkert, *Weisheit und Wissenschaft* (Nürnberg 1962), translated as *Lore and Science in Ancient Pythagoreanism* (Cambridge Mass. 1972), 83-96.

29. See Holger Thesleff, *An Introduction to the Pythagorean Writings of the Hellenistic Period* (Åbo 1961); Thomas Alexander Szlezák, *Pseudo-Archytas über die Kategorien*, Peripatoi vol. 4 (Berlin and New York 1972).

30. Plotinus e.g. 4.8.1; 5.1.8 (10-27); 5.1.9.

31. See Dominic O'Meara, *Pythagoras Revived: Mathematics and Philosophy in Late Antiquity* (Oxford 1989).

Greek philosophy by presenting it as a continuous clarification of divine revelation[32] and Simplicius argued for the same general unity in order to rebut Christian charges of contradictions in pagan philosophy.[33]

Later Neoplatonist commentaries tend to reflect their origin in a teaching curriculum:[34] from the time of Philoponus, the discussion is often divided up into lectures, which are subdivided into studies of doctrine and of text. A general account of Aristotle's philosophy is prefixed to the *Categories* commentaries and divided, according to a formula of Proclus,[35] into ten questions. It is here that commentators explain the eventual purpose of studying Aristotle (ascent to the One) and state (if they do) the requirement of displaying the harmony of Plato and Aristotle. After the ten-point introduction to Aristotle, the *Categories* is given a six-point introduction, whose antecedents go back earlier than Neoplatonism, and which requires the commentator to find a unitary theme or scope (*skopos*) for the treatise. The arrangements for late commentaries on Plato are similar. Since the Plato commentaries form part of a single curriculum they should be studied alongside those on Aristotle. Here the situation is easier, not only because the extant corpus is very much smaller, but also because it has been comparatively well served by French and English translators.[36]

Given the theological motive of the curriculum and the pressure to harmonise Plato with Aristotle, it can be seen how these commentaries are a major source for Neoplatonist ideas. This in turn means that it is not safe to extract from them the fragments of the Presocratics, or of other authors, without making allowance for the Neoplatonist background against which the fragments were originally selected for discussion. For different reasons, analogous warnings apply to fragments preserved by the pre-Neoplatonist commentator Alexander.[37] It will be another advantage of the present translations that they will make it easier to check the distorting effect of a commentator's background.

Although the Neoplatonist commentators conflate the views of Aristotle with those of Neoplatonism, Philoponus alludes to a certain convention

---

32. See Christian Guérard, 'Parménide d'Elée selon les Néoplatoniciens', forthcoming.

33. Simplicius *in Phys.* 28,32-29,5; 640,12-18. Such thinkers as Epicurus and the Sceptics, however, were not subject to harmonisation.

34. See the literature in n. 2 above.

35. ap. Elian *in Cat.* 107,24-6.

36. English: Calcidius *in Tim.* (parts by van Winden; den Boeft); Iamblichus fragments (Dillon); Proclus *in Tim.* (Thomas Taylor); Proclus *in Parm.* (Dillon); Proclus *in Parm.*, end of 7th book, from the Latin (Klibansky, Labowsky, Anscombe); Proclus *in Alcib. 1* (O'Neill); Olympiodorus and Damascius *in Phaedonem* (Westerink); Damascius *in Philebum* (Westerink); *Anonymous Prolegomena to Platonic Philosophy* (Westerink). See also extracts in Thomas Taylor, *The Works of Plato*, 5 vols. (1804). French: Proclus *in Tim.* and *in Rempublicam* (Festugière); *in Parm.* (Chaignet); Anon. *in Parm* (P. Hadot); Damascius *in Parm.* (Chaignet).

37. For Alexander's treatment of the Stoics, see Robert B. Todd, *Alexander of Aphrodisias on Stoic Physics* (Leiden 1976), 24-9.

when he quotes Plutarchus expressing disapproval of Alexander for expounding his own philosophical doctrines in a commentary on Aristotle.[38] But this does not stop Philoponus from later inserting into his own commentaries on the *Physics* and *Meteorology* his arguments in favour of the Christian view of Creation. Of course, the commentators also wrote independent works of their own, in which their views are expressed independently of the exegesis of Aristotle. Some of these independent works will be included in the present series of translations.

The distorting Neoplatonist context does not prevent the commentaries from being incomparable guides to Aristotle. The introductions to Aristotle's philosophy insist that commentators must have a minutely detailed knowledge of the entire Aristotelian corpus, and this they certainly have. Commentators are also enjoined neither to accept nor reject what Aristotle says too readily, but to consider it in depth and without partiality. The commentaries draw one's attention to hundreds of phrases, sentences and ideas in Aristotle, which one could easily have passed over, however often one read him. The scholar who makes the right allowance for the distorting context will learn far more about Aristotle than he would be likely to on his own.

The relations of Neoplatonist commentators to the Christians were subtle. Porphyry wrote a treatise explicitly against the Christians in 15 books, but an order to burn it was issued in 448, and later Neoplatonists were more circumspect. Among the last commentators in the main group, we have noted several Christians. Of these the most important were Boethius and Philoponus. It was Boethius' programme to transmit Greek learning to Latin-speakers. By the time of his premature death by execution, he had provided Latin translations of Aristotle's logical works, together with commentaries in Latin but in the Neoplatonist style on Porphyry's *Isagôgê* and on Aristotle's *Categories* and *de Interpretatione*, and interpretations of the *Prior* and *Posterior Analytics*, *Topics* and *Sophistici Elenchi*. The interruption of his work meant that knowledge of Aristotle among Latin-speakers was confined for many centuries to the logical works. Philoponus is important both for his proofs of the Creation and for his progressive replacement of Aristotelian science with rival theories, which were taken up at first by the Arabs and came fully into their own in the West only in the sixteenth century.

Recent work has rejected the idea that in Alexandria the Neoplatonists compromised with Christian monotheism by collapsing the distinction between their two highest deities, the One and the Intellect. Simplicius (who left Alexandria for Athens) and the Alexandrians Ammonius and Asclepius appear to have acknowledged their beliefs quite openly, as later

---

38. Philoponus *in DA* 21,20-3.

did the Alexandrian Olympiodorus, despite the presence of Christian students in their classes.[39]

The teaching of Simplicius in Athens and that of the whole pagan Neoplatonist school there was stopped by the Christian Emperor Justinian in 529. This was the very year in which the Christian Philoponus in Alexandria issued his proofs of Creation against the earlier Athenian Neoplatonist Proclus. Archaeological evidence has been offered that, after their temporary stay in Ctesiphon (in present-day Iraq), the Athenian Neoplatonists did not return to their house in Athens, and further evidence has been offered that Simplicius went to Harrān (Carrhae), in present-day Turkey near the Iraq border.[40] Wherever he went, his commentaries are a treasurehouse of information about the preceding thousand years of Greek philosophy, information which he painstakingly recorded after the closure in Athens, and which would otherwise have been lost. He had every reason to feel bitter about Christianity, and in fact he sees it and Philoponus, its representative, as irreverent. They deny the divinity of the heavens and prefer the physical relics of dead martyrs.[41] His own commentaries by contrast culminate in devout prayers.

Two collections of articles by various hands have been published, to make the work of the commentators better known. The first is devoted to Philoponus;[42] the second is about the commentators in general, and goes into greater detail on some of the issues briefly mentioned here.[43]

---

39. For Simplicius, see I. Hadot, *Le Problème du Néoplatonisme Alexandrin: Hiéroclès et Simplicius* (Paris 1978); for Ammonius and Asclepius, Koenraad Verrycken, *God en wereld in de Wijsbegeerte van Ioannes Philoponus*, Ph.D. Diss. (Louvain 1985); for Olympiodorus, L.G. Westerink, *Anonymous Prolegomena to Platonic Philosophy* (Amsterdam 1962).

40. Alison Frantz, 'Pagan philosophers in Christian Athens', *Proceedings of the American Philosophical Society* 119 (1975), 29-38; M. Tardieu, 'Témoins orientaux du *Premier Alcibiade* à Harrān et à Nag 'Hammādi', *Journal Asiatique* 274 (1986); id., 'Les calendriers en usage à Harrān d'après les sources arabes et le commentaire de Simplicius à la *Physique* d'Aristote', in I. Hadot (ed.), *Simplicius, sa vie, son oeuvre, sa survie* (Berlin 1987), 40-57; id., *Coutumes nautiques mésopotamiennes chez Simplicius*, in preparation. The opposing view that Simplicius returned to Athens is most fully argued by Alan Cameron, 'The last day of the Academy at Athens', *Proceedings of the Cambridge Philological Society* 195, n.s. 15 (1969), 7-29.

41. Simplicius *in Cael.* 26,4-7; 70,16-18; 90,1-18; 370,29-371,4. See on his whole attitude Philippe Hoffmann, 'Simplicius' polemics', in Richard Sorabji (ed.), *Philoponus and the Rejection of Aristotelian Science* (London and Ithaca, N.Y. 1987).

42. Richard Sorabji (ed.), *Philoponus and the Rejection of Aristotelian Science* (London and Ithaca, N.Y. 1987).

43. Richard Sorabji (ed.), *Aristotle Transformed: the ancient commentators and their influence* (London and Ithaca, N.Y. 1990). The lists of texts and previous translations of the commentaries included in Wildberg, *Philoponus Against Aristotle on the Eternity of the World* (pp. 12ff.) are not included here. The list of translations should be augmented by: F.L.S. Bridgman, Heliodorus (?) in *Ethica Nicomachea*, London 1807.

I am grateful for comments to Henry Blumenthal, Victor Caston, I. Hadot, Paul Mercken, Alain Segonds, Robert Sharples, Robert Todd, L.G. Westerink and Christian Wildberg.

English-Greek Glossary

abide: *menein*
above: *anô*
abstract: *aphairein*
absurd: *atopon*
accidental(ly): *kata sumbebêkos*
account: *logos*
accurate: *akribês*
acquire: *apolambanein*
act: *poiein*
actual: *energeiai*
actuality, actuation: *energeia*
actuate: *energein*
add: *epagein, prostithenai*
addition: *prosthesis*
adduce: *paralambanein*
adjacent: *parakeimenos*
affect (n.): *pathos*
be affected: *paskhein*
affection: *pathêsis*
affirmation: *kataphasis*
agency: *poiêsis*
agent: *ho poiôn, to poioun*
agree: *homologein, sunkhorein*
aim: *skopos*
air: *aêr*
all: *pas*
alter: *metaballein*
alteration: *metabolê*
alternatively: *allôs*
altogether necessary: *pasa anankê*
amend: *metharmozein*
amount: *plêthos*
analytic: *kat' analusin*
ancient: *arkhaios, palaios, palai*
animal: *zôion*
annihilate: *katanaliskein*
appear: *phainesthai*
appellation: *prosrhêma*
apply: *harmozein, epharmottein*
approach: *prospelazein*
arbitrary: *apoklerôtikos*
arbitrator: *diaitêtês*
argument: *logos*
arrive: *katantan*

assign: *apotithenai*
assume: *prolambanein*
assumption: *lemma*
attack: *epilambanein*
axiom: *axiôma*

bastard: *nothos*
be: *einai*
begin: *arkhesthai*
beginning: *arkhê*
believe: *huponoein*
below: *katô*
bisect: *dikhotomein*
bisection: *dikhotomia*
black, etc.: *melas, etc*
blend: *sunklôthein*
body: *sôma*
book: *biblion*
breadth: *platos*
bring, etc.: *agein, anagein, pherein*
build, etc.: *oikodomein*
bulk: *onkos*

call: *kalein, prosagoreuein*
category: *kategoria, kategorêma*
cause: *aitia, aition*
centre: *kentron*
change (n.): *kinêsis*
change (v.): *kinein*
changeable: *kinêton*
changelessness: *akinêsia*
circle: *kuklos*
circumference: *periphereia*
circumscribe: *perigraphein*
clear: *saphês*
coercive: *anankastikos*
colour: *khrôma*
column: *sustoikhia*
combination: *sunkrima, sunduasmos*
combine: *sunduazein*
come to an end: *epileipein*
come to be: *gignesthai*
commentator: *exêgêtês*
common: *koinos*

community: *koinônia*
commutative: *alloiôtikos*
compel: *anankazein*
complete: *teleios*
completeness, completion: *teleiotês*
compose: *sumplêrein*
composition: *sunthesis*
compound (v.): *suntithenai*
compound, composite: *sunthetos*
compression: *pilêsis*
comprise: *sumplêroun*
conceive: *noein*
conception, conceptualisation: *noêsis*
conclude: *epitithenai*
conclusion: *sumperasma*
concomitant: *parakolouthêma*
concrete: *sunkekhumenos*
conduce: *suntelein*
confirm: *pistoun*
confirmation: *pistis*
conjunction: *sundesmos*
consequence: *akolouthon, hepomenon*
conserve: *phulattein, diaphulattein*
consider: *episkeptein*
consideration: *ennoia*
constitutive: *sumplerôtikos*
construct: *anagraphein*
consume: *katadapanein*
contact (n.): *haphê, hapsis*
in contact: *haptomenos*
continuity: *sunekheia*
continuous: *sunekhês*
contrary: *enantios*
contrast: *antidiastellein*
contribute: *sumballein*
conventionally: *thesei*
converse: *antestrammenôs*
conversely: *empalin*
coolness, etc.: *psukhrotês, etc.*
correct (v.): *diorthoun*
correctly: *kalôs, diorthountes*
corruption: *phthisis*
countless: *murioi*
cut: *temnein*
cut off: *aphairein, apotemnein*

dampness, etc.: *hugrotês, etc.*
deceive: *apatan*
defect: *elleipsis*
define: *horizein*
definition: *horismos, horos*
delete: *perigraphein*

demiurge: *demiourgos*
demonstration: *epikheirêma, epikheirêsis, kataskeuê*
demonstrative: *apodeiktikos*
deny: *arneisthai*
deprived: *esterêmenos*
depth: *bathos*
derivative: *parôpnumos*
destroy: *phtheirein*
destruction: *phthora*
determinate, determined: *hôrismenos*
devoid: *erêmos*
differ: *diapherein*
difference: *heterotês*
different: *diaphoros, heteros*
difficulty: *aporia*
digress: *parekbainein*
digression: *parekbasis*
dimension: *diastasis*
diminish: *meioun*
disappear: *aphanizesthai*
discrete: *diorismenos*
discuss: *dialegein*
dispensation: *apoklêrosis*
dispersion: *skedasmos*
dissection: *tomê*
dissolution: *dialusis, epilusis*
dissolve: *dialuein, epiluein*
distance: *diastasis, diastêma*
distinguish: *diairein*
divide: *diairein*
dot: *stigmê*
downward: *katantes*
draw: *graphein*
draw (pull): *helkein*
drive: *ôthein*
dryness, etc.: *xêrotês*

earth: *gê*
efficient: *poiêtikos*
element: *stoikheion*
elemental: *stoikheiôdês*
eliminate: *anairein*
elliptically: *ellipôs*
embrace: *enapolambanein*
enclose: *perilambanein*
end: *telos*
endure: *hupomenein*
ensouled: *empsukhos*
entelechy: *entelekheia*
entirety: *holotês*
ephemeral: *spanios*

equal: *isos*
equality: *isotês*
error: *planê*
essence: *ousia*
essential: *ousiôdês*
establish: *kataskeuazein*
eternal: *aïdios*
ethereal: *aitherios*
even: *artios*
every: *pas*
everywhere: *pantakhou*
examine: *dialambanein, skopein*
example: *paradeigma*
exceed: *huperballein*
excess: *huperokhê*
exist: *einai, huphistasthai, huparkhein*
existent: *on*
explain: *exêgêtein*
extend: *ekteinein*
extension: *ektasis*
extraneous: *allakhothen*
extreme: *eskhaton*

false: *pseudês*
fiery sphere: *hupekkauma*
figure: *skhêma*
final: *telikos*
find: *heuriskein*
fire: *phlox, pur, purkaia*
first: *prôtos*
fixed sphere: *aplanês*
flame: *phlox*
follow: *akolouthein, hepesthai,*
    sumbainein
force (n.): *bia, iskhus*
form: *eidos*
formal: *eidikos*
formative: *diaplastikos*
formless: *aneideos*
formula: *logos*
full: *plêrês*
function: *ergon*

generally: *katholou*
generate: *gennan*
generated: *genêtos*
generation: *genesis*
genus: *genos*
geometry, etc.: *geômetria, etc.*
germane: *oikeios*
give: *apodidonai*
go: *pheresthai*

grasp: *lambanein*
great: *megas*
greater: *meizôn*
greatest: *megistos*

handle (proof): *epikheirein*
have: *ekhein*
healthy, etc.: *hugiês, etc.*
heavenly: *ouranios*
heavens: *ouranos*
heavy: *barus*
henad: *henas*
heterogeneous: *heteroeidês*
hold in: *eirgein*
homogeneous: *homoeidês*
homoiomery: *homoiomereia*
homonymous: *homônumos*
hypothetical: *hupothetikos*

idea: *idea*
imagination: *phantasia*
imagine: *phantazesthai*
imitate: *apomimeisthai*
imitation: *mimêma*
immaterial: *aülos*
immediate: *amesos*
immediately: *euthus*
immobile, immovable: *akinêtos*
impossible: *adunaton*
impulse: *hormê*
incidental: *parakolouthon, (kata)*
    sumbebêkos
incomplete: *atelês*
incorporeal: *asômatos*
increase (n.): *auxêsis*
increase (v.): *auxanein*
indefinite: *aoristos*
indestructible: *aphthartos*
indicate: *emphainein*
indivisible: *adiairetos*
inequality: *anisotês*
infer: *epagein*
inference: *akolouthia*
inferior: *kheirôn*
information: *historia*
inhere: *enuparkhein, huparkhein*
inquire: *zêtein*
inquiry: *zêtêsis*
inscribe: *katagraphein*
inseparable: *akhôristos*
intelligible: *noêtos*
intense: *sphodros*

intention: *dianoia*
intermediary, intermediate: *metaxu*
interval: *diastasis, diastêma*
interweave: *sumplekein*
introduce: *eisagein, eispherein*
invisible: *aoratos*
ipso facto: *euthus*
irrational: *alogos*
isolated: *apotetmêmenos*

just any: *tukhon*
juxtapose: *paratithenai*
juxtaposition: *parathesis*

kindle: *haptein, sunaptein*
know: *gignôskein, eidenai*
knowledge: *eidêsis, gnôsis*

large: *megas*
larger: *meizôn*
learn, etc.: *manthanein, etc.*
least: *elakhistos*
leave off: *apolegein*
left (opp. right); *aristeros*
be left: *leipesthai*
length: *mekos*
less: *elattôn*
light (adj.): *kouphos*
light (n.): *phôs*
like (adj.): *homoios*
limit (n.): *peras*
limit (v.): *perainein*
limited: *peperasmenos*
line: *grammê*
locomotion: *phora*
logical: *logikos*
look on: *aphoran*
look to: *apoblepein*

magnitude: *megethos*
make: *poiein*
man (= human): *anthrôpos*
manifest: *phaneron*
mark off: *aphorizein*
mass: *onkos*
material: *hulikos*
mathematical, etc.: *mathêmatikos etc.*
matter: *hulê*
mean (v.): *legein*
mention: *mnasthai*
method: *methodos*
middle: *meson*

mind: *nous*
minimum: *elakhiston*
mixture: *krasis, migma*
mobile, movable: *kinêtos, phorêtos*
monad: *monas*
motion: *kinêsis*
move (trans.): *kinein*
move (intrans.): *kineisthai, pheresthai*
multiplicity: *plêthos*
multiply: *pollaplasiazein*
mutate: *alloioun, alloiousthai*
mutation: *alloiôsis*

name (n.): *onoma*
name (v.): *onomazein*
natural: *phusikos, kata phusin*
naturally: *phusei*
is naturally liable: *pephuken*
nature: *phusis*
necessarily: *ex anankês*
necessary: *anankaios*
necessity: *anankê*
negate: *aphairein*
negation: *apophasis*
negation with inversion: *sun
    antithesei antistrophê*
neighbouring: *prosekhês*
next: *ephexês*
now (in argument): *toinun*
number: *arithmos*
numerable: *arithmêtos*

object (n.): *pragma*
object (v.): *enistasthai*
objection: *enstasis*
oblong: *heteromêkes*
observe: *theôrein*
obvious: *dêlon*
obviously: *dêlonoti*
occupy: *katekhein*
odd: *perittos*
often: *pollakis*
once: *pote*
opinion: *doxa*
opposite: *antikeimenos*
order (n.): *taxis*
origin: *arkhê*
originally: *ex arkhês*
own (adj.): *idios, oikeios*

part: *meros*
partake: *metekhein*

partial(ly): *kata meros*
partless: *amerês*
passible: *pathêtikos*
past: *parelêluthos*
patent: *enargês*
patent fact: *enargeia*
patently: *enargôs*
perceive: *aisthanesthai*
perceptible: *aisthêtos*
permanence: *monê*
perpetual generation: *aeigenesia*
persuasion: *peithô*
persuasive: *pithanos*
pervade: *khôrein*
physicist: *phusikos*
physics: *ta phusika*
place: *topos*
plane: *epipedon*
plausible: *eulogon*
point (n.): *sêmeion*
pointless(ly): *mataios, matên*
portion: *morion*
posit: *theinai*
position: *thesis*
possess: *ekhein*
possession: *hexis*
possible: *dunaton*
posterior: *husteros*
postulate (n.): *aitêma*
potential: *dunamei*
potentiality: *dunamis*
power: *dunamis*
precede: *proêgeisthai*
predicate: *katêgorein*
premiss: *protasis*
preserve: *sôzein, diasôzein*
prevent: *koluein*
primarily: *proêgoumenos, prôtos*
primary: *prôtos*
prior: *proteros*
privation: *sterêsis*
privative: *sterêtikos*
problem: *problêma*
proceed: *proerkhesthai*
procession: *proödos*
produce: *ekballein* (geom.), *poiein*
productive: *poiêtikos*
proof: *apodeixis*
properly: *kuriôs*
propose, propound: *hupotithenai*
proposition: *hupothesis*
prove: *apodeiknunai*

quality: *to poion, poiotês*
quantity: *to poson*

raise: *meteorizein*
rational: *logikos*
ready: *epitêdeia*
really: *toi onti*
reason: *aitia, aition*
reasonably: *eikotôs*
reasoning: *logismos*
receive: *dekhesthai, epidekhesthai, lambanein*
receptive: *dektikos*
receptivity: *epitêdeiotês*
refutation: *elenkhos*
refute: *elenkhein*
regress: *anapodizein*
related, relative: *pros ti*
relation: *skhesis*
remain: *menein*
remainder, rest: *loipon*
remaining: *loipos*
reproach (v.): *enkalein*
resist: *antibainein*
resolve: *analuein*
resolution: *analusis*
response: *apantan*
rest (n.): *êremia*
rest (v.): *êremein*
restore: *apokathistanai*
resume: *analambanein*
return: *epanerkhesthai*
ridiculous: *katagelastos*
right (opp. left): *dexios*
rightly: *kalôs*
road, route: *hodos*
room: *khôra*

say: *legein, phanai*
scheme: *taxis*
science: *epistêmê*
secrete: *ekkrinein*
section: *tomê*
see: *horan*
seem: *dokein*
segment: *tmêma*
separate (adj.): *kekhôrismenos*
separate (v.) *diakrinein*
set-square: *gnômôn*
shape: *morphê*
show: *deiknunai*
side: *pleura*

sideways: *plagia*
sign (n.): *sêmeion*
significant: *sêmantikos*
signification: *sêmainomenon*
signify: *sêmainein*
similar: *homoios*
similarity: *homoiotês*
simple: *haplous*
simpliciter, simply: *haplôs*
simultaneously: *hama*
solution: *lusis, epilusis*
solve: *luein*
soul: *psukhê*
sound (adj.) *hugiês*
sound (n.): *phonê*
spatial: *topikos*
speak: *legein, phanai*
specific: *idios*
specifically: *idiai*
speech: *dialektos*
sphere: *sphaira*
square: *tetragonos*
stability: *stasis*
stay, stop: *histasthai*
straight: *euthus*
study: *theôria*
subject, substratum: *hupokeimenon*
subsequent: *ephexês*
subsist: *huparkhein, hupostasthai*
subsistence: *huparxis*
subsume: *perilambanein*
subtract: *aphairein*
subtraction: *aphairesis*
sufficiently: *hikanôs*
superior: *kreittôn*
supervene: *episumbainein,*
    epigignesthai
surface: *epiphaneia*
surprising: *thaumastos*
suspend: *kremazein*
sustain: *stêrizein*
syllogism: *sullogismos*
symbol: *sumbolon*
symbolically: *sumbolikôs*

take: *lambanein*
take shape: *sunistasthai*
teach, etc.: *didaskein, etc.*
temporal: *khronikos*
term: *phônê, horos*
text: *lexis*

then (in argument): *oun*
theorem: *theorêma*
therefore: *ara*
thing: *pragma*
think: *nomizein*
time: *khronos*
timelessly: *akhronôs*
token: *tekmêrion*
touch (n.), touching: *thixis*
touch (v.): *thinganein*
transcribe: *graphein*
translation: *metaphora*
transparent: *diaphanes*
traversable: *diexitêtos*
traverse: *diexelthein*
true: *alêthês*
truth: *aletheia*
understand: *akouein, epistasthai,*
    lambanein
undertake: *protithenai*
unequal: *anisos*
ungenerated: *agenêtos*
uniform: *monoeidês*
unit: *to hen*
universe: *kosmos*
unknowable: *agnôstos*
unlimited: *apeiron*
unlimitedness: *apeiria*
untraversable: *adiexitêtos*
upward: *anantês*
usage: *khrêsis*
use (v.): *khrêsthai*
vehicle: *bastazôn*
vicissitude: *anakampsis*
visible: *horatos*
void: *kenon*

walk: *badizein*
warmth, etc.: *thermotês, etc.*
water: *hudôr*
way: *tropos*
weakness: *astheneia*
weight: *rhopê*
white, etc.: *leukos, etc.*
whole: *holos*
wish (v.): *boulesthai, thelein*
witness (n.): *martus, marturia*
word: *logos, rhêton*
work (v.): *dran*
workmanship: *dêmiourgia*
worthy: *axios*

Greek-English Index

adiairetos: indivisible, 481,12ff.; 487,5ff.

adiarthrotos: (of an argument, sentence) disconnected, 431,3

adiastatos: without dimension, 401,30

adiexitêtos: untraversable, 409,18; 413,9; 459,16; 467,23; 468,7

adunaton: [is] impossible, 436,8; 463,1; 464,9

aeigenêsia: perpetual generation, 395,18; 405,4; 432,16; 484,9 (cf. 341,10, 493,28)

aeikinêton: always in motion, 444,27

aêr: air, 378,20; 395,17; 415,20; 427,21; 431,2; 433,6f.

agenêtos: ungenerated, 398,26; 404,2

agnoein: not to know, 339,15

agnôstos: unknowable, 476,6; 479,27

agnôstoteros: less known, 369,16

agôn: contest, 459,13

aïdios: eternal, 400,6; 406,9; 408,15; 435,4; 467,6; 490,14

ainittesthai: to say, speak enigmatically, 391,27; 392,19

aiôn: eternity, 458,2

aisthanesthai: to perceive, 439,9

aisthêsis: perception, 433,19; 438,15

aisthêton: perceptible, 413,2; 413,15; 426,18; 441,3; 462,21

aisthêtos: perceptibly, 425,18

aitêma: postulate (pejorative), 421,33

aitherion: ethereal, 340,31

aitia: reason, cause, 346,12; 361,23; 389,15; 479,4; 402,8

aitiaton: caused, 381,20

aition: reason, cause, 364,21; 375,3; 411,25; 457,20; 483,15; 483,24

akinêsia: changelessness, immobility, 362,14; 451,15

akinêtos: unchangeable, immobile, immovable, 355,17; 442,4; 451,23; 464,16

akhôristos: inseparable, 489,18

akhronôs: timelessly, 340,6; 368,24; 401,20; 458,21

akolouthein: (of conclusion) to follow, be a result, 400,7; 427,6; 444,21; 481,22; 485,19

akolouthos: 486,17

akolouthia: inference, 374,17f.

akouein: to understand (a passage), 346,17f.; 355,15; 391,12

akribestatos: most accurate, 482,28

akribesteros: more accurate, 367,28; 385,16; 454,5; 468,10; 495,6

akribôs: accurately: 353,7

alêtheia: truth, 493,24

alêthês: true, 351,23; 372,16; 381,5; 477,23

allakhothen: extraneous, 356,17

alloiousthai: to mutate, 355,11, 403,15

alloiôsis: mutation, 350,13; 368,19; 378,8; 403,15

alloiôtikos: commutative, 384,27; 424,22

alloiôtos: mutable, 350,13

allôs: otherwise, alternatively, 339,17; 347,5; 384,5

allotrios: foreign, 447,2f.

alogos: irrational, unreasonable, 371,5; 372,10; 421,33

amegethos: without magnitude, 401,4f.; 401,33

amerês: partless, 391,29; 401,31; 465,10f.

ameristos: without parts, 415,26; 416,3

amesos: immediate, 428,29

ametablêtos: unalterable, 434,17

ametria: disproportionality, 418,22

amphô: both, 375,13; 376,16; 378,1

amphoteroi: both, 371,21f.; 475,13

amudra: weak, 423,9

amudroteros: weaker, 423,11

apatan: to deceive, 479,5
apeikazein: to liken, 389,8
apeinai: to be absent, 474,18; 478,4
apeirakis: an unlimited number of
 times, 412,16; 415,6
apeiria: unlimitedness, 489,14; 24
apeiros: unlimited, 339,21; 340,12ff.;
 345,5; 387,25; 388,8ff.; 389,13ff.;
 390,20ff.; 394,29; 395,1f.; 396,3;
 399,19ff.; 409,9ff.; 410,2ff.;
 413,18f.; 414,20f.; 416,20; 418,16;
 428,17ff.; 432,15; 436,8; 466,10;
 478,19; 479,3f.; 482,8; 483,8; 489
ep' apeiron: (of a process) without
 limit, 340,1; 345,12; 389,12
apeiroplasion: in an unlimited
 degree, 419,22
apeirôs: 426,23
aphairein: to subtract, cut off, take
 away, 405,5; 470,10; 470,24f.; to
 negate, 482,19; 483,2f.; 491,21
aphairesis: abstraction, 482,21
aphanizesthai: to disappear, 459,28
aphoran: to look on, 402,15f.
aphorizein: to allot, mark off, 454,18;
 462,15; 493,20
aphthartos: indestructible, 398,25;
 407,10
hê aplanês: the fixed sphere, 441,31;
 485,13; 494,5
apoballein: to rid oneself [of], 342,18;
 469,26f.
apoblepein: to look to, 403,13;
 407,13f.
apodeiknunai: to prove, 353,21;
 482,17
apodeiktikos: demonstrative, 346,19
apodeixis: proof (esp. in geometry),
 482,20ff.; 483,2ff.; 492,4
apodidonai: to give (reason, account
 etc.,), 353,22; 363,17; 450,2ff.;
 452,3f.; 453,16
apodosis: giving (of proof), 350,7,
apogignôskein: to deny, 438,12,
apokathistanai: to restore, 421,15f,
apoklêrôsis: dispensation, 405,24f.;
 408,8; 429,27
apoklêrôtikos: (of argument)
 arbitrary, 408,11
apolambanein: to receive, 353,31;
 354,1; 358,16-17

apolêgein: to leave off; come to an
 end, 407,6; 409,27
apoleipein: to abandon, 434,15-16
apolêpsis: acquisition, 363,3
apomattein: to model, 402,19-20
apomimeisthai: to imitate, 402,16
apoperatoun: to limit, 413,8
apophasis: negation, 456,19; 457,14
apophatikôs: negatively, 454,25
apoptôsis: aberration, 479,5
aporia: a difficulty, 368,29; 376,6;
 380,25; 383,7, (cf. *aporon* at
 493,23)
aporein: to raise a difficulty, wonder,
 369,22; 372,16; 374,27; 378,16;
 440,19
apotelein: to arrive at (result), 389,3
apotelesma: result, 376,12
apoteleutêsis: termination, 385,2
apotemnein: to cut off, isolate, 370,1;
 371,1; 372,30; 381,10
apôthein: to drive away, 403,24
apotithenai: to assign, 347,22;
 361,22; 416,9-10; 480,13
apsukhos: unsouled, 468,26
ara: therefore (usu. in formal proof),
 339,17 and *passim*
aristeros: left (opp. right), 368,2ff.;
 440,8; 454,8f.
arithmêtikos: arithmetician, 393,6
arithmêtos: numerable, 428,13f.;
 489,17
[*ho*] *arithmôn*: [the] numerator,
 428,15
arithmos: number, 414,5; 428,12ff.;
 467,13ff.; 481,6ff.; 481,28; 487,6;
 488,7; 488,21ff.
arkhaios: ancient, 421,15; 473,22;
 493,12
arkhê: basis, beginning, origin,
 principle, (logically) premiss,
 339,3; 340,19; 344,8; 360,23f.;
 361,3; 386,16; 387,2; 388,3;
 397,3ff.; 399,17; 400,7ff.; 401,25f.;
 404,3; 406,29; 407,26f.; 427,7;
 432,6; 483,19f.; 492,22
arkhesthai: to begin, originate,
 346,24; 370,9; 393,23; 396,17;
 397,15
arneisthai: to deny, 458,23
arrên: male, 360,27; 389,4

artios: even, 360,26; 389,3ff.; 391,2; 391,20

artos: bread, 355,27; 371,3; 478,12

asômatos: incorporeal, 391,3; 401,10

asphalesteron: safer, 488,5

astheneia: weakness, 457,30; 458,3; 490,26

asthenês: weak, 418,28; 419,3

asthenesteros: weaker, 420,13; 421,17

atelês: incomplete, 341,32; 344,26

athroos: all together, all at once, 368,21; 407,8; 420,7

athrooteros: more sudden, 379,3

atmis: steam, 371,18

atoma: individuals, 439,4ff.; 446,15; 447,10; 468,25

atomoi: (Democritean) atoms, 396,11; 398,11; 14f.; 494,21

atomos: indivisible, 456,3ff.

atopon: [it is] absurd, 380,23; 381,22; 372,26; 418,7; 476,14

atopôs: absurdly, 448,13

aülos: immaterial, 340,8

autognôsis: proper knowledge, 476,16

autoousia: an essence in itself, 387,25; 416,2

aux(an)ein: to increase, 345,12; 410,24; 420,22; 481,9

auxêsis: increase, increment, 345,16; 350,23f.; 473,6f.; 480,29; 481,14

axiôma: axiom, 343,22; 347,14; 347,28; 348,6

axios: worthy, 376,7; 406,22

badisis: walking, 383,24

badizein: to walk, 424,8

baros: weight, 420,9f.; 453,2ff.

barus: heavy, 379,23; 417,26; 452,17; 453,7; 462,11

barutês: heaviness, 424,23; 437,16

bastazein: to be a vehicle, (of scale pan) 423,24f.

bathos: depth, 417,16; 454,3

bia: force, 451,18

biai: by force, 355,5

biaios: enforced, 449,13; 450,1

biblion: book, 339,8; 386,16; 389,20; 409,6; 440,17

boêtheia: help, 422,27

boêthein: to help, 421,25

bolos: clod, 436,18; 442,10

boulesthai: to wish, 397,13; 410,16; 439,12; 460,5

braduteros: slower, 379,3

brakhutatos: shortest, 427,3

daktulikos: countable, 394,5 (see 428,14)

daktulion: finger-ring, 392,4; 474,4

daktulos: finger, 360,2; 428,14

deiknunai: to show, 343,24; 344,6; 366,6; 368,26; 369,6; 395,19-20; 399,20ff.; 404,13; 418,17; 432,7; 436,20; 492,3

deka: ten, 369,18

dekaplasiôn: tenfold, 431,11

dekas: decad, 388,29; 473,17

dekhesthai: to receive, admit, 406,1; 434,16

dektikos: receptive, 406,1; 408,18

dêlon: obvious, 360,18; 364,13; 377,1; 419,28; 462,4; 483,22

dêlonoti: obviously, it is obvious that, 466,5; 485,13

dêloun: to make obvious, 376,10; 400,5

dêmiourgia: workmanship, 403,31; 491,1

dêmiourgos: workman, the Demiurge, 402,5ff.

dêpou: presumably, 352,33; 360,18; 376,14; 436,18

dexamenê: receptacle, 419,30

dexios: right (opp. left), 368,2ff.; 440,7; 454,7f.

diairein: to divide, distinguish, 350,4; 412,14; 440,10; 477,8; 488,4

diairesis: division, 345,15; 413,20; 459,17; 464,21; 481,20

diairetos: divisible, 412,11

diaitan: to act as arbiter, arbitrate, 459,1; 464,22

diaitêtês: arbiter, 456,12; 464,16

diakonikos: domestic (of fire), 420,1

diakrinein: to secrete (from a mixture); isolate, distinguish, 398,2f.

diakrinein: to separate, 349,17; 438,27

diakrisis: separation, 397,25f.; 398,3

diakritikon einai: to penetrate, 402,1

diakubernan: to govern, 407,13-14

dialambanein: to examine, 339,10; 340,14; 387,2

dialampein: to be eminent, 387,1

dialegein: to discuss, 339,10; 340,15; 387,5

dialektos: speech, 411,18f.

dialuein: to dissolve, 427,17; 432,17

diametros, diametron: diameter, diagonal, 359,32-360,1; 483,9

dianeimai: to distribute, 440,26

dianoia: intention, 473,22

diaphanês: transparent, 358,5-6

diapherein: to make a difference, differ, 371,11; 396,10; 398,10; 492,16

diaphora: difference, 463,5

diaphoros: different, 371,10; 376,4f.; 377,7; 378,10ff.

diaphulattein: to conserve, 342,27f.

diaplastikê: formative (always with *tekhnê*), 353,30; 354,2

diarthroun: to subjoin, 346,27; to articulate, 352,18

diasôzein: to preserve, 368,19

diaspasthai: to be pulled asunder, 437,19

diastasis: distance, interval, 374,8; 376,2f.; (geometrical) dimension, 426,22f.; 454,16

diastêma: interval, distance, 455,6f.; radius, 410,15

diastolê: contrast, 458,11

diatêrein: to maintain, 434,14

didagma: tuition, 380,7

didaskalia: teaching process, 383,29

didaskalos: teacher, 373,16; 381,10ff.

didaskein: to teach, 372,3ff.; 373,12ff.; 382,2ff.; 383,19

didaxis: teaching, 373,16; 380,4; 383,14f.; 384,2; 387,14

diêkein: to spread out, 443,5

diexelthein: to traverse, 409,26; 413,7f.; 461,17

diistanai: be distant, be extended, 425,3; 431,25; 454,16; (causative) 475,13

dikê: justice, 388,30

dikhôs: in two senses, 349,27

dikhotomein: to bisect, 410,26; 461,23; 470,3f.; 492,8f.

dikhotomia: bisection, 389,12;

391,26; 395,3; 408,23; 466,29; 477,18

diorismenos: discrete, 345,13; 345,17; 464,13

diorthoun: to correct, 418,3

diplasiazein: to duplicate, 418,6; 440,1; 441,2

diplasiôn: double, 369,10; 376,3

diplôs: of two kinds, 344,7

dittos: double, of two kinds, 341,29; 349,30; 366,19; 433,11

dokein: to seem, 344,20; 355,20; 364,21; 384,18; 439,27

doxa: opinion, 366,16; 395,18

dran: to work [on], 421,20; 423,5f.; 424,2f.; 428,19

drastêrios: operative, 421,23; 424,17

drastikos: operative, 424,22

drastikoteros: more potent, 421,29

duas: dyad, 393,22; 394,11

dunamei: potentially, in potential, in potentiality, 340,28; 342,11; 347,18; 350,9; 354,27f.; 352,4f.

dunamis: potentiality, power, 340,27; 341,8; 342,16; 357,18; 403,22f.; 436,11

dunasthai: to be possible (variously translated), 349,26; 359,11; 409,21

dunaton: [it is] possible, 361,28; 366,11; 371,9

duo: two, 364,6; 375,26; 473,5; 473,11; (the number) 488,17

dusbatos: difficult of passage, 410,1

eidenai: to know, 339,13; 433,19; 457,6; 471,27

eidêsis: knowledge, 485,20

eidikos: formal, 414,20

eidopoieisthai: to undergo formation, 493,11-12

eidopoiia: production of form 394,29

eidos: form, class, 340,22; 341,17; 353,32; 369,17; 402,5; 446,14; 493,2f.

eikôn: image, 355,26; 371,2

eikotôs: reasonably, 349,20; 481,22; 486,20

eilêmmenon: presumed, 354,14

eilikrinôs: strictly, 361,21; 368,3

einai: to be, 339,3 (copula); 464,20 (existential); etc.; see esp. 456,17ff. (on tense), and *onta, mê on, tôi onti*; to be possible, 466,27; 474,1; 476,27

eiôthe: he was accustomed, 361,5; 388,24

eirgein: to hold together, 449,22; 451,22

eisagein: to introduce, 405,14; 465,12

eisbolê: introduction, 363,18

eiskrinesthai: to enter, 391,9-10

eispherein: to introduce, 365,18

ekbainein: to exceed (boundary) 403,32; to come to pass, pass into, 459,30; 460,2; 490,13

ekballein: to produce (a line), 455,6f.

ekhein: to have, possess (variously translated), 359,3; 390,19; 399,24; 400,12; 413,20; 453,9; 462,17

ekkrinein: to secrete, 396,28; 398,2

ekkrisis: secretion, 396,19; 397,29

ekleipein: to come to an end, 403,16; 489,11

ekphusan: to abhor, 403,24

ekpureisthai: to suffer combustion, 433,6; 436,5

ekstasis: departure, 364,13

ektasis: extension, 409,27; 411,12; 413,12; 416,10f.; 436,25-6; 480,24; 483,18; 492,17

ekteinein: to extend, 426,24

elaion: olive, 423,11

elakhistos: smallest, least, minimum, 447,10; 481,6; 486,27; 488,16

elatton: less, shorter, smaller, 379,2; 398,16; 404, 19; 408,3; 425,9; 421,2; 481,4

elenkhein: to refute, 343,18; 408,11; 417,28

elenkhos: refutation, 372,17; 413,27; 427,4

ellampsis: illumination, 403,14

elleipein: to fall short, be vacant, be missing, 423,3; 446,22; 453,11f.

elleipsis: defect, 341,14ff.; 343,18

ellipesteros: more elliptical, 446,22

ellipôs: (of argument) elliptically, 363,16

emballein: to throw into, 419,30

empalin: conversely, 348,4; 381,24; 463,16

emperiekhein: to embrace, 488,2

emphainein: to indicate, 380,11f.

emphainesthai: to be seen, 345,5

emphrôn: intelligent, 364,12

emprosthen: before, previously, 347,17; 368,14; 369,8; 400,29; 440,7; 444,9f.

empsukhos: ensouled, 348,16; 468,26

enapolambanein: to enclose, 391,18; 392,7

enantios: contrary, 357,13; 364,7; 430,13; 435,19; 473,23; 475,10; 490,1

enantiôs ekhein: to be contrary, 481,28

enantiotêtes: contrarieties, 418,2ff.; 432,17; 434,13; 435,2

enantioun: to contradict, 493,26

enargeia: patent fact, 419,28; 422,12; 437,20; 445,7

enargês: patent, 438,15

enargôs: patently, 371,2; 424,25; 425,8

endekhesthai: to be able, possible (variously translated), 358,22; 433,14; 464,6; 480,21

[ta] endoxa: admitted premisses, 417,14

energeia: actuality, actuation, 340,24ff.; 342,12f.; 345,4; 351,12f.; 353,9ff.; 370,12; 372,29f.; 377,5

[to] energeiai: actually, in actuality [the] actual, 343,5; 347,15ff.; 350,9; 352,4f.

energein: to actuate, be actual, be active, 356,1; 358,19; 367,9; 381,21

energêtikon: actuating, 375,21

engignesthai: to come to be in, 401,23

eniautos: year, 458,24

enistanai: to object, 368,1

enkalein: to reproach, 473,12

enkosmios: in the world, 476,19

ennoein: to conceive, 455,21

ennoia: conception, consideration, 360,16; 364,22; 417,27; 455,23; 480,3

enokhlein: to cloud (understanding), 484,7

enstasis: objection, 420,27; 423,17; 442,24

entelekheia: entelechy, 340,29ff.; 342,11ff.; 351,12f.; 375,13

entelesteros: more complete, 430,9

exisazein: to be equal, 422,25-6; 426,8; 431,13
exô: outside, beyond, 383,3; 472,27; 474,1; 476,27
exôthen: from without, externally, 356,17; 391,9

gamos: marriage, 389,1
gê: earth, 359,29f.; 379,22; 451,19
gelôs: ridicule, 457,7; 458,29
genesis: generation, coming-to-be, 340,30; 355,13; 362,11f.; 409,7; 437,22; 493,28; 495,20
genêtos: generated, 407,7
gennan: to engender, generate, 345,15; 389,4; 394,14
gennêtikos: generative, 355,12
genos: genus, 348,15f.; 349,1; 363,1; 454,28f.; 463,16; generation, 429,7f.
geômetrês: geometer, 404,13; 417,1; 465,7; 482,19f.; 491,25; 492,16
geômetria: geometry, 455,5
geômetrikos: of geometry, 429,24; 455,4
gignesthai: to come to be, come into being, arise, 346,5; 375,10; 381,14; 393,14; 401,14; 433,19; 466,6
gignôskein: to know, 340,1; 387,7f.
gnômôn: (in geometrical sense only) set-square, 392,21ff.
gnôrimos: knowable, 369,14
gnôrimôteros: more knowable, 369,15; 386,1
gnôsis: knowledge, 479,28f.; 480,3f.
grammatikos: grammarian, 359,7; 382,2
grammê: line, 399,15; 465,8; 468,3; 477,9
graphê: text, 356,3.8
graphein: to write, draw, 356,7; 379,4; 410,15; 468,3
gumnê: devoid, 340,26

hagein: to train, (perf. pass. part.) 455,4
hama: simultaneously, at the same time, 370,4; 373,2; 438,8; 445,7f.; 466,24
haphê: contact, 458,20; 484,31

haplos: simple, 401,21; 403,2; 414,15; 419, 27; 432,6; 447,8
haplôs: simply, simpliciter, 341,32; 346,20; 351,13; 355,11; 380,14
haptesthai: to be in contact, 438,28; 439,1; 446,5; 453,23; to kindle, 420,9; 422,13; to address (a study), 387,12
haptomenos: in contact, contiguous, 362,22; 446,5; 484,26
harmozein: to apply, be applicable, 384,18; 385,23; 427,1; 472,3
hêgeisthai: (logically) to precede, [*to*] *hêgoumenon*: the antecedent, 490,16
heis, mia, hen: one (masc.; fem.; neut.), 349,3; 371,11; 376,5; 378,30f.; 380,3; 381,27; 382,12; 432,6; 481,13
hekatonplasion: a hundredfold, 431,12
hêlios: the sun, 384,28; 402,32; 425,5; 454,12; 455,12
helkein: to draw, 403,23; 424,4ff.
hêmera: day, 466,5; 471,4
hêmikuklios: semicircle, 378,18
hêmisphairios: hemisphere, 454,18
hêmisu: half, 456,16; 462,11; 469,11
to hen: the unit, 487,5
henas: henad, 481,11.23
hepesthai: (logically) to follow, 371,23; 374,3; 381,2f.; 383,9
[*to*] *hepomenon*: [the] consequence, consequent, 372,16f.; 382,26; 490,15
heteroeidês: heterogeneous, 440,24; 446,3-4
heteromêkês: oblong, 360,28
heteros: different (with def. art. = the other), 354,5; 358,1; 360,2; 419,2; 457,2f.
heterotês: difference, 359,21f.; 360,13; 361,12
hêttôn: less, 420,9
heuriskein: to find, 377,10; 393,25; 429,8
hexis: (contrasted with privation) possession, 365,14; 390,3; proficiency, 386,28
hikanos: sufficient, 458,16
hikanôs: sufficiently, 426,20; 465,1

himation: cloak, 374,2; 384,25
hippos: horse, 359,30; 429,14; 454,29
histasthai: to stop, stay, 357,7;
    433,17; 442,14; 442,14; 444,25;
    445,23; 473,16; 487,10; 488,8;
    495,12
historein: to inform, 360,25
historia: information, 360,25
hodos: road, (metaphorical) route,
    349,25; 350,1; 378,33; 373,18
holikôteros: more universal, 346,26
[*to*] *holon*: as a whole, 419,27
holos: whole, 425,26; 477,2
holôs: in general, comprehensively,
    overall, at all, 383,14, (flatly)
    368,18
holotês: entirety, 419,18f.; 424,25;
    436,19; 442,15
homoeidês: (of parts) similar, (of
    wholes) homogeneous, 442,7f.;
    444,16; 450,8; 474,9
homoiomereia: homoeomery,
    396,5ff.; 397,17ff.
homoios: like, 386,11; 423,31
homoiôs: similarly, likewise, equally,
    373,16; 440,17; 443,19; 444,10
homoiotês: similarity, 341,11; 474,10;
    476,20
hômologêma: (thing) agreed, 403,20
hômologoumenon,
    hômologêmenon: agreed, 369,8;
    491,18
homônumos: homonymous, 343,26;
    377,4; 349,6; 409,15
homônumôs: homonymously, 348,18;
    402,11
homoulos: having the same matter,
    362,26
hôra: hour, 455,11
horan: to see, 358,8; 366,1; 424,25;
    425,8; 439,6; 446,3
horatos: visible, 352,23; 358,1f.
horizein: to define, 350,14; 385,4
hôrismenos: determined,
    determinate, 365,18; 365,20;
    446,26; 472,20f.; 473,3; 489,8f.
hôrismenôs: determinately,
    definitely, 361,22
horismos: definition, 344,1; 350,6;
    351,3f.; 356,19; 363,5; 381,24
hormê: impulse, 445,10
horos: definition, term, 345,23;

360,18; 475,10; 480,28; border,
    455,21
horos: mountain, 378,13
hosakhôs: in as many ways as, 348,8
hudôr: water, 395,17; 419,5f.; 419,32;
    432,25
hugiainein: to be healthy, 353,1;
    357,17; 23
hugiês: sound, 405,3
hugiôs: soundly, 366,7
hugros: damp, 417,25
hugrotês: dampness, 418,19
hulê: matter, 339,6; 340,26; 354,7;
    395,4; 399,6; 401,4; 402,2;
    471,13f.; 473,20; 476,6; 479,29;
    482,20; 484,8
hulikos: material, 400,11; 483,28
huparkhein: to exist, inhere, be
    present, constitute, 370,2; 449,1;
    452,9; 456,14; 466,24; 471,22;
    476,26
huparxis: subsistent entity,
    subsistence, 457,24
to hupekkauma: the fiery sphere,
    378,25; 384,19f.; 449,7
huperballein: to exceed, 431,19-20;
    495,2
huperbatos: as a hyperbaton, 356,10
huperkosmia: above the world,
    476,18
huperokhê: excess, 341,14ff.; 343,18;
    347,26
huperphuôs: preternaturally, 378,26
hupertithenai: to communicate,
    355,24
huphasma: skein, 390,22
huphesis: subordination, 402,24
huphistasthai: to subsist, be
    present, be there, 374,22; 412,4;
    414,9f.; 435,11
hupodokhê: reception, 403,17
hupographikos logos: sketch, 344,1
hupokeimenon: (grammatical,
    logical) subject, (physical)
    substratum, 345,7; 352,32f.;
    357,25f.; 381,24; 382,10
hupokeisthai: to underlie, 395,20
hupomenein: to endure, 468,18
huponoein: to believe, 361,8; 391,9;
    395,14
hupôpteuein: to conjecture, 407,22f.;
    465,12

khôristos: separable, 391,1; 413,11; 489,18
khôrizein: to separate, 349,18; 391,3; 428,12
khortos: straw, 355,28; 371,3
khous: pitcher, 426,6
khrêsis: usage, 377,11; 390,27
khrêsthai: to use, employ, practise, 358,3; 377,11; 404,15; 427,4; 463,21
khrôma: colour, 352,23; 358,3; 463,26
khronikos: of time, temporal, 399,22; 456,20
khroniôteros: more gradual, 421,29
khronos: time, 339,7; 386,15; 400,5; 456,16ff.; 457,21; 466,10; 467,29; 489,14; temporal phase, 353,25ff.
kinein: to change, move, 351,23; 355,9ff.; 379,8f.
kinêsis: change, motion, 339,7ff.; 342,3; 348,13f.; 349,1f.; 356,3; 357,2; 369,23; 378,18; 452,15
[*to*] *kinêtikon*: the source of change, motion, 348,1
[*to*] *kinêton*: [the] changeable, movable, 355,1; 356,1; 369,23
to kinoumenon: the subject of change, motion, 352,10; 370,22f.
to kinoun: the cause of change, motion, 355,1; 370,22f.; 377,26
klêroun: to assign, 440,5
koinônia: [something] in common, community (of properties etc.), 402,12f.; 467,1; 468,27
koinos: common, 346,11f.; 347,2f.; 395,14; 472,12; 474,3, (of argument) 427,13; 428,3
koinôs: commonly, with common scope, 466,23; 482,7
kôluein: to prevent, 381,27; 431,27; 440,24; 454,2
kosmos: universe, 429,26; 472,22; 478,6
kouphos: light, 379,22, 417,27; 453,8f.
kouphotês: lightness, 424,22-3; 437,17; 453,6
krama: mixture, 418,21
krasis: mixture, 403,30; 425,28; 426,1
kratêr: crater, 447,3
kremasthai: to be suspended, 451,8
kreittôn: superior, 341,29f.; 342,4f.; 360,29; 361,7

krikos: hoop, 474,7
krustallos: ice, 420,2; 426,17
kuklos: circle, 378,17; 379,11; 390,20; 410,15; 413,6ff.; 438,7ff.
kurios: lord, 485,25
kuriôs: properly, 343,30; 380,20; 383,15f.; 478,5; 481,27
kuriôtatos: most proper, 337,20; 440,6; 453,26
kuriôteron: more proper, 475,22

laburinthon: labyrinth, 410,4-5
lambanein: to acquire, get, take, accept, 405,12; 409,19; 410,12; 443,24; 444,17; 458,7; 459,12; 489,8; to grasp, apprehend (meaning, etc.), 366,4; 445,7; 454,17; 465,17; 466,7
lampas: lamp, 419,29-30
lebês: cauldron, 475,21
legein: to say, mean, speak, call, 348,2; 352,17; 358,13; 358,20; 367,11; 369,1; 377,1; 381,1; 406,26; 476,21
leipetai: it remains (as the last alternative or task), 399,2; 400,31; 446,13; 465,14
lêmma: assumption, 343,13; 349,29; 350,5; 441,14
leukainein: to whiten, 371,32; 372,32f.; 373,12; 384,15
leukansis: whitening, 371,31; 373,12
leukos: white, 342,1; 371,17; 379,2
leukotês: whiteness, 378,9
lexis: text, 388,23
linon: flax, 478,19f.
lithos: stone, 351,4; 403,23f.; 487,24
litra: pound, 423,25
litriaion: [of] a pound [weight] (often in combination), 420,11ff.
logikos: (of argument) logical, 376,6; 379,19; 417,1; (of intellect etc.) rational, 355,4; 402,7
logikôs: logically, 416,8ff.
kata logon: according to reason, 480,14
logôi: verbally, notionally, in the account, 370,6; 382,20; 384,4; 456,16
logos: word, account, argument, discussion, (mathematical) ratio, (ontological) formula, principle,

339,20; 340,11; 357,9; 370,6; 381,18; 401,31; 403,29; 426,9; 428,10; 433,17; 475,12; 494,2

[*to, ta*] *loipon, loipa*: the rest, remainder, 353,19; 359,11; 454,22

loipon: (adverb, variously translated), 350,6; 493,18

loipos: remaining, 343,26f.

lôpion: cape, 374,2

luein: to solve, 465,4

lukhniaia: of a lamp, 422,13f.; 423,6

lusis: solution, 372,22

magnêtês: magnet, 403,23

to mallon: a fortiori, 411,32; 412,9; 414,17

manthanein: to learn, 373,30f.; 372,4f.; 374,1ff.

marturia: witness, 483,22; 493,1

martus: witness, 439,12

mataios: pointless, 406,8; 435,3f.

matên: pointlessly, 398,24f.; 406,28f.; 407,1f.

mathêmata: mathematics, mathematicals, 412,30

mathêmatika: mathematicals, 416,28

mathêsis: learning, 380,4; 383,3ff.

mathêtês: learner, 381,10

to mega kai to mikron: the great and the small, 389,17; 395,1f.; 480,6f.

megas: large, great, 421,18; 422,1

megethos: magnitude, 331,19; 413,17f.; 414,5; 466,13f.; 469,11; 490,1; 491,7; 495,7

megistos: greatest, 480,23; 492,6f.

meignunai: to commingle, 396,23

meioun: to diminish, 469,10; 470,6; 472,18

meizôn: larger, greater, 341,15; 398,16; 419,8; 424,17; 469,12; 470,14; 472,26; 487,3; 489,5; 490,11

mêkos: length, 417,16; 454,3

melansis: blackening, blackness, 371,17

melas: black, 342,1

menein: to abide, 385,3; 438,3; 443,14; 445,19

menos: month, 467,27

meros: part, 415,7; 426,2; 429,27; 442,22f.; 443,5; 452,4

kata meros: part by part, in parts, gradual, 379,3; 385,26; 460,3; 466,7

merikos: particular, 347,6; 454,8

merizesthai: to be partitioned, 401,32

meson: middle, medium, mean, 379,26; 449,22; 462,7f.; 475,4

mesotês: medium, 427,29

[*to*] *mesouranema*: [the] mid-heaven, 455,10.12.15

messothen: from the midpoint, 475,3

metabainein: to turn to (a subject etc.), 379,30; 382,11; 411,14; 414,6; 417,22; 447,9

metaballein: to alter, 351,9; 353,16-17; 368,3; 385,11; 435,19

metabolê: alteration, 350,25; 363,4; 371,4; 379,25; 403,16; 435,6

metaphora: translation, 383,25

metaxu: between, in the middle, intermediate, 353,28; 379,22; 413,26-7; 455,8; 455,14

[*to*] *metaxu*: [the] intermediary, 387,21; 432,10; 435,2; 484,3

metekhein: to partake of, 361,21ff.; 366,14; 477,31

meteôrizein: to raise, 449,7

meteôros: mid-air, 451,6

metharmozein: to amend (a definition), 369,1

methodos: method, 344,17; 379,19; 435,1

metron: bounds, 403,32

migma: mixture, 396,13f.; 448,17

mikros: little, 398,8 (but cf. *merikas* at 397,21)

mikron: a little, 419,28

mikroteros: small, 341,15

mimêma: imitation, 402,18

mnasthai: to mention, 344,10; 455,3

molis: barely, 413,4

monakhou: in one place, 408,7

monas: monad, 389,20; 393,22ff.; 473,16; 487,9; 488,12; single instance, 429,2

monê: permanence, 385,2; 445,17

monoeidês: uniform, 392,1; 444,17f.

monon: only (adv.), 357,10; 365,19

monos: only (adj.), 355,14; 378,30

monôs: only (adv.), 340,24; 341,11; 353,20f.; 358,20

morion: portion, 398,4; 398,10;

441,24; 437,20f.; 450,14; 453,18;
471,5; trans. "limb" at 377,2
kata morion: partially, 423,21-2
morphê: shape, 340,29; 343,2; 349,28
murias: (figure of) ten thousand,
419,19-20
murioplasiôn: tenthousandfold,
419,17
murios: ten thousand, 419,21;
(countless) 456,3f.
murmêx: ant, 378,31

neikos: (Empedoclean) strife, 407,26
neuein: to incline, 443,3f.; 449,23
nikan: to overcome, 419,8
noein: to conceive, 443,1; 484,12f.;
485,22
noêsis: conception, conceptualisation,
455,4; 484,11f.; 486,10; 494,25f.;
495,3
noêtos: intelliegible, 476,12-13; 480,7
nomizein: to think, entertain [an
opinion], 366,16; 381,5f.; 433,2
nosein: to be sick, 357,13ff.
nothos: bastard, 463,23; 480,1
nous: mind, 397,13f.; 398,2; 414,25

oiesthai: to think, 432,15; 476,4
oiêteon: must be thought, 475,1
oikeios: germane, [of] its own, 390,24;
401,22; 436,28; 437,2ff.; 438,7ff.;
442,19; 444,19; 445,6
oikia: house, 354,7
oikodomein: to build, 351,4; 354,7;
359,9; 424,8
oikodomêsis: building (process),
354,8ff.
oikodomêtos: buildable, 351,1f.; 354,5
oikodomos: builder, 354,6
ôkeanos: ocean, 410,6
oligon: a little, 351,9
on, onta: being, existents, what is,
things that are, 342,4; 360,27;
361,18; 409,29
mê on: non-being, not-being, what is
not, non-existent, 341,31; 342,4;
359,29; 363,14; 364,4
tôi onti: really, in fact, 359,28; 386,6;
488,6
onkos: bulk, mass, 418,28; 422,10;
423,23f.; 431,16

onoma: name, 342,12; 350,23; 376,11;
377,5ff.; 428,19
onomazein: to have a name for,
365,17
onos: ass, 355,28; 371,3
opisthen: before, behind, 368,14;
429,6; 440,7; 444,10f.
opsis: sight, 390,1; 402,1; 417,16
orektos: object of desire, 355,26
organikon: organ, 404,4
orthogônios: (of triangle)
right-angled, 404,26
orugma: excavation, 443,10
ôthein: to drive, 424,4
oun: then (as next stage of argument),
339,9 and *passim*
ourania: heavenly (bodies etc.)
347,20f.; 355,6; 355,16f.; 417,19
ouranos: the heavens, 379,22; 384,21;
391,5; 391,12; 405,19; 472,26
ousia: essence, 356,17; 411,6-7;
414,13; 415,17; 416,1
kat' ousian: in essence, essentially,
399,22; 399,31; 400,3
ousiôdês: essential, 402,12
ousiôdôs: essentially, 391,13

palai: ancient, 407,13
palaios: ancient, 356,8; 390,27; 483,22
palaioteros: more ancient, 398,20
palê: wrestling, 459,15; 471,6
to pan: the All, 446,1; 469,16
pandokeion: inn, 378,13
panspermia: seminal mixture of all,
396,10
pantakhou: everywhere, in every
place, 408,7; 445,19
pantêi: in every way, in every place,
on every side, 347,19
pantelôs: utterly, 409,22; 459,4
pantôs: ubiquitously, in every case,
352,12; 367,5; 368,15; 399,19;
421,20; 454,29
paradeigma: example, 343,4; 351,3;
358,1; 375,27; 403,19; 463,21
paradekhesthai: to allow, 456,9
paradidonai: to offer, 459,2
paragein: derive, 388,1; emit,
407,25-6
paragignesthai: to arrive, 475,19-20
parakeimenon: adjacent, 422,28f.;
423,5

phthisis: corruption, 350,20f.
phthôra: destruction, 340,30; 355,13;
   409,8; 435,22; 493,28
phulattein: to conserve, 362,4;
   393,1ff.; 393,24; 426,14; 470,15
phusei: naturally, 399,17
ta phusika [pragmata]: [subject
   matter of] physics, 339,4; 340,20;
   346,31
phusikoi: physicists, 339,11; 340,8;
   346,14; 387,5; 388,17; 395,12;
phusikos: natural, 378,22; 436,11;
   441,14, 453,25
phusikôs: naturally, 355,1
phusiologos: physical theorist, 407,13
phusis: nature, 339,3; 343,29; 395,8
phuton: plant, 404,4; 429,14
pilêsis: compression, 423,26
pistoun: to confirm, 351,3; 480,6
pistis: confirmation, 422,12
pithanos: persuasive, 376,7f.
pithanôs: persuasively, 416,26
pithanotês: persuasiveness, 405,15
plagia: sideways, 378,27; 379,7f.
planê: error, 365,24; 475,7
plasmatôdês: factitious, 432,2
platos: breadth, 417,16; 454,3
plattein: to imagine, 457,2
pleiô; pleiona: many, more, a
   plurality, 346,29; 418,11
plêrês: full, 479,4; (plenum) 340,3
plêrôma: constitutive element, 402,22
plêroun: to fill, 405,25
plethos: amount, multiplicity,
   aggregate, 360,26; 413,7; 413,17f.;
   418,8; 420,6; 430,15; 489,9
pleura: side, 359,32; 404,17; 408,4
ploion: ship, 399,3
poiein: to act, make, produce, 367,26;
   370,27; 393,11; 401,24; 404,27;
   410,16
poiêma: action, 376,13
poiêsis: agency, 370,9f.; 376,13
poiêtês: the poet, i.e. Homer, 454,10
poiêtikos: productive, efficient,
   397,30; 400,24
ho poion, to poioun: the agent,
   372,4; 380,1
[to] poion: quality, 341,27; 349,9;
   365,22; 420,28
poios: of what kind, 360,16; 367,11

poiotês: quality, 347,24; 409,24;
   411,10; 418,6; 420,8
polis: city, 422,12
pollakhôs: in many ways, senses,
   409,9
pollakis: often, repeatedly, 345,20;
   454,33
pollaplasiazein: to multiply, 389,2;
   446,14; 454,22; 468,1
pollaplasiôn: many times (more)
   422,31
poreia: passage, 410,3
posakhôs: in how many ways, 409,9
posos: how many, 340,22
[to] poson: quantity, 341,27; 364,16;
   365,22; 402,6; 420,28; 422,6 (see
   esp. 463,21f.)
pote: once (quoted term), 458,1
pous: foot, 390,22; 424,7
pragma: thing, object,
   subject-matter, 339,5; 340,20;
   475,21
pragmateia: subject, (literary) work,
   367,8; 389,20; 412,29
pragmateiodês: belonging to objects,
   399,21ff.; 400,4ff.
pragmatikos: of, belonging to
   objects, 399,6f.
proagôgê: (lit. bringing forward:
   variously translated), 385,4; 407,8
proagein: to carry on, 417,17
proaktikê dunamis: capacity for
   generation, 391,5
proballein: to advance, lay down
   (theorem, etc.), 385,4-5
problêma: problem, 363,19; 386,21
prodêlon: patently obvious, 359,3;
   399,20
proêgeisthai: to be prior, 346,18
proêgoumenos: par excellence, 345,10
proerkhesthai: to progress, proceed,
   374,22; 381,11; 402,26-7; 459,25
[to] prokeimenos: [the] present
   (subject, etc.; variously
   translated), 369,24; 375,6; 394,1;
   413,1
prokheirizein: to handle, 381,13
prokheiroteros: more easy (to
   conceive) 455,4
prokopein: to proceed [with], 469,4
prolambanein: to lay down, assume,

340,23; 349,29; 351,27; 425,14; 464,22f.

proödos: procession, 403,6; 403,13; 383,1

proöimion: proemium, 346,23

pros ti: relation, related thing, 358,7; 368,13; 380,28; 484,26

prosagoreuein: to give a name, 392,25

prosallêla: mutually, 368,14

prosbolê: application, 381,12

prosekhês: neighbouring, 384,27

prosôpon: person, 397,9

prospelazesthai: to approach, 367,24

prosrhêma: appellation, 456,20

prosthesis: addition, 410,20; 468,22; 469,5; 471,2

prostithenai: to add, 359,19; 363,28; 441,4; 469,7; 471,1; 472,1; to set forth, 347,4

protasis: premiss, 379,17

proteros: former, prior, previous, 343,29; 344,3f.; 362,34; 363,1; (adverbial) 351,26

prôtistos: most primary, 440,6

protithenai: to undertake, 416,17; 466,18

prôtôn: first (adv.), 347,14; 427,15

prôtôs: first (adj.), 343,13; 351,11; 373,5; 380,25; 397,2; 407,21; 417,9

prôtôs: first (adv.); primarily, 345,12; 345,16; 377,26; 491,14

prôtotupon: prototype, 403,3-4

prumnê: prow, 399,3

psekades: drizzle, 422,24

pseudês: false, 351,22f.; 377,25; 379,17; 423,18; 449,5; 451,7

psukhê: soul, 344,3f.; 355,4; 414,19; 380,9

psukhein: to cool, 352,7; 357,14

psukhron: cool, 352,5ff.; 354,20; 422,23; 433,7

psuxis: cooling, 350,21; 420,1

pugmê: boxing, 471,6

pur: 419,5ff.; 426,18; 431,1; 431,14; 433,21; 446,21

puramoeides: pyramidal, 398,12

purkaia: bonfire, 421,18f

rhanis: oil, 423,11

rhephanis: radish, 422,2

rhêton: word, 347,1; 388,26; 415,21

rhiza: root, 404,5

rhônnunai: to strengthen, 420,23

rhopai: weights, 420,8; 423,20

rhopê: weight, tendency, 417,26; 423,23; 442,3; 444,1; 452,14

saphês: clear, 385,27; 453,9

saphesteros: clearer, more obvious, 346,26; 386,3

saphôs: clearly, 384,31

sarx: flesh, 400,1; 404,4; 475,31

sbennunai: to extinguish, 423,7

selêniakos: lunar, 443,1

sêmainein: to signify, 345,6; 404,13; 409,8f.; 409,21; 413,5; 458,10; 464,25; 473,20; 491,4

sêmantikos: significant, 445,1

sêmeion: sign, 390,24; 392,9; 394,4; (geometric) point, 409,21; 410,16; 455,6

semnotês: lofty diction, 479,1

semnunein: to speak in a lofty manner, 474,16

sidêron: iron, 403,23

siôpein: to suppress (word), 458,1

skedasmos: dispersion, 475,10-11

skeptein: to consider, 408,22

skeuê: artefact, 475,18

skhedon: almost, 469,2

skhesis: relation, 368,13f.; 373,27; 375,26; 376,1-5; 454,6

skhêma: figure, 396,11; 398,14f.; 402,17; 424,4; (of syllogism) 373,3; 417,4f.; 483,14

skhêmatizein: to shape, 353,26

skholazein: to be interested in, 395,1

skholê: study, 458,31

skia: shade, 425,5

skopein: to inquire, 436,1

skopos: aim, 340,14

skolios: tortuous, 410,4

skoliotês: tortuosity, 410,2

skotos: darkness, 360,27

sôma: body, 340,31; 347,8; 405,29; 436,8; 438,14; 442,15; 446,5; 450,13; 485,31

sôzein: to preserve (a quality, etc.), 343,8; 354,8; 430,25; 432,24; 460,11

spanios: ephemeral, 398,25

sperma: sperm, 399,34; 475,27

sphaira: sphere, 429,14; 443,2; 485,13

telos: end, 367,14; 399,17; 400,27;
    483,27
temnein: to cut, 465,9; 470,6; 470,11;
    492,1
tetragônos: square, 360, 27; 392,22f.;
    393,2; 455,20
tetrainein: to perforate, 391,8-9
tetrakhôs: in four ways, 348,9
tetraktus: the tetraktys, 388,2
tettares: four, 380, 6; 395, 24; 400,9;
    413,19; 432,17; 433,12; 434,9;
    483,20
thalatta: sea, 410,10; 426,7
thattôn: more rapidly, 420,420,19;
    421,18
thaumastos: surprising, 375,26;
    490,13
theios: divine, 407,17; 457,23
thelein: to wish, 426,6; 446,22
thêlus: female, 360,27; 389,3
theologia: theology, 395,11
theôrein: to observe, discern, study,
    340,29; 349,30-350,1; 368,22;
    386,25; 454,29
theôrêma: theorem, 373,13f.; 483,9;
    491,9
theôria: study, theory, 346,17;
    346,23; 390,24
theos: God, 458,8
thermainein: to warm, 352,5; 357,14
thermansis: warming, 350,22; 359,11
thermos: warm, 352,4f.; 354,20;
    422,1f.
thermotês: warmth, 422,2
thesei: by convention, 399,17; 454,6
thinganein: to touch, 362,20; 367,19;
    484,31
thixei: by touch, 367,16
thnêtos: mortal, 402,4; 415,4
thrix: hair, 360,3

tithenai: to posit, assign (to class),
    341,17; 362,1; 363,13; 381,1
tmêma: segment, 370,20; 458,7f.;
    477,11
tode [*ti*]: this [in particular], 414,21
toinun: now (as next stage of
    argument), 343,9 and *passim.*
tomê: cutting (process), 470,23;
    473,11; 475,14; 487,17; 489,2;
    section, 467,4
topikos: (of motion) in place, 341,2
topos: place, 339,7; 340,3; 345,25f.;
    346,2; 347,6; 437,18; 439,24;
    441,23; 446,1; 447,8; 450,20-1;
    452,12
trakhus: rough, 410,1
tria: (the number) three, 488,17
trigonon: triangle, 404,16ff.; 405,1f.;
    455,20
tripous: tripod, 357,7
tropis: keel, 399,3
tropos: sense, way, (metaph.) route,
    366,12; 376,27; 401,18; 423,18;
    458,3
tukhon: just any, 477,11; 478,8
tuphlos: blind, 390,4
tuphlotês: blindness, 390,2

xêrotês: dryness, 418,19
xestês: pint, 419,12ff.
xulon: wood, 420,18; 421,20; 470,16;
    475,27f., 478,11

zêtein: to seek, inquire, 344,17;
    365,10; 369,13; 387,7; 405,20;
    460,11; 461,10; 491,27
zêtêsis: inquiry, 416,1
zôion: animal, 346,21; 348,16; 378,26;
    379,8; 400,1; 414,23; 454,30

Subject Index

body
  ethereal, 340,31
  always continuous, 347,7
  sought outside universe, 405,20
  'unlimited body' postulated, 408,10;
      454,17
  determined by plane, 417,2
  the unlimited not a body, 434,1ff.
  place cannot exceed body, 447,2
  cannot be unlimited, 448,6ff.;
      462,1ff.; 463,2ff.
  always has weight, 453,3
  always in place, 462,21
  never greater than universe, 472,22
categories
  of essence, quality, quantity, 341,25
  of quantity, 344,22
  of change, 348,14; 349,1
  and genus, 348,15; 463,25
  and homonymity, 348,17; 349,4
  are of completed things, 349,2
  interwoven, 349,15ff.
  have form and privation, 349,30f.
  no category of privation, 365,11
  ten categories, 369,18
change
  originates in nature, 339,3
  not apart from categories, 348,21
  no common genus, 348,23
  depends on objects, 349,1-2
  by desire, 355,26f.; 377,25f.
  defined, 356,3
  and entelechy, 357,2
  indefinite, 361,14
  in the changeable, 369,23; 370,22
  subject of physics, 386,15
continuous
  in change, 339,20; 344,21
  divisibility and, 340,1; 345,15f.
  requires unlimited in definition,
      345,19
  of bodies, 347,7
  forms of, 349,26

  in argument, 463,12
  primarily in magnitude, 491,15
elements
  and Empedocles, 395,26
  elemental form, 402,2
  four elements, 403,20
  resolution of, 405,7
  fire versus water, 419,8f.
  elemental heat, 420,2
  intensity of fire, 420,4
  cooling of air, 422,12ff.
  quenching of fire, 422,23ff.
  no one unlimited, 426,19; 447,23ff.
  and Anaximander, 432,22f.
  air is warm, 433,8-9
  fire never called unlimited, 446,21
  in foreign places, 447,2f.
  immobility of earth, 449,5f.; 451,19f.
entelechy
  of all that has shape, 340,29
  of ethereal body, 340,31
  of the potential, 342,11; 357,2
  = actuality, 342,12-13
  double, 342,17ff.; 351,12ff.
  and change, 357,2
form
  subject of physics, 339,7
  of change, 340,22; 341,17
  and categories, 344,25; 369,17
  formative art, 353,32
  brought by change, 369,17
  formal origin, 400,10
  cause of limit and definition,
      400,21; 475,17; 493,2-3
  as end, 400,29
  in matter, 402,2
  in Demiurge, 402,5
  and individuals, 446,14
  matter formless, 479,27
geometry
  square, 360,27; 392,21ff.; 455,20
  oblong, 360,28
  circumference, 379,10f.

Index of Citations

Because it is often difficult to distinguish between a quotation and a significant allusion in the text of Philoponus, the numerals in bold refer to the notes.